The Uses of Memory

The Critique of Modernity in the Fiction

of Higuchi Ichiyō

Harvard East Asian Monographs 275

The Uses of Memory

The Critique of Modernity in the Fiction

of Higuchi Ichiyō

Timothy J. Van Compernolle

Published by the Harvard University Asia Center
Distributed by Harvard University Press
Cambridge (Massachusetts) and London 2006

PL
808
.I4
Z93
2006

Printed in the United States of America

The Harvard University Asia Center publishes a monograph series and, in coordina-
tion with the Fairbank Center for East Asian Research, the Korea Institute, the Reis-
chauer Institute of Japanese Studies, and other faculties and institutes, administers research projects designed to further scholarly understanding of China, Japan, Vietnam,
Korea, and other Asian countries. The Center also sponsors projects addressing mul-
tidisciplinary and regional issues in Asia.

Library of Congress Cataloging-in-Publication Data

Van Compernolle, Timothy J., 1968–
    The uses of memory : the critique of modernity in the fiction of Higuchi Ichiyō /
Timothy J. Van Compernolle.
        p. cm. -- (Harvard East Asian monographs ; 275)
    Includes bibliographical references and index.
    ISBN-13: 978-0-674-02272-0 (cl : alk. paper)
    ISBN-10: 0-674-02272-6 (cl : alk. paper)
    1. Higuchi, Ichiyō, 1872–1896--Criticism and interpretation. I. Title. II. Series.
    PL808.I4Z93 2006
    895.6'342--dc22

                                                                            2006007662

Index by the author

⊗ Printed on acid-free paper

Last figure below indicates year of this printing
16 15 14 13 12 11 10 09 08 07 06

To the memory of

Robert Lyons Danly

Discourse lives, as it were, on the boundary between its own context and another, alien context.

— Mikhail Bakhtin, "Discourse in the Novel"

The innate dynamism of the modern economy, and of the culture that grows from this economy, annihilates everything that it creates—physical environments, social institutions, metaphysical ideas, artistic visions, moral values—in order to create more, to go on endlessly creating the world anew. This drive draws all modern men and women into its orbit, and forces us all to grapple with the question of what is essential, what is meaningful, what is real in the maelstrom in which we move and live.

— Marshall Berman, *All That Is Solid Melts Into Air*

The greatest consolation it is to sit alone underneath the lamplight, spread a book out, and make the acquaintance of people of long ago.

— Yoshida Kenkō, *Tsurezuregusa*

Acknowledgments

This book argues that underneath the authorial insignia of Higuchi Ichiyō lies a creative dialogue with the literary ancestors. Likewise, my book is unequivocally the result of a creative dialogue with many people, and it seems somewhat disingenuous for my name alone to appear on the cover. It is with great pleasure, then, that I acknowledge the others who contributed to its development. I owe my largest intellectual debt to Ken K. Ito of the University of Michigan. His contributions run the gamut from his willingness to engage in a patient, exacting critique of my work at every stage of its development, to the model of excellence in scholarship that he himself provides. Put in the simplest terms, he taught me how to read modern Japanese literature. I spent nearly a year and a half researching this project under the skillful guidance of Komori Yōichi of the University of Tokyo, whose vast erudition and intellectual generosity are unparalleled. From him, I learned that the world of Meiji Japan lies not behind the words on the page, but *in* those words. With Watanabe Eriko, a fellow graduate student at the University of Tokyo, I read scores of works from the Meiji period, both canonical and obscure. This book is richer for that experience. I would also like to thank the teachers and friends who gave so generously of their time and wisdom while this project was at the dissertation stage: Leslie Pincus, Esperanza Ramirez-Christensen,

David Rolston, and Seki Reiko. Ann Sherif read the entire draft of the manuscript and wrote comments that were so valuable they were never far from my notebook computer. A number of people read individual chapters and willingly, even enthusiastically, offered comments and critiques: Alex Bates, Rachel DiNitto, David Henry, Jason Herlands, Peter Kalliney, Jan Leuchtenberger, Hoyt Long, Mimi Plauché, Bob Rama, Rafael Reyes-Ruiz, Jeremy Robinson, Richi Sakakibara, Atsuko Ueda, Kristina Vassil, and Jonathan Zwicker. I thank John Ziemer, William Hammell, Julie Perkins, and the staff at Harvard's Asia Center—it was truly a pleasure to work with them—as well as the two anonymous readers for the press, each of whom provided invaluable comments for the final stage of preparing the book.

· I received a Fulbright graduate research fellowship with which to conduct research in Japan for fifteen months, which I gratefully acknowledge. Between that time and the completion of the manuscript, I received financial support from the Rackham School of Graduate Studies and the Center for Japanese Studies at the University of Michigan, as well as consecutive faculty summer grants from the College of William and Mary. Most of the labor of drafting the manuscript was done with the luxury of time and good companionship while I was a postdoctoral fellow in the East Asian Studies Program at Oberlin College. I carried out the final revisions of the manuscript surrounded by inspiring scholar-teachers in the Department of Modern Languages and Literatures at the College of William and Mary. I was able to explore some of the ideas in this project at the Midwest Japan Seminar, held at Washington University in St. Louis in February 2001, and at the East Asian Studies Faculty Lecture series at the College of William and Mary in 2003. This book is better for my having had those forums. I would also like to single out three institutions in Tokyo and to thank them for their generosity and hospitality: the Taitō Kuritsu Ichiyō Kinenkan in Taitō Ward, the Nihon Kindai Bungakukan in Meguro Ward, and the Meiji Shinbun Zasshi Bunko at the University of Tokyo in

Hongō. Each provided wonderful resources for exploring Higuchi Ichiyō's life and times.

The fourth chapter of this book originally appeared as "Happiness Foreclosed: Sentimentalism, the Suffering Heroine, and Social Critique in Higuchi Ichiyō's 'Jūsan'ya,'" *Journal of Japanese Studies* 30:2 (Summer 2004). I thank the journal for permission to reprint.

Finally, a personal memory: I arrived in Ann Arbor in the autumn of 1995 as a new graduate student in the Department of Asian Languages and Cultures at the University of Michigan. I was scheduled to TA for Bob Danly in his survey of premodern Japanese literature. On the first day of class, he was immediately surrounded by admiring students, each of whom wanted to tell him about their summer in Japan, their internships, and other experiences. Sadly, I only worked with him for a few class sessions before he was forced to withdraw from the university, having been diagnosed with the illness that would eventually claim his life. In those few sessions, though, I witnessed firsthand what an incredibly gifted teacher he was. Those gifts in teaching were matched by his amazing abilities as a scholar and a prose stylist, as anyone who has read his marvelous biography of Ichiyō can attest. At that time, I never imagined working on the same subject, but during the course of researching and writing this book and teaching my own classes, the example of Bob Danly has been a constant source of inspiration. I dedicate this book to his memory.

Contents

Note to the Reader

Except where otherwise indicated, I have used the following edition of Higuchi Ichiyō's writings because it is the most widely available to readers: Wada Yoshie, ed., *Higuchi Ichiyō shū, Nihon kindai bungaku taikei*, vol. 8 (Tokyo: Kadokawa shoten, 1970). Throughout this book, page numbers for citations from Ichiyō's works are given parenthetically in the body of each chapter, while references to all other sources are given in the notes. Because the aim of the critic is different from that of the translator, I have used my own translations of Japanese texts throughout, with a few exceptions that are indicated in the notes. Each of Ichiyō's stories examined in detail herein has been beautifully rendered into English by Robert Lyons Danly in his *In the Shade of Spring Leaves: The Life and Writings of Higuchi Ichiyō, a Woman of Letters in Meiji Japan* (New York: W. W. Norton, 1992). So marvelous are Danly's translations of Ichiyō that a felicitous phrase or two has no doubt crept into my own versions.

All names are given in Japanese style, surname first, given name last, and I refer to most people by their family name. Most Meiji-era authors, however, used pen names, and I follow convention in referring to authors by those pen names (e.g., Higuchi Ichiyō is referred to as Ichiyō, Mori Ōgai as Ōgai).

Note to the Reader

The following abbreviations are used for serials and collected works.

MBZ: Meiji bungaku zenshū. Chikuma shobō, 1965–1985, 100 vols.
NKBT: Nihon koten bungaku taikei. Iwanami shoten, 1957–1968, 102 vols.
NKBZ: Nihon koten bungaku zenshū. Shōgakukan, 1970–1979, 51 vols.
RHI I: Ronshū Higuchi Ichiyō I. Ed. Higuchi Ichiyō kenkyūkai. Tokyo: Ōfūsha, 1996.
RHI II: Ronshū Higuchi Ichiyō II. Ed. Higuchi Ichiyō kenkyūkai. Tokyo: Ōfūsha, 1998.

The Uses of Memory

The Critique of Modernity in the Fiction

of Higuchi Ichiyō

ONE

Literary Memory in Modernity

The desire to speak with the dead — to make the acquaintance of people of long ago, as Yoshida Kenkō so wonderfully put it — is central to the fiction of Higuchi Ichiyō (1872–1896), a desire inscribed in the very letter of her texts. For Ichiyō, to put writing brush to paper, whether crafting a short story, composing a verse, or recording the day's events in her elegant and very literary diary, was necessarily to summon an anterior literary corpus and to breathe new life into it. Literary writing was first and foremost the art of literary memory, and each of Ichiyō's meticulously fashioned sentences became a site where a vital literary tradition could be remembered and renewed, even as the tradition itself was modified to accommodate new concerns and themes. For someone like Ichiyō — a woman who had stunning command of the linguistic and rhetorical riches of Japan's written heritage — the memory of traditional images, motifs, plot elements, and turns of phrase was so much a part of the composition process that it possessed her very writing brush, even as she struggled to develop her own idiom and grappled with a world that would have been utterly alien to those long-dead writers who exerted so much power over her.

Ichiyō's unswerving commitment to the practices and conventions of her literary ancestors should not lead us to conclude that her writing is so absorbed in the past that it exhibits no engagement with the problems of modern life, that is, with the very world that was changing frantically around her. This book investigates the social dimensions of her artistic imagination, and I will argue in these pages that the Japanese literary tradition is creatively reworked by Ichiyō in order to engage and understand and, more often than not, to confront and critique modernity. In this somewhat unorthodox sense, this book is concerned with stylistics, but with a stylistics in which the linguistic texture of fiction is firmly secured to the social world while also being embedded in a dense literary-textual network with roots thrust deep into the soil of classical literature. My approach to Ichiyō's oeuvre is thus also calculated to broach larger theoretical issues of historicist criticism, the relationship between literature and the surrounding social world, nation-building in Japan's modernization, and the politics in and of literary texts.

Above all, however, this project is designed to overcome what I see as an impasse in current scholarship in the interpretation of Ichiyō's fiction. Simply put, criticism has never really reached a consensus on how to situate Ichiyō in relation to Japanese modernity. She is regularly included in the canon of modern Japanese literature, but this is probably only because she wrote at the cusp of the twentieth century: modern times, after all, were supposed to have begun in 1868 with the Meiji Restoration, and modern literature is widely held to have its origins in the mid-1880s. Interestingly, there is a cautious revival of older notions about Ichiyō's place in Japanese literature. An annotated volume devoted to Ichiyō's writings has recently appeared in a series devoted to *premodern* Japanese literature, the implication being that anything written in classical Japanese and relying so heavily on old rhetorical modes and allusions to ancient texts should properly be considered part of the long tradition of classical literature, a sensible enough view in some respects.[1] With the broad periodization of Japanese history into modern and premodern, which is the very foundation for the way Japanese literature is organized academically as an object of research and teaching, we can only either hesitatingly position Ichiyō in one camp or the other, or with a sense of resignation declare her to be on the fence between epochs — which is only to acknowledge that her writings point to the inadequacy of our own historical and critical categories.[2]

Until fairly recently, the image of "the last woman of old Japan" (*furui Nihon no saigo no onna*), which finds its roots in the reception of Ichiyō's works by some of her contemporaries, had clung rather tenaciously to her, an image easy enough to construct given the obvious rootedness of her texts in the classical tradition and Ichiyō's own affiliations with the conservative, backward-looking poetic circles of the day. Yet it was also an act of image construction that was inseparable from the way literary writing was gendered in Ichiyō's time. Women writers of the era were figured by their male peers as the keepers of the literary traditions of the Heian court, especially the halcyon days of the eleventh century, not as people engaged in a serious way with contemporary society and new ideas. Although there were more than a few nineteenth-century Japanese women who were conversant with Western literature and thought, the would-be writers among them were supposed to follow in the footsteps of their sisterly forebears and continue the ancient women's tradition of *belleslettres*, which to late-nineteenth-century sensibilities meant elegance, modesty, and decorum, for both the author and her prose.[3] Male writers could then comfortably flirt with the new Western learning knowing that at least someone was cultivating the old ways. In this context, the representation of Ichiyō as "the last woman of old Japan" certainly expresses a patronizing attitude toward her art, which could sometimes slide over into a pejorative or dismissive stance, but paradoxically it could also be an act of literary appreciation by those who recognized the intricate and skillfully constructed network of allusions to classical literature and thus believed Ichiyō was admirably fulfilling the mandate of a properly "feminine" textual practice.

This image of "the last woman of old Japan" was strengthened (perhaps unwittingly) by the first generation of postwar

Ichiyō critics. Admittedly, these scholars concentrated less on interpreting Ichiyō's stories than on the reconstruction of her life, and even when they did analyze the texts, exegesis occasionally took the form of biographical reduction, in which both the conception for and themes in a work were sought solely in the events of Ichiyō's own life (a practice, incidentally, by no means alien to broader trends in Japanese literary criticism of that era). This group of scholars accomplished the necessary and significant task of annotating Ichiyō's stories, which by that time had become quite difficult to read, increasing the sense of her distance from modernity.[4] All of her stories have been fully annotated—and the most acclaimed pieces have received this attention several times over—thus giving collections of Ichiyō's writings the look and feel of modern printed editions of Japanese classics. This is where postwar critics inevitably contributed to the image of Ichiyō as a holdover from premodern times. After all, the task of annotation necessitates, in addition to seeking out the meaning of long-dead words and unfamiliar customs, hunting down the ubiquitous allusions to classical works and elucidating their full meaning in the scholarly apparatus to the printing. However, postwar critics did not ask about the purpose or function of these allusions to ancient texts. Their unspoken assumption seems to have been that allusion served Ichiyō's artistic intentions and reflected her passion for the literature of old.

In contrast to these scholars, most of whom began working before the mid-1970s, the current generation of Ichiyō critics has concentrated almost exclusively on the task of teasing out the modern themes in Ichiyō's works (which also reflects a broader shift toward the study of a textuality largely divorced from the author's life experiences); using primarily feminist and historicist methodologies, they have been concerned to demonstrate Ichiyō's engagement with the important social issues of her day so as to situate her squarely in Japanese literary history as the first significant modern woman writer in the country.[5] A welcome consequence of this work has been that the image of "the last woman of old Japan" has been systematically dismantled over the years, though it remains a compelling trope in some circles. Having thus concentrated so overwhelmingly on Ichiyō's relationship to her present, however, more recent scholars have not on the whole done a satisfying job of analyzing her appropriation of the literary past, a phenomenon that I hope to show is the very center of Ichiyō's craft of fiction.[6]

Critical discourse, then, seems unable to think simultaneously about Ichiyō as an author with roots in the Japanese literary tradition and as a writer engaged with problems in modern society. As soon as the term "modernity" is made the dominant framework for thinking about literature and history, a formidable barrier appears in the late nineteenth century, which demarcates the largely mutually exclusive domains of the modern and the premodern. When we think in these terms, all we end up accomplishing is discussing where exactly to set this protective border: should it be closer to the 1850s or closer to 1900? This historical demarcation is not merely an imaginary entity or a convenient critical construct; it is connected to important social ideologies and thus carries real force, as I discuss shortly. Once this barrier becomes naturalized, Ichiyō can be considered a modern author only by ignoring her roots in classical Japanese literature and disregarding the role of literary memory in her textual practice. In a reverse dynamic, Ichiyō can be considered a holdover from the premodern tradition only by an act of stubborn inattention or willing blindness to the thematic concerns of her stories.

This leads to the first of three aspects of the impasse in Ichiyō criticism that I wish to highlight: the fissure between the literary (analysis of rhetorical and formal design) and the social (often a thematic or historicist-oriented analysis). If we concentrate on matters of language and style, her allegiance to the native tradition tends to dominate our perspective on her writing; if we focus on the themes in her stories, she appears as one of the moderns, as a woman grappling with social issues with which everyone in the era was concerned. The term "modernity" is in need of some interrogation, it seems.

Otherwise style and theme, language and content will forever be held apart in our search to find a suitable niche for Ichiyō in our literary histories.

As I hinted in mentioning the recent appropriation of Ichiyō by the editors of premodern anthologies, the second aspect of the current impasse can be attributed to the complex nature of her writing style—classical Japanese grammar in polished sentences that ceaselessly appropriate, allude to, and echo the literature of old—and to the widely held view, ever since the late nineteenth century, that such a style cannot constitute a modern literary language. Arguments about the first modern Japanese novel, after all, have been based overwhelmingly on an assessment of which was the first to use vernacular prose throughout the narrative, a style usually called *genbun itchi* (literally, the unification of the spoken and written words). A historical view that insists on a total rupture between the modern and what went before, wherever we ultimately decide to place the boundary, became the central fiction around which late-nineteenth- and early-twentieth-century Japanese literature was organized as an object of study, and the term *genbun itchi* could be waved about as the absurdly reductive yardstick for assessing the modernity of an author or a work. Once vernacular fiction came to be rather simplistically equated with a truly modern fiction in critical discourse on Japanese literature, then most Meiji-era writers who experimented with other styles—that is, most writers before about 1900—were left in a rather ambiguous relationship both with Japanese modernity and with the classical tradition, meaning, of course, that, apart from a handful of authors such as Ichiyō, they went unread.

The third aspect, which is intricately connected to issues of language, concerns gender. Ichiyō received a rigorous education in the Japanese classics at the Haginoya poetry conservatory, an institution that served as a kind of finishing school for girls from good families. I will have more to say about this shortly, but for now it is sufficient to emphasize that Ichiyō was highly conversant with literature in classical Japanese and, of course, with contemporary works in her native tongue. Ichiyō was no Mori Ōgai fluent in German, nor a Futabatei Shimei with facility in Russian, nor a Nagai Kafū conversant with French and English. She seems to have had some exposure to classical Chinese, but it is doubtful that she could read it with the understanding of a Natsume Sōseki. Like many women writers and poets, then, Ichiyō's own literary creativity depended greatly on the existence of a *tradition* conceived not in nationalistic but in linguistic terms, that is, on a corpus of anterior works in classical Japanese that collectively form an intertextual field. Ichiyō did not have a strong sense of being a national subject, but she was acutely aware of being the heir to a rich literary heritage and did her best to further it. This is not exclusively a matter of one girl's somewhat idiosyncratic education, for as I mentioned, Meiji-era women writers were supposed to be the keepers of the classical tradition of literary writing and were thus viewed as being outside the main line of modern fiction. Such views are uncritically passed along and then internalized within Japanese literary studies. Furthermore, the gender configurations of literary production in Meiji Japan are worth bearing in mind in this age of globalization and comparative, transnational literary study. There is now a welcome trend toward transgressing national boundaries and situating national literatures in the global circulation of texts and ideas, and I have no wish to apply the brakes to this movement; but we should keep in mind that a writer like Higuchi Ichiyō, who worked within a single linguistic tradition, cannot be easily situated in a transnational context because the kind of education she received limited the kind of literature available to her and shaped her attitudes toward it. The Japanese context—both in terms of linguistics and the project of nation-building—is important for Ichiyō's fiction; one of the things this book does is show that a woman writer could occupy the gendered antiquarian role and still be engaged with contemporary ideas and even lodge a forceful critique of institutions arising with the emerging modernity of the Meiji period.

Apart from the sheer pleasure Ichiyō gives us through her fiction—which is considerable, as she is, in my opinion, the most accomplished short-story writer in the Meiji period—she also compels us to interrogate conceptualizations of gender and language, the boundaries between tradition and modernity, the literary and the social, and also forces us to develop reading strategies that can simultaneously grasp these aspects of her texts, strategies that I hope others will find productive in examining writers of other periods and places. My goal in this book will be to illustrate the "worldliness" of Ichiyō's stories,[7] to take hold of some of the threads that radiate out from her fiction and trace their connections to a range of texts from different times and from different culturally demarcated zones. I wish to transgress the boundaries between the literary and the social and between modernity and its shadow, the premodern, in order to read Ichiyō's fiction in a new light. I wish to show especially that the Japanese literary tradition was for Ichiyō *productive* of new literary creation; the classical canon was a reservoir of tropes and paradigms that could be reshaped and renewed in an encounter with Japanese modernity. This agenda can only be accomplished through a thoroughgoing critique of formalism. While I have learned a great deal from formalist criticism in Japanese and English (as the chapters that follow will make abundantly clear), I wish to emphasize that a reading methodology that severs the literary text from the surrounding social world is completely arbitrary and, while not necessarily egregious in and of itself, lacks a satisfactory theoretical foundation and generally leads, in the study of Ichiyō's fiction at least, to many of the problems I have been discussing in the preceding pages. If we wish to read Ichiyō as a modern writer with strong roots in the classical tradition, we cannot implement such a methodology. I want to stress, however, that my project is not to renounce attention to formal and linguistic design, but to view these elements as inescapably intertwined with the surrounding social world. In order to fulfill these mandates, I center this study on the intersection of different kinds of discourse, and I locate the act of interpretation on the boundary between theme and rhetorical design, that is, between content and form.

ii

In this introductory chapter, I wish to interrogate the connections between literary memory and Japanese modernity. While this book is above all a record of my own engagement with and immersion in Ichiyō's marvelous fictional world, at the same time, I want to suggest how we can situate her writings in the broader contexts of both modern institutions and the ideology of the modern.

One of the fringe benefits of the preoccupation in academia with postmodernity over the last couple of decades is that it has done much to clarify our thinking about that which has supposedly been surpassed. Whereas little agreement has been reached on the meaning of modernity at the level of institutions and social practices in a global context beyond acknowledgment of the rise of capitalism and the nation-state form, a surprising consensus exists regarding the ideology of the modern. A few examples will suffice to illustrate how this transcultural concept has been conceived in contemporary criticism. Paul de Man, reading the texts of Nietzsche, Baudelaire, and others, describes it as follows: "Modernity exists in the form of a desire to wipe out whatever came earlier, in the hope of reaching at last a point that could be called a true present, a point of origin that marks a new departure."[8] David Harvey, also drawing on the writings of Baudelaire, but also on the previous work of Marshall Berman, who is quoted in one of the epigraphs on page vii, describes a modern world of fragmentation and ephemerality loosed of its moorings in the past, a world that adhered and continues to adhere to the motto of creative destruction, the clearing away of what went before in order to make way for the new.[9] Harry Harootunian, writing of interwar Japan, has made a similar observation in the context of narratives of history: "One of the more widely agreed upon characteristics of modernity, where none practically exists, is the fact that modernism—the ideology of the modern—has subsumed all preceding histories as prefigurations of moments that now have been surpassed."[10] The ideology of the modern, the urge to constantly make it new, entails a willful suppression, even a savage destruction at times, of everything that has gone before in order to clear space for a new beginning unburdened by the past, tradition, and the way things have always been done. That which has been surpassed can then be dismissed as premodern and thus as something with little or no hold on the concerns of the present; the premodern becomes, in effect, the Other of modernity, or that against which modernity defines itself, and the one has no meaning without the other.

In a nineteenth-century Japan dominated by Euro-American encroachment on the emperor's soil, unequal treaties, and the vivid memory of Perry's smoke-belching black ships, conjoined with internal domestic difficulties and sometimes-violent eruptions of social unrest, there was a sense of crisis. There was a widespread feeling that radical change, even revolutionary upheaval, was imminent.[11] Just how radical the changes were that got underway after the Meiji Restoration of 1868 is certainly debatable, but it is worth recalling that by 1933, Kobayashi Hideo (1902–1983) could famously remark that those who nostalgically scratched below the surface of modern life would find nothing left of old Japan.[12] When modernization began in the middle of the nineteenth century, the project of clearing away space for new ways of thinking and acting must have seemed to many an urgent enterprise indeed. For them, the only conceivable course of action was to jettison the past and follow the ways of Europe and America in order to avoid becoming a subservient, colonized land. For others, all this newness must have seemed the bewildering loss of a foothold in the familiar with each successive wave of ideas and institutions. This is the context in which the ideology of the modern took root in Japan; it is a transcultural phenomenon that books passage on imperial gunboats and takes hold during a time of crisis.

The sense that radical transformation was afoot in the larger social world reinforced calls for aesthetic change among artists, even though those artists did not necessarily occupy the same social space as those propagating change and may or may not have been sympathetic to the ideological projects and institutions that arose. The sense of crisis and imminent transformation of the world turned the literary imagination outward, amplified the urge to create new kinds of art, and even aroused the desire among many for a complete break with past aesthetic practices, which were viewed by avant-garde artists as a straitjacket and were even perceived as partly responsible for Japan's sudden sense of backwardness and belatedness. In the sphere of Meiji letters, new narrative apparatuses, new modes of representation, and, above all, the new literary language of *genbun itchi* were developed to repress the classical literary tradition and to create a new origin for Japanese literature, a world freed from the influence of the (Japanese and East Asian) past and instead affiliated with the contemporary literature of Europe and America. Many of the Meiji writers, especially those who received a first-class education in the new school system and who had significant contact with Western books and ideas, were completely enveloped in the ideology of the modern, even if their ways of accomplishing its mission of suppression varied.

Consider the example of Kunikida Doppo (1871–1908), who sought an active forgetting of his country's literary heritage, especially its practices of writing about the natural world, in his short piece, "Musashino" (The Musashi Plain, 1898). Doppo encountered a new way of representing the natural world when he read Futabatei Shimei's "Aibiki," a translation of a Turgenev story from *Sportsman's Sketches*, which incorporates lush descriptions of nature.[13] Inspired by Futabatei's translation, Doppo attempted a renovation of the literary representation of the Musashi Plain. By engaging a different representational system, he was trying to suppress the classical *utamakura* (pillow word), which attached specific natural images and a fixed literary vocabulary to certain poetically charged places, among which was the Musashi Plain, made famous by Ariwara no Narihira (825–880) and others. By following the lead of Japanese translations of Russian literature, he could thus sever his own textual practice from his country's literary tradition in his quest for new modes of representation, a quest Doppo's narrator makes quite explicit during the course of the essayistic story. In doing this, however, he shifted his literary citations from the Japanese poetic tradition to Europeans such as Ivan Turgenev (in Japanese translation) and William Wordsworth, whose poem "The Fountain" is partially quoted in "Musashino" in English. One way to read Doppo's text, then, is as a battle between two different methods of representing nature, with the "modern" one prevailing.[14] This is closely allied to Doppo's appropriation of the avant-garde experiments with *genbun itchi* in the 1880s and 1890s. When Doppo wrote in the *genbun itchi* style, he gained a great deal of freedom and could avoid the involuntary rush of poetic imagery and diction that adheres to the very language of classical Japanese in general and to the *utamakura* in particular. In fact, it becomes extraordinarily difficult, if not practically impossible, to incorporate citations of *waka* into a running line of prose (a common practice, incidentally, in Ichiyō's early writings) once the classical literary language and its rhythms have been replaced with the newer literary language of *genbun itchi*.

Another prominent example is Tsubouchi Shōyō's (1859–1935) manifesto, *Shōsetsu shinzui* (The Essence of the Novel, 1885–1886). Within the space of a few short pages at the beginning of his treatise, Shōyō manages to incorporate the entire prose tradition of Japan into a grand story that is nothing but a prefiguration for his new structure, *shōsetsu* = novel, which will represent (in all senses of that word) the new world of modern life.[15] Since it is nothing but a prefiguration, Shōyō can then declare this tradition to be inadequate for moderns in his Darwinian framework of the evolution of genres with the advance of civilization, and claim that the modern *shōsetsu* has surpassed and replaced all previous Japanese narratives. Once Shōyō had freed himself from his country's literary heritage, he then made use of his new equation in order to displace the standards for judging the modern Japanese *shōsetsu* onto the Western novel in a bold maneuver from which criticism has never really recovered to this day.[16] Interestingly, language is crucial for Shōyō, too: he calls for classical Japanese in the narrative discourse and colloquial Japanese for the dialogue (the style on which Ichiyō and many others settled), but only until a sufficiently literary form of vernacular Japanese could be created to free Japanese literature once and for all from the hold of the past. This may be the conservative side of Shōyō on display, for he was essentially urging would-be authors to continue doing what writers of the playful *gesaku* tradition had been doing for a hundred years, at least until a literary messiah came along.

In standard literary histories, that messiah is Futabatei Shimei (1864–1909): one way to read his *Ukigumo* (Drifting Clouds, 1887–1889) is as a struggle between a premodern rhetoric rooted in *gesaku* and a *genbun itchi* style heavily indebted to Futabatei's own translations of Russian fiction, with the latter gaining more and more ground as the novel progresses until, in the final book, the text looks like the quintessential *genbun itchi shōsetsu*.[17] Indeed, the drama of this battle or progression is one of the chief pleasures in reading Futabatei's pioneering novel. We could go on citing other examples and then arrange the authors into a narrative of the ideological underpinnings of the development of modern Japanese fiction, but that would be a very different book. As a parenthetical aside, though, I will add that it is fascinating how the suppression of the country's literary traditions among many of these canonical authors, regardless of their degree of success, necessitated a turn to other writings (no one creates art in a vacuum, after all), especially those of contemporary Western writers, such as Turgenev, Dumas, Zola, Maupassant, and, as strange as it may seem to us nowadays, the Englishman Bulwer-Lytton, among many others. Given the way precedent and inspiration was shifted within an imperialist context to Western authors who were largely contemporaries of the Meiji-era writers, the frameworks of postcolonial theory and translingual practice continue to be highly productive, even necessary, for the study of the rise and development of the canonical *shōsetsu* in Japan and the displacement of other writings to the margins of literary history.[18]

Acknowledgment of these aspects of certain texts does not imply that we should denigrate the accomplishments of their authors nor undermine the gravity of the mission they set for themselves. It is, rather, to apprehend the fact that there were a great many literary responses to crisis and modernity and an immense variety of narrative and representational strategies designed to capture some significant part of the maelstrom. Indeed, if I were to use one phrase to represent the literature of the Meiji period, it would be *linguistic experimentation*. The rise of the institution of modern Japanese literature from within this literary and cultural ferment and the eventual dominance of *genbun itchi* prose within that institution were by no stretch of the imagination inevitable. The project of suppressing the (Japanese) literary past creates affiliations among a select group of the (overwhelmingly male) writers of the era, which plays a substantial, if underappreciated, role in shaping what we have received as the canon of modern Japanese prose. I have no desire to instate a reductive dichotomy between two opposing literary camps, those demanding a radical break with past aesthetic practice and those clinging to the old ways; the range of experimentation in the writings of the era would show such a formulation to be a lie anyway. The task is to read Meiji-era texts critically and to understand how a sense of crisis creates new aesthetic practices, which may break with the past to a greater or lesser degree, or may, in the case of Ichiyō and others, reconfigure the past. The literary map needs to be redrawn, as it has proven immensely difficult to insert the writings of many Meiji-era authors into the staid framework of modern Japanese literature, including the fiction of Higuchi Ichiyō, even though Ichiyō herself remains a perennial favorite among the Japanese reading public and has thus escaped being consigned to the margins of the canon.

The project of creating new aesthetic practices by suppressing the literary tradition would have been utterly alien to Ichiyō, who found in its works little cause for anxiety and a great deal of creative inspiration. This is only to say that she was not completely enveloped in the ideology that fetishized the new or the West. Instead of situating her in relation to some of the canonical male authors I have been discussing, I prefer to see Ichiyō's oeuvre as an alternative path opened up for modern Japanese literature, a path that depends on the act of literary memory, which I define as the appropriation of the literary heritage in order to confront the present, with the consequent revision and renewal of the literary past in the process. While her stories have been admired ever since her own day, the particular path Ichiyō opened up was left largely untrodden, though certainly not unappreciated, for a long while as *genbun itchi* prose became dominant. Yet Ichiyō continued to be an inspiring pioneer to many women writers, including several gathered around the journal *Seitō* (Blue Stockings) at the beginning of the twentieth century and later writers such as Sata Ineko (1904–1998) and Setouchi Harumi (b. 1922). In addition, engagement with the country's literary heritage is a strong current in contemporary Japanese women's writing, the most prominent examples perhaps being Enchi Fumiko (1905–1986) and Ōba Minako (b. 1930); and although I would hesitate to draw a direct line from Ichiyō to these later women writers, she is no doubt part of the mix of influences on them. In her own time, Ichiyō's dependence on her heritage for her own creativity loosely affiliates her with a host of writers who have usually been viewed as insufficiently modern because of their indebtedness to premodern language and tropes: authors such as Kōda Rohan (1867–1947), Ozaki Kōyō (1867–1903), and Izumi Kyōka (1873–1939), among others.[19]

Ichiyō's distance from an emergent ideology of the break between the premodern and the modern has much to do with her unique, intense education in the Japanese classics and with her almost complete lack of exposure to both modern educational institutions and Western literature. It thus has precious little to do with some kind of nostalgia for the past in the face of the on-slaught of foreign ideas and practices.[20] Her passion for the lit-erature of old was present even when she was a girl, when she was already reading some of the Edo-period writers like Taki-zawa Bakin (1767–1848). There is a delightful anecdote from her childhood, no doubt apocryphal, in which a friend marvels over the boast that the seven-year-old Natsu (Ichiyō's real name) had polished off in only a few days the 98 volumes of Bakin's massive *Hakkenden* (Chronicle of Eight Dogs, 1814–1842), which had taken the irascible Edo master nearly three decades to write. When her friend asked how it was possible to make one's way so quickly through the old texts, the young Natsu was said to have wittily replied that as she had two eyes, she could read two lines at once. Whether the anecdote is true or not, it certainly indicates that her family and friends were well aware of how much time she spent among her books, devour-ing volume after volume of the old literature. I might also add that this was just an extreme example of a phenomenon that was not at all uncommon in her day; Edo-period writers such as Bakin, Tamenaga Shunsui (1790–1843), Ryūtei Tanehiko (1783–1842), and Jippensha Ikku (1765–1831) still commanded a large readership in the Meiji period, and even worked their charms on the pens of those writers who were trying to shed such in-fluence and create a fresh start for Japanese literature.[21]

Ichiyō's enthusiasm was immeasurably strengthened while she was a student at the Haginoya, or Bush Clover poetry conservatory, where she studied for many years from the age of fourteen after her formal schooling ended at about age eleven. She spent only a few years in modern schools because her mother, Taki, like many middle-aged women of the era, believed that too much of the newfangled education was unbecoming for a young woman and therefore forced her daughter to withdraw. Taki later consented to Natsu's enroll-ment at Nakajima Utako's Haginoya after some arm-twisting by Natsu's father, Noriyoshi, who recognized early on what a gifted daughter he had. Her mother could at least be persuaded that education in a poetry academy among the daughters of privileged families would not jeopardize Natsu's chances of a good marriage (in fact, she never married) and might even make a finishing school suitable to the middle-class yearnings of the Higuchi family. The Haginoya stressed a thorough literary education: a deep familiarity with classical works and a textual practice striving for continuity with the traditions of old. Put simply, at the Haginoya Ichiyō learned poetic composition. But this was poetic practice in the old style, especially composition on fixed topics (*daiei*), which necessitated intensive study of Japan's rich literary tradition in order to craft densely allusive and wittily learned verse. Here she encountered in a formal way and with an eye toward composing such elegant, allusive poems, the writers, especially the Heian-period women writers, who would inspire her fiction-writing throughout her career. She eventually acquired sufficient knowledge to lecture on the Heian classics at the Haginoya and to tutor young women in the art of composing 31-syllable *waka* poetry. Her education at a poetry conservatory provided more fuel for a voracious literary appetite that, as is amply recorded in her diary, drove her week after week during her short adulthood to the women's reading room of the newly established Tokyo Public Library in Ueno, where she consumed whatever was left untaught at the Haginoya.[22]

Yet despite her intensive education in the classical tradition, Ichiyō was by no means ignorant of the literary and cultural ferment going on around her. Only a few years into her fleetingly brief writing career she already counted some of Japan's preeminent writers, critics, and publishers of the day her acquaintances, friends, and admirers, including men as diverse as the translator and critic Baba Kochō (1869–1940), the publisher Ōhashi Otowa (1869–1901), the writer and critic Saitō Ryoku'u (1867–1904), and the formidable man of letters Mori Ōgai (1862–1922). She worked hard to keep up with the latest fiction and criticism from these Meiji luminaries and others, buying more than a few literary journals and, when she could not afford them, borrowing extensively from her

growing circle of literary friends. The new literary world that
was taking shape in mid-Meiji influenced Ichiyō's own writing, causing her, among other things, to jettison the extensive
citation of poetic fragments in her prose—a practice that dominated her first eleven stories, but that seemed hopelessly
old-fashioned to her literary mentors—and instead to search
for new ways of joining her devotion to the literary past to the
renewed emphasis in Meiji letters on social engagement and
mimetic realism.

The experimentation with new modes of representation
found its way into Ichiyō's fictional world, too. *Takekurabe*
(Child's Play, 1895–1896) is just one example of this. This
novella is situated in the Yoshiwara prostitution district,
which had a history that stretched back to the seventeenth
century and which was a crucially important institution in
the cultural production of the Edo period. Yet, while it may
be credibly argued that the narrator's scrupulous attention
to the authentic diction of the quarter is inherited from earlier,
linguistically fastidious genres such as the *sharebon* and
ninjōbon, the narrator's ethnographic style of representing the
environs of the Yoshiwara bears no resemblance to this body
of fiction and is more fruitfully traced back to the reportage
literature that flourished from the early 1890s until well into
the Taisho period. Many of the early reportage pieces, such
as Sakurada Bungo's work in 1890 or Matsubara Iwagorō's
Saiankoku no Tōkyō (Darkest Tokyo, 1893), were written by journalists who were assigned to report in great detail on the
conditions in the city slums (which seemed to have emerged
almost overnight in the eyes of many) for a bourgeois newspaper audience simultaneously fascinated by and terrified of
an emergent lumpenproletariat. The narrative discourse of
these early reportage pieces, regardless of the writer's political
sympathies, positions the journalist as a knowledgeable mediator between the newspaper reader and the city slum in
a way that strongly resembles the narrator's stance in the later
Takekurabe. The novella can thus be read as a kind of demimonde reportage.

What we have in Higuchi Ichiyō, then, is a figure who was familiar with and certainly not unenthusiastic about current developments and experiments in the contemporary literary world, but who was educated in such a way as to make an allusive classical style the most natural and compelling form of literary discourse. Her writings exist in that gendered no-man's land between eras, and this is what has made her fiction, to say nothing of her poetry, so difficult to situate in our histories of modern Japanese literature. Yet, if we are willing to subject our literary and historical paradigms to critical scrutiny, we will discover that Ichiyō allows us to gain some valuable critical distance on the ideology of the modern itself, and even to ruffle the staid map of Meiji letters a little.

iii

Modernity, as troublesome and slippery as the term has been, remains invaluable as a kind of narrative shorthand for the maelstrom of destruction, construction, and transformation that occurred in Japan beginning in the second half of the nineteenth century. I actually use the word sparingly in the chapters that follow, as I prefer to investigate the historical specificity of Ichiyō's texts without always feeling obligated to kick my readings up to a higher level of generality or abstraction. However, as a preliminary step, it is worth spending some time unpacking the term "Japanese modernity" as I understand it, because it reveals a great deal of coherence in Ichiyō's thematic concerns and choice of protagonists, a coherence that I believe has not been fully addressed in Ichiyō scholarship. This will ultimately allow us to place her legitimately alongside other Meiji writers who enacted a critique of the creative destruction raging around them and of the new institutions that were the result.

It is widely agreed that Japanese modernity involves the construction of the Japanese nation-state under the banner of the emperor and the eventual bureaucratization of politics, with those very bureaucrats being imagined as the emperor's loyal servants. There is some consensus on other features as well. We witness the reorganization of the past into a history of this new imagined community of the nation-state (a history that was preparatory but that has been surpassed), which then allows the new state to pose as if it were of ancient pedigree and had a distinguished record of accomplishments. The state tries to accommodate and support a nascent industrial capitalism, which makes its way into the urban centers of the country beginning in the final decades of the nineteenth century via an elite group of entrepreneurs, many of whom came out of the great family enterprises of the Tokugawa period. Japanese modernity will ultimately be connected to Japanese imperialism as big capital begins to chase after opportunities and resources beyond Japan's self-assigned borders, although this process only began in mid-Meiji and one is hard pressed to find much awareness of it in Ichiyō's writings, apart from occasional diary entries about international political intrigues glimpsed in the newspapers or celebrations and war memorials in the aftermath of Japan's victory in its first imperialist adventure, the Sino-Japanese War of 1894–1895.

In the broadest terms, then, Japanese modernity encompasses the construction of the nation-state and the expansion of capitalism within the archipelago, but such large-scale transformations cannot be felt as direct presences in Ichiyō's writings. They are changes of enormous scope and scale, which nonetheless animate more minute and local metamorphoses, those that directly affected the lives of people away from the center of power. The experience of modernity for someone like Ichiyō involves elements that are necessarily felt closer to home. Each of these will receive detailed attention in the appropriate chapters, so here I will just draw up a brief inventory as a kind of preface to the discussions that follow. Modernity involves the transformation of forms of subjectivity within the context of a nascent industrial capitalism and an emergent imperial nation-state. An often overlooked aspect of modern subjectivity is the discourse on ambition and success (*risshin shusse*), which fills the social void after the collapse of the Tokugawa-period status system by helping to articulate the contours of a new social order in which ambition is linked both to the national good and to a new distribution of wealth and power. The newly formed subject, brimming with the desire to succeed in government, business, or other endeavors, gravitates toward the city, accelerating to breakneck speed the process of urbanization that had begun over two centuries before. The city is the place of opportunity as industrial capitalism claims more and more urban space in these decades, leading to the commodification of work, and of social relations more generally. Also crucial in any discussion of modernity are the reorganization of the traditional sprawling household into the nuclear family and the emergence of new ideologies about the appropriate spheres of men's and women's activities. The nuclear family then becomes one of the primary sites in which people are made into national and imperial subjects and programmed for life and work in the new world of industrial capitalism. The creation of the modern subject also entails the construction of Others against which it can define itself—mistresses, prostitutes, the insane, the destitute, all marginal social figures who densely populate much of Ichiyō's best fiction and who will be one of this book's most consistent preoccupations.

Of course, the rise of new institutions and the construction of subjects who can successfully function in them did not occur overnight. These are all interlocked elements of a massive and convoluted process of change, a process that resists neat untangling and summation, but as others have richly documented, the third decade of Meiji (1888–1897)—the very time when Ichiyō was writing—was a decisive period, when the nation-state came into its own with the Meiji Constitution, the emperor system took its characteristic prewar shape, capitalism began to shape the urban environment profoundly and imagined the larger world as a place where raw materials could be obtained, the country acquired its first colonial possessions, and most of the local aspects of modernity I outlined above moved to the forefront of social life.[23] Almost all of the social transformations against which I read Ichiyō's stories acquired hegemonic stature just after this decade, when the saturating power of the state over society began to be forcefully felt at the level of individual existences and destinies. Before these various discourses acquired such power and became embedded in social practices, they were hotly contested. Each of the social transformations I mentioned in my outline of modernity was enacted only after bitter sparring, always discursive and frequently accompanied by more overt methods of violence, control, and discipline, as I will discuss in the following chapters.

These struggles, which are part and parcel of any political community undergoing energetic and disorienting transformations, are obscured if history is conceived in linear, evolutionary terms as a *transition* to modernity. In the context of Asian Studies pursued within a postcolonial problematic, recent works by Prasenjit Duara and Dipesh Chakrabarty are especially instructive.[24] Duara has demonstrated that the transition narrative of modernity, which is a kind of evolutionary paradigm rooted in Enlightenment models, privileges the nation-state as the subject of History. The transition story is so tied to the nation and its unitary narrative of development that it has occluded the struggles and violence that attended modernity and the forceful propagation of certain ideals of political community in East Asia. Duara's caution is worth heeding in this study because most of the social discourses that animate Ichiyō's fiction did not originate with the state, but with individuals or groups of different stripes, some of whom were affiliated with state organs, to be sure, but many of whom proposed a very different agenda from that of the emperor's ideologues. Many of these views were eventually appropriated by the government as part of official ideology, but they became dominant only through discursive and other struggles.

Along somewhat different lines, Chakrabarty has persuasively argued that the transition narrative of capitalist modernity invariably invokes a host of critical categories and concepts that have their roots in a phantasmal or virtual Europe that is always considered to be the source of modernity. In a world shaped by imperialism and colonialism, Europe remains the sovereign subject and theoretical root of modernity, and histories of areas such as south (or east) Asia, especially when grasped using an evolutionary transition model, tend to become variations on a European master narrative of modernization such that so-called latecomers merely repeat a process earlier experienced by Europe. This conceptualization erases the conflicts and discursive struggles that occurred during the experience of modernity in the non-European world. Chakrabarty writes that "the idea is to write into the history of modernity the ambivalences, contradictions, the use of force, and the tragedies and ironies that attend it."[25] For Chakrabarty, modernity is best conceived not as transition, but as translation, in which the transnational, global tendencies of capitalist modernity have to vie with local conditions in a conflict-wrought encounter that is never fully resolved, and thus the theories of modernity derived from study of the European archive cannot be applied to the non-European world in unaltered form, without critical scrutiny and modification.

The arguments of these two historians have far-reaching implications for the study of the modern literatures of Asia. Most importantly, we should acknowledge that there was nothing inevitable about the form of modernity or its specific institutions, literary or otherwise. In addition, these views give us a perspective whereby we can read fictional and other artistic texts as socially engaged, rather than view literature as passively "reflecting" or "responding to" modernity. This would give us a satisfying base that aligns well with the received wisdom that the Meiji-era *shōsetsu* was a very socially engaged form. I would like to push the standard view further and argue that the new *shōsetsu* was, over the course of the Meiji period, being refashioned into an instrument of incisive social critique and that a woman writer could take part in the process of transforming the nature of fiction through acts of literary memory. This is possible only if we consider a given literary text as taking part in the discursive struggles that attended modernity rather than consider modernity the text's decorative historical backdrop. I will approach Ichiyō's fiction in this spirit as I elucidate how past and present are brought into contact in her writings. This provides us with guiding principles, but not with a methodology for reading the literary text.

The Russian literary and cultural theorist Mikhail Bakhtin remains one of the great theorizers of discursive struggle and has given us the requisite tools for apprehending various forms of conflict at the level of individual signifying practices, especially that of literary production. I have found his concept of dialogism to be a most productive way to approach Ichiyō's fiction from within the problematic I have been outlining.[26] Dialogism, which poststructuralist critics somewhat problematically appropriated as intertextuality, exists whenever multiple semantic positions, or ideological points of view, interact within a given medium, whether in conflict or in agreement and affirmation; dialogic interaction exists between different words, utterances, language styles, texts, or anything else that can take shape within any signifying material, such as artistic images or music. Bakhtin is perhaps most well known for his theorization of that specific form of dialogism he calls double-voiced discourse, in which two conflicting points of view inhabit a single utterance, but it is a mistake to confine his concept to the collision of voices within the individual word or phrase.[27] In fact, I inflect the concept of dialogism in a variety of ways in the pages that follow, connecting it to tropological revision, genre theory, modes of literary imagination, and subjectivity, as well as making use of double-voiced discourse. I am consistently interested in examining how traditional rhetoric and literary devices are dialogically engaged with discourses associated with modernity within the pages of Ichiyō's narratives. A dialogically conceived concept of literary memory is theoretically productive and polemically useful in that it offers a model of a motivated, creative troping on texts of all kinds while rejecting too strict a distinction between literary discourse and social discourse. The discourses of the Meiji period against which Ichiyō's fictional world is constructed—those that posited the ambitious imperial subject striving to succeed and the Others of this discourse, which created the bourgeois nuclear family and explicitly commodified all other relationships—are rejoinders in a dialogic encounter. They are rejoinders that have been forgotten, however, as time has done its work of scouring the historical landscape and as the transition narrative of modern history has worked to obscure them by creating a unitary, inevitable story of the rise of the capitalist nation-state. As we enter the first decade of the twenty-first century, the dialogic context of Ichiyō's fiction must be reconstructed through a historicist criticism. Once this context has been reenacted, we can view Ichiyō's ceaseless gestures toward classical literature in a new light; we begin to see how premodern tropes and narrative paradigms can be, as I keep stressing, *productive* of literary creation in a world confronting crisis.

My intent in this book is to restore to literary-critical memory the dialogical context and forgotten interactions between the modern and the premodern, the literary and the social so as to grasp Ichiyō's texts as occupying a site at which the literary past is appropriated as a way to explore transformations that were in the process of being formed and contested during the 1890s. Moreover, I will argue that in this dynamic the literary past is necessarily renewed and revised; literary memory is repetition but repetition with a difference.[28] The literary past, after all, cannot itself remain unchanged once it has been put into contact with the emerging modernity of the Meiji era, with all its dislocations and with all its social and political contradictions. To be as clear as possible here, I consider Ichiyō's gestures toward past literature to be socially engaged with the contemporary world.

The widespread sense of crisis, the dawning conviction that radical change is in the air, means that the entire Meiji-era literary imagination is turned resolutely outward toward the social world and is engaged with social and political ideas in a substantial way. The most obvious examples are the political novels (*seiji shōsetsu*) that flourished during the 1880s, staking out the positions of the various political parties in operation at the time. Even before this, the works of Kanagaki Robun (1829–1894) and the so-called "poison woman" stories (*dokufumono*) of the 1870s explored contemporary issues, especially social hierarchy. Ichiyō's career was contemporaneous with the *hisan shōsetsu* and the *kannen shōsetsu*, or tragic and conceptual novels respectively, two kinds of fiction that grappled with serious social problems. Canonical novelists from Futabatei and Ōgai in mid-Meiji to Sōseki, Shimazaki Tōson (1872–1943), and the Naturalist writers in the early twentieth century explored the tensions and contradictions of modern society.[29] The world of Meiji letters is a very socially engaged corpus of fiction—to some extent this is acknowledged in our paradigms about modern Japanese literature, but I try in this book to push this view further. Moreover, although I unapologetically devote more space to uncovering Ichiyō's acts of literary memory than to the contemporary literary scene, I know of no better way to situate her in the literary landscape of her time than to argue that her work is also turned outward and is socially engaged and to insist that Ichiyō, despite her youth and relative inexperience, be given, in words Claudia Johnson uses to describe Jane Austen, "the dignity and the activity of being a warrior of ideas."[30] Ichiyō's fiction takes part in the communal project of fashioning the *shōsetsu* into an instrument of social analysis and critique, and, as untenable as it first sounds, literary memory in Ichiyō's fiction supports this endeavor; her fiction is best read as an appropriation of past literature in a hard-edged analysis of the human costs of modernization. A major leitmotif of these chapters is that most of Ichiyō's characters are the cast-aside figures of modernity. Ultimately, this will give us the means to see Ichiyō's fiction in a more complex, nuanced, and satisfying way, rather than to go on trying to situate her either with the moderns or in the camp of the premodern.

What follows are five chapters, each devoted to producing a reading of one work from the later phase of Ichiyō's career: "Ōtsugomori" (On the Last Day of the Year, 1894), "Nigorie" (Troubled Waters, 1895), "Jūsan'ya" (The Thirteenth Night, 1895), *Takekurabe* (Child's Play, 1895–1896), and "Wakaremichi" (Separate Ways, 1896). In my reading of "Ōtsugomori" – the story of a servant who steals money from her employer in a desperate attempt to help her family – I employ dialogism to demonstrate how Ichiyō transforms premodern tropes and motifs in a textual engagement with the commodification of work. In my reading of "Nigorie," a story set in the gritty world of unlicensed prostitution, I connect dialogism and genre theory in order to demonstrate that the interaction of heterogeneous, ideologically charged narrative archetypes, especially those concerning the classical love suicide and modern stories of ambition, compels Ichiyō to resolve the narrative tension in an ambiguous way. In the chapter on "Jūsan'ya" – the story of a woman who unsuccessfully seeks a divorce from her husband – I explicate how a classical rhetoric pressed into the service of sentimentality is dialogically engaged with an emergent ideology of the bourgeois nuclear family. The penultimate chapter concerns *Takekurabe*, Ichiyō's acclaimed story of children growing up near the licensed prostitution district of the Yoshiwara. I use dialogism to elucidate the text's preoccupation with subjectivity and desire. The text gives us a model of how institutions and discourses compete over the subject and how the gaze in the prostitution district works to stifle one girl's subjective desires, figured with a variety of classical tropes and topoi. Finally, in the chapter on "Wakaremichi" – the story of the end of a friendship between a young man and an older woman – I use Bakhtin's concept of double-voiced discourse in order to demonstrate that Ichiyō confronts the gender and class implications of the ideology of ambition and success, an ideology that finds a new source of strength in the recirculation of old folk tales in the Meiji period.

These five works are Ichiyō's most well-known and most frequently discussed stories. They are also the most interesting examples from her oeuvre of the potential for interanimation between past and present and between the literary and the social. Before "Ōtsugomori," Ichiyō's works did not exhibit a sustained engagement with the problems of modern society, although such issues were not entirely absent either. From "Ōtsugomori" on, an abrupt and quite noticeable shift emerges in the thematic content of her stories toward a direct engagement with contemporary social issues such as marriage, children, sexuality, prostitution, patriarchy, and the status of women, as well as a preoccupation with marginal social figures who turn out to be, as we will see in each of these chapters, the Others of the normative modern subject. I will take up the reasons for this frequently observed change in more detail in the next chapter.

First, though, it is well worth warning the reader at the outset that this study is not intended to be an exhaustive handbook of allusions to traditional literature in Ichiyō's fiction, an exercise in list-making that, while desirable in a reference work, would not make for the most stimulating monograph; nor do I pretend to trace every sociopolitical reference in her stories, which would be a futile effort in any case. This means that many intertextual strands go unrecognized or unacknowledged, and thus unexplored here. I offer instead close readings of five marvelous stories by Ichiyō that seek to understand how past and present are brought into contact in her fictional worlds as part of a concerted effort at social critique. In the end, there can never be an exhaustive account of dialogic contexts in any text, for what we notice in a writer's works will forever change as our dialogue with that writer continues and changes, and indeed, as our dialogue with the literary past itself changes.

TWO

A Thousand Coins of Gold

"Ōtsugomori" (On the Last Day of the Year) is generally regarded today as the first of a series of masterpieces from Higuchi Ichiyō's brush, although the story attracted little attention when it was first published in *Bungakukai* (Literary World) in 1894 and it even received some unfavorable reviews from several prominent literary figures when it was reprinted in *Taiyō* (The Sun) in 1896. Mori Ōgai's review in the February 1896 issue of *Mezamashigusa* was one such unfavorable reaction: "This is a previously published story by Ichiyō that has been revised. Despite being a work by this author, it has few outstanding merits." Miyazaki Koshoshi, reviewing the story for *Kokumin no tomo* (February 15, 1896), concludes similarly: "No doubt because it is an older work, neither the conception nor the style invite comparison to the author's 'Jūsan'ya,' and one feels that it falls well short of 'Wakaremichi' as well."[1] Reactions to the story have changed substantially over the years. The brilliance and polish of the stories from the final years of her life are what have earned Ichiyō the enormous admiration she now commands in Japan, and the fact that the most acclaimed pieces appeared over the course of a mere fourteen months only adds to the sense of sheer wonder that is invariably associated with her writing career. A phrase attributed to the writer and critic Wada Yoshie—"the unforgettable fourteen months"—is reproduced time and again in reference to the second half of Ichiyō's brief, four-year professional writing career, and "Ōtsugomori" is nowadays held up by most not as a mere transitional story, but as *the* decisive break with the works in the first half of her career, most of which are read today only by Ichiyō specialists.

Scholars are nearly unanimous in their judgment of the crucial stimuli for this new stage of literary production in Ichiyō's career, and I am not inclined to disagree with them. The first factor was her move from the Hongō district of Tokyo to the plebeian area on the eastern flatlands of the capital, the *shitamachi*, or "low city." With financial worries pressing in on all sides, Ichiyō, her mother Taki, and sister Kuniko (the father and one brother were already deceased) gave up trying to maintain appearances as a respectable middle-class family and moved in the summer of 1893 to an area called Ryūsenji in present-day Taitō Ward, where they lived in tenement housing and operated a sundries shop from the front of their new home. This area of Tokyo was worlds apart from those in which the family had previously lived. Ryūsenji was in the shadow of the venerable Yoshiwara, the premier licensed prostitution district in the city, and every manner of business and tradesperson congregated in its vicinity to serve its economic and material needs. By living and working in such an area, Ichiyō was exposed to people from all walks of life, thus providing her with raw materials for "the unforgettable fourteen months." In the spring of 1894, after having lived in Ryūsenji for nine months, but having so little success with their shop that they were teetering on the edge of insolvency, the Higuchi women returned to Hongō, this time to an area called Maruyama-Fukuyama, and Ichiyō, relieved of the burden of shop-related chores and errands, at last regained both the time to write and a critical distance from the sights and sounds of Ryūsenji.

However, she still needed exposure to writing that depicted the kind of people she had encountered in the plebeian district; her heroines up until then had been, with a few exceptions, women of vaguely "aristocratic" background, if only in attitude and demeanor. She also needed to develop narrative strategies suitable to combining her desire to commune with her literary ancestors and her newfound interest in society's outcasts. The other crucial stimulus on Ichiyō's development as a writer, then, was her encounter with the early-modern author Ihara Saikaku (1642–1693), a man who died two centuries before Ichiyō began publishing her first stories.

Although Saikaku is now considered one of the masters of prose fiction in Japan, in the first half of the Meiji period he had been largely forgotten, overshadowed by writers from a later age such as Jippensha Ikku, Takizawa Bakin, Ryūtei Tanehiko, and Tamenaga Shunsui, each of whom was still immensely popular with all manner of readers well into the Meiji period. However, spurred on by the antiquarian Awashima Kangetsu, a Saikaku boom of sorts began in the early 1890s, reaching a zenith in the summer of 1894 with the appearance of Saikaku's complete works (*Saikaku zenshū*) in two volumes in the publisher Hakubunkan's *Teikoku bunko* (Imperial Library) series.[2] *Saikaku zenshū* was edited by Ken'yūsha members Ozaki Kōyō, arguably the leading literary figure of the 1890s, and Ōhashi Otowa, who had actually married into Hakubunkan and was in charge of the entire *Teikoku bunko* project, as well as several of the publisher's house journals. Many writers of the day, Kōyō included, had fallen under the spell of Awashima's enthusiasm for Saikaku and were emulating the Genroku iconoclast in some of their own fiction. Initially the publication of the complete works was met with a ban from the authorities (presumably the erotic content of Saikaku's *kōshokubon* [the "amorous books"] was still potent after 200 years), and it took some effort for the two volumes to see the light of day. Eventually they did find their way into print in May and June of 1894. It has long been known that Ichiyō was reading Saikaku for the first time just before she started "Ōtsugomori."[3]

Ichiyō's encounter with the seventeenth-century chronicler of the fiscal practices and erotic escapades of early-modern Japanese townsfolk presented her with a new vision of what fiction writing could be, for here was an author who was demonstrably familiar with the Japanese classics through his training in poetry, yet who could convincingly portray the lives of people from every social stratum, from lofty samurai to lowly actors. Indeed, scholars attribute enormous significance to Ichiyō's fateful encounter with Saikaku. Robert Danly, Ichiyō's English-language biographer, calls the seventeenth-century writer Ichiyō's "true mentor."[4] Maeda Ai sees Saikaku as the main inspiration driving Ichiyō toward polyphony in her fiction.[5] Kamei Hideo, while acknowledging the complexity and richness of Ichiyō's mature style, also sees its roots in the prose of the early-modern master.[6]

It is not my goal here to debate these various scholarly views point by point; I only wish to show the importance attached to Saikaku in discussions of Ichiyō's later fiction.[7] I do this because in this chapter and in those that follow I intend to de-emphasize to some extent the relationship between Ichiyō's fiction and Saikaku's works so that I can demonstrate a much richer connection between her stories and the classical literary tradition. In contrast to the conventional pieties of source hunting, I draw connections between Ichiyō's acts of literary memory and social transformations in her own time.

Literary memory is the reactivation of language, tropes, or narrative paradigms from the past. Memory is different from influence in that it emphasizes the appropriation and creative negotiation with antecedent texts more than the impact of the precursor literary figure on the latecomer. The concept of memory has recently been taken up by Miryam Sas in her study of the Japanese Surrealist poets. She draws on a tradition, with roots in Freudian psychoanalysis and Walter Benjamin's studies of Baudelaire, of treating memory as shock or trauma.[8] As illuminating as this is in her study, I do not ground this book in that context; literary memory in Ichiyō's writings requires a rather different understanding: it is the result not of shock, but of the more prosaic process of reading and rereading, of memorization and repeated citation during bouts of poetic composition.

Ichiyō's supremely polished classical-language sentences, which effortlessly and spontaneously appropriate past literary forms and diction, link her fiction to a corpus of anterior texts in Japanese literature. Sometimes the gesture is toward a specific work that can be identified, while at other times it is toward a more broadly conceived literary discourse in one genre or another. Traditional ideas of allusion stop here; critics have been content to identify the works toward which any given text gestures and to duly record them. Those working within this paradigm did not pursue the issue further because the worlds of literature and society were rarely brought together in such a way that the question of the social significance of literary memory could be fruitfully posed. However, if we consider that borrowing also implies a transformation and repetition a difference, we can pry open a space for situating the act of literary memory in a social field, for we must inevitably inquire about the impetus for the act of rewriting. In the case of Ichiyō, I view the acts of literary memory as being anchored in the social world rather than as acts internal to some entirely self-contained literary sphere.

The stakes of this approach are higher than they might at first appear to be and certainly go well beyond the study of a single author. As I argued in the introductory chapter, to re-conceive literary memory in modernity offers the possibility of producing a revised reading of Ichiyō's oeuvre; but it also offers the possibility of rewriting our literary histories of the Meiji era and interrogating a critical discourse that can only conceive of the time before 1868 as the spectral Other of modernity and that can only imagine gestures toward the classical canon as nostalgia.

To be sure, Ichiyō had something of a worshipful attitude toward her literary forebears, but literary memory is not just an academic exercise in allusion; rather, I show that memory implies both repetition and transformation and can occur as part of an engagement with modernity. We can then make the claim that Ichiyō's allusive fiction participates in its own way in the process of remaking the *shōsetsu* into a form of social and cultural analysis and that Ichiyō could occupy the inevitable, gendered role of antiquarian yet still say something about the wrenching transformations of the age and the people cast aside during the relentless march forward.

The concept of literary memory can be developed along these lines by drawing on Mikhail Bakhtin. Through the concept of dialogism, Bakhtin was able to posit the linguistic space of fiction as a plane of interacting discourses. The distinctiveness of the novel lies in its linguistic diversity and its astonishing capacity to incorporate surrounding discourses, genres, and tropes: "Diversity of voices and heteroglossia enter the novel and organize themselves within it into a structured artistic system." Bakhtin goes on to emphasize the intentional hybridity — the presence of heterogeneous discourses and the illumination of one language by means of another — of dialogic fiction:

Every novel, taken as the totality of all the languages and consciousnesses of language embodied in it, is a *hybrid*. But we emphasize once again: it is an intentional and conscious hybrid, one artistically organized, and not an opaque mechanistic mixture of languages (more precisely, a mixture of the brute elements of language). *The artistic image of a language* — such is the aim that novelistic hybridization sets for itself.[9]

Bakhtin's paradigm de-emphasizes fiction as narrative to some extent, and one of my goals is to correct this oversight and demonstrate that a dialogically conceived literary memory is fundamentally connected to the unfolding of a story's plot and the development of its themes. On the other hand, Bakhtin's model has the singular advantage of allowing the critic to situate the text in a field of competing discourses, precisely what we need in order to grasp the *shōsetsu* as a socially engaged form in the Meiji era, one that incisively analyzes Japanese modernity.

Approaching Ichiyō's fiction with an awareness of the historically specific, highly charged discourses of an emergent nation-state and a capitalist system in the process of inventing themselves allows us to glimpse how her oeuvre is crisscrossed with the traces of modernity. In this I follow and build on the work of the current generation of Ichiyō scholars, who have consistently pointed to the modern themes in Ichiyō's fiction, even if they have accomplished this by failing to consider her gestures toward past literature. If we view literary memory as the appropriation and transformation of earlier texts, we can profitably view the plane of expression in Ichiyō's fiction as staging the interaction of past and present in such a way that prior modes of literary discourse function as a kind of commentary or critique of the discourses put into circulation by the Meiji-era project of modernization. It is important to underscore that a concept such as "the literary past" is by no means unproblematic: hybridization implies that the past is not on quite an equal footing with the present, for it is always rewritten with the concerns of the here and now in mind.

One major ambiguity in Bakhtin is especially relevant to my reading of Ichiyō's fiction, and this concerns the status of the author or authorial voice. One of the unavoidable conclusions about language is that it is communal. While we may shape language to some extent with our individual use of it, it shapes us much more; to a great extent, it makes us. At times Bakhtin seems to treat language as an entity that has its own subjectivity and that speaks through us, radically undermining the notion of the author as transcendental subject. Indeed, in places Bakhtin seems to imply that a true dialogic novel possesses no organizing center, being merely a collection of competing voices. At other times, as in the above quotation, Bakhtin pulls back from this position and emphasizes an author who organizes for artistic effect the voices that enter the novel. If we wish to read the Meiji *shōsetsu* as an instrument of social critique, we need a tolerably strong and willful subject capable of taking positions, and thus I prefer the latter formulation of dialogism. Such a conception of the author also prevents us from reducing literary memory to mere imitation and instead allows us to view it as the starting point for an author's exploration of new terrain.

My reading of Ichiyō's oeuvre suggests that the author, while certainly not a controlling center in the sense of being the transcendental subject so feared by some theoretical schools, is a presence who cannot be easily dismissed. Nor should we wish to, for to erase the authorial persona of a woman writer is to contribute to the age-old marginalization of women's writing. Given the dense history of most literary tropes available to Ichiyō, we must acknowledge some limitation on her ability to improvise and renovate, but we should not swerve to the other extreme and view the history that clings to past tropes and figures as being so sedimented as to be unmalleable. In this chapter, I isolate precursor texts as disparate as the writings of Ihara Saikaku, the Sukeroku figure from the kabuki tradition, and the poetic discourse on dreams. Each of these elements has been modified across time to a greater or lesser degree, and Ichiyō inherited past literary discourse in all of its richness and complexity. However, I also show that Ichiyō's acts of literary memory partially detach each trope from its prior contexts, even as they necessarily preserve aspects of traditional figures, and systematically orient these borrowings around the concerns of family and economic hierarchy, thus revising the tropes in the process and adding another layer of meaning. This dynamic of revision and renewal is connected to the changing economic relationship between servants and their mistresses in Meiji Japan, as we shall see.

I should emphasize that none of my remarks about dialogism or past scholarship are meant to suggest that we should dismiss the importance of Saikaku to Ichiyō's textual practice, only that we can view the relationship between Saikaku and Ichiyō in a new light. It has long been argued that the title of Ichiyō's story, "Ōtsugomori" (On the Last Day of the Year), alludes to Ihara Saikaku's *Seken mune zan'yō* (Worldly Reckonings), which carries the subtitle "The Last Day of the Year, a Day Worth a Thousand Coins of Gold" (*Ōtsugomori wa ichi-nichi sen-kin*).[10] However, the idea of allusion fails to adequately capture the nature of Ichiyō's appropriation of and creative negotiation with Saikaku's text or the function memory serves. *Seken mune zan'yō*, first published in 1692, is a collection of stories and anecdotes, sometimes supported by only the barest narrative framework, loosely connected by the fact that everything in the book occurs during the final few days of the year, when all outstanding debts were to be repaid.

Taken as a whole, *Seken mune zan'yō* is a great drama of rich and poor on a busy day that is simultaneously festive (it heralds the arrival of spring in the traditional lunar calendar) and tense (it is the biggest day of financial reckoning in the year), and the busiest people of all are the moneylender and his agents. In the stories collected in *Seken*, we are introduced to moneylenders trying desperately to recover the money due to them from loans, cash-strapped debtors inventing ingenious plans for deceiving the moneylenders, and still other moneylenders too smart and experienced to be deceived. We are witness both to innumerable schemes for getting rich quick — some brilliant but most flawed — and to the great variety of festivals and customs for celebrating the coming of spring.

But perhaps more vivid than all of these are the stories of desperate people at the pawnshops trying to secure enough money from the meager possessions they have remaining to repay the loans they took out to see them through the trying times of the year. Money, the coin itself, becomes the central unifying symbol in the text. In the story called "Koban wa nesugata no yume" (Dreams of Gold Coins), for example, we hear that the greatest hope among the poor is stumbling across money by the side of the road. We are then introduced to a woman who awakens on the last day of the year to find a heap of gold coins in her home, but alas, this was nothing but a dream; she awakens for real to find nothing but the same haunting debts.[11]

Seken does not shy away from the issues of class it raises either, for the text acknowledges that the end of the year is really only festive for the rich, and that the anxiety associated with the day tends to be lopsided, falling largely on the shoulders of the poor. Nonetheless, *Seken* is not a gloomy work. The beginning tells us that the last day of the year is dark, but once it is past everyone is witness to a bright spring.[12] Throughout its pages *Seken* is punctuated by staccatos of irony and humor, and we sense our narrator standing high above the hustle and bustle, looking down on the great drama and showing us the comic nature, and maybe even the absurdity, of the whole business.

Although it is certainly a more unified work than vintage Saikaku, "Ōtsugomori" could find a comfortable niche in *Seken mune zan'yō*. In Ichiyō's story, we are introduced to the wealthy Yamamura family, who lend money and rent property, and to their maid, the protagonist Omine, whose own family is struggling to make ends meet because Omine's uncle Yasubei has been forced to give up his green-grocery due to a protracted illness. The fallen merchant family cannot make ends meet, so they have been forced to take out a loan, and this loan has to be paid back before the New Year unless they can come up with the money for an extension, one yen and fifty sen. Even this relatively small amount is beyond the family's means, so Yasubei makes a request of Omine: could she ask the Yamamuras for an advance on her wages, a couple of yen to see them through the year? Omine agrees, saying she will have the money ready for her brother Sannosuke to pick up by noon on the last day of the year. On that day, Omine, having received only a vague reply when she inquired about the possibility of an advance before, presses her mistress once again, but this time is flatly refused. Desperate and with no more options, she steals two yen from a packet of money in a writing desk. Later in the day, Omine is worrying: she is certain that she will be caught and terrified that blame will fall on her uncle, so she resolves to confess her crime. However, it turns out that the Yamamuras' profligate son, Ishinosuke, took the stack of money with the missing two yen, leaving only a note stating that he has "borrowed" it. No one will know that Omine ever took the money. Omine is saved, and she is not hesitant about concluding that Ishinosuke is her benefactor. The narrator, however, refuses to say if Omine is right or wrong, merely stating teasingly at the end of the story, "would that we could know what happened next" (152).

Like the majority of stories in Seken mune zan'yō, Ichiyō configures the drama of "Ōtsugomori" around the dichotomy between rich and poor, the Yamamura family and Omine's family; and the climax unfolds on the last day of the year, the time when the chasm between the haves and the have-nots surfaces with stark clarity. "Ōtsugomori" reveals the same truth about the end of the year as does Saikaku's text: far from being a time of celebration, poverty and debt make ōmisoka a time of tremendous anxiety for those without means; the only people who can afford to be festive on this day are those who are free from concerns about money because they have it in abundance. In the most telling example of this, when Omine sees firsthand the shabby circumstances in which her family has been forced to live since her uncle took to his sick-bed, a tear comes to her eye as she recalls that the Yamamura family is on an outing to the kabuki theater that day (142).

In addition, Ichiyō implicitly critiques Saikaku in that her story gestures toward an uncertain future, which the narrator hints will not be quite as bright as the Seken narrator has led us to believe of the New Year: while the problem of the interest on Yasubei's debt is momentarily resolved—thereby allowing the family to keep going for a few more months and perhaps even to enjoy a modest New Year celebration—the problem of the debt itself is far from being solved.[13]

Ichiyō's literary debt is extensive, for she rather directly appropriates certain tropes and thematic concerns from Saikaku. At the same time, she transforms her borrowed material in order to meet her own narrative requirements. The two texts share a concern with debt and the fiscal world to be sure, but we can glimpse in the recesses of Ichiyō's story a confrontation with the ethical and economic issue of commodification, which is specific to modernity and which would therefore have been alien to the likes of Saikaku. Commodification becomes the center around which all of the acts of literary memory will turn.

ii

Beginning around 1880, and continuing for the next 20 years or so, there was a radical transformation of master-servant and mistress-servant relations in the major urban areas of Japan. A relationship that had once been seen as quasi-familial — and thus intentionally misrecognized as being non-economic — came to be seen after about 1900 as blatantly economic: a domestic servant who lived and worked in her master and mistress's home received a wage in exchange for her labor. This transformation — what we can call the commodification of master-servant relations — accompanied the penetration of capitalism into the urban centers of Japan. Before the 1880s, service in a household was quite common for women of good family, which would not be the case in a later age. Before the transformation, the daughters of the well-to-do were frequently sent to live and work in a distinguished and wealthy household, for it was seen as an opportunity for them to absorb the etiquette and cultural niceties that were crucial for married life in the upper strata of society. In fact, women typically served in a household only until they reached marriageable age, and the master and mistress were usually instrumental in the matchmaking. Since the master-servant relationship was seen as quasi-familial, the servant had all of her material needs filled as did anyone else in the household; pocket money might be doled out, but there was no question of wages in the sense of selling labor for money. This is not to say that there were no economic interests involved; the cultural accoutrements of civilized life that could be attained by serving in a good family had economic and class implications on the marriage market. Also, the household itself gained by using the labor of these people as servants, and those servants had their immediate material needs met by their master. However, the economic aspect of the relationship was disguised by the patina of the acquisition of cultural refinement and polite graces. This form of service was still held as an elusive ideal well into the Taishō period (1912–1926), but it was clear by about 1900 or so that wages were a ubiquitous, indeed increasingly an expected, part of service in a household, and thus the economic aspect of the master-servant relationship became bluntly apparent to all concerned.

A major factor behind the transformation of master-servant relations in the Meiji period was the rise of a middle class beginning in the final decade of the nineteenth century. With its emergence came an increase in the number of people wishing to employ servants—doctors, university professors, high-level bureaucrats, wealthy businessmen—and we see the blossoming of a full-fledged labor market for *jochū* (maids), the new word for female domestic servants, who had been called *gejo* or *hashita* before. Given that service in a household was one of the few kinds of work available to women in the Meiji period, the rise in demand for domestic help meant that there were increasing opportunities for women from poor families in all parts of the country to find work in the cities, and they began to displace women from well-to-do families. With the appearance of a labor market, it became increasingly common for maids to change jobs (sometimes frequently) in the hopes of improving their lot.[14] Between the 1880s and the early 1900s—the time when "Ōtsugomori" was written—these two systems coexisted in a state of extreme tension; old-fashioned service of the quasi-familial kind was still valorized, but the existence of a blatant economic relationship symbolized by the wage could no longer be denied.

The infrastructural elements that accompanied the commodification of master-servant relations are evident in the first pages of "Ōtsugomori." Omine found her position with the Yamamura house through the good offices of a woman at the *ukeyado* (in later times more commonly known as a *kuchi-ireya*), the forerunner of the employment agency (139). This woman informs Omine that the Yamamuras are "the wealthiest family in the neighborhood," adding (no doubt with a wry smile indicating a connection) that "they're also the stingiest" (139). The *ukeyado* functioned as a mediator between families seeking domestic help and women seeking positions. Its appearance signals both a new convenience for families seeking to employ domestic servants and a new mobility for women who are looking for employment, or who are looking to better their lot with a different employer. This new mobility, which scandalized those holding to the ideals of an earlier time, is fully expressed when the woman at the *ukeyado* tells Omine, "if the job gets disagreeable, just send me a note—no need for details—and I'll do my best to find you another position" (139). Details are not needed by the woman because she is already intimately familiar with the problems at the Yamamura house, problems the narrator is eager to relate to the reader: "There were many in the city who employed servants, but no house had the turnover of the Yamamuras. Two servants in a month was the normal situation, but there were some who left after four or five days, and even some who fled after only a night" (140).

The woman at the *ukeyado* is no doubt kept agreeably busy by this rather extreme rate of turnover. It indicates that at the margins of our text we have the trappings of an emergent labor market for women, at least one revolving around domestic service. However, in our story the commodification of master-servant relations is not yet complete, for though we know Omine lives and works in the Yamamura house and gets a wage, there seems to be no concept yet—as there would be in the next generation—of quantifying the labor of the servant and her wage in terms of time spent working; the servants in "Ōtsugomori" literally work all day.[15] What we glimpse in Ichiyō's text, then, is a historical transformation in the making, not a static, decorative historical backdrop, and "Ōtsugomori" is a potent bearer of social anxiety regarding this transformation.

The change in the material conditions of domestic service was naturally accompanied by discourse on it, a discourse against which "Ōtsugomori" can be fruitfully read. The story was originally published in the December 1894 issue of *Bungakukai* and appeared again as a reprint in February 1896 in *Taiyō*. A remarkable cultural document called *Kijo no shiori* (Handbook for Ladies) was published in 1895 between the appearances of these two versions of our text. I hasten to add that there is no evidence that Ichiyō was familiar with *Kijo no shiori*. Nor do I wish to imply that there were changes in the two versions of "Ōtsugomori" that would indicate a direct engagement with the ideas in *Kijo*; there are no significant content changes in the two versions of Ichiyō's text.[16] However, Ichiyō's knowledge of *Kijo* is not the issue here. Both texts are bound up in the same discourse on mistress-servant relations, and to a remarkable degree they even share the same language.

Maeda Ai made *Kijo no shiori* known to scholars in his outstanding essay on "Ōtsugomori," and others have used it after him, for it is a text that exemplifies one powerful discourse on women and female ideals in mid-Meiji.[17] In my opinion, *Kijo* remains a valuable document against which to juxtapose "Ōtsugomori," but here I want to utilize *Kijo* differently from the way in which it has been put to use in the past. Maeda implicitly treats *Kijo* as a unified, homogeneous text, one that articulates a single, overarching vision about women. I want to read *Kijo* as a heterogeneous site of discursive conflict by deploying a Bakhtinian concern with the dialogic nature of utterances so that I can highlight the issue of wages, a problem that is invisible in Maeda's approach. *Kijo no shiori* can be read as a heterogeneous site in which the two systems of logic concerning mistress-servant relations I outlined above—the quasi-familial relationship and the wage-based economic relationship—forcefully collide, producing within the pages of the section of *Kijo* dealing with servants the same tension that existed in real relations between servants and their mistresses. Once the language and stakes of this conflict are understood, this same collision of systems can be teased out of Ichiyō's text.

Kijo no shiori was compiled by Kuniwake Misako, a woman who became an instructor at the Tokyo Women's School, and appeared in December 1895 in two weighty volumes. It is a massive and ambitious compilation, both a household manual and a conduct book aimed at upper-class and upper-middle-class women, organized around nearly every conceivable topic, from etiquette and letter-writing, through flower-arranging and poetry composition, to domestic economy, the education of children, and even hygiene. Perhaps no other text in that decade so relentlessly and graphically situates women within the contours of nation, marriage, and home. The first volume opens with a series of maps of decreasing scale: a map of the world; a map of Japan (including the recently acquired colony of Taiwan); and maps of the metropolitan centers of Tokyo, Kyoto, and Osaka; an illustration of cultured, well-to-do women at a marriage ceremony comes after these. These graphics are accompanied by poems from the Empress, the "Imperial Rescript on Education" (*Kyōiku chokugo*), and a preface asserting that the overall task of *Kijo no shiori* is to help create educated and cultured women for the benefit of the nation.[18] In addition, illustrations of specific points of etiquette made in the text appear throughout the two volumes.

The section on mistress-servant relations is part of the chapter dealing with wifely duties toward other family members, and it is instructive that servants find their place in the same textual space as parents, husbands, husband's siblings, children, stepparents, and stepchildren. This places *Kijo* squarely in the logic of the great household of early modern times, in which everyone under the same roof is accorded either familial or quasi-familial recognition. This is not the logic of the bourgeois nuclear family, which was coming into its own in mid-Meiji, though the bourgeois woman would no doubt find herself nodding in agreement over many of the passages in *Kijo*.

There are three sections in the chapter dealing with mistress-servant relations: a prefatory section called "On Service" (*Miyazukae no koto*); a section addressed largely to servants themselves called "Rules toward One's Mistress" (*Shujin ni taisuru kokoro-e*); and finally, a section called "Rules for Those Employing Servants" (*Hōkōnin o tsukau kokoro-e*). The inclusion of the word *kokoro-e* (rules, expectations, attitudes) in nearly every section of the chapter, whether the referent is one's servant, husband, or stepson, is important, for the text argues that there should be a proper atmosphere of harmony among different family members in the sprawling household, and it is the responsibility of the mistress of the home to see to this: "We must conclude that seeing that the day passes well in a home—with good will toward all and no stirring of wind and waves—is the fulfillment of wifely duties."[19]

The prefatory section "On Service" is quite brief, and I quote about half of it in order to illustrate the lofty tone employed in the text:

After a woman has finished the regular course of education, it is desirable for her, regardless of wealth or position, to serve for a time in another household. This will allow a more rounded education and give her the opportunity to absorb elevated customs. . . . If one does not learn the feminine arts such as playing the *koto*, composing verse, and flower-arranging through such service, then one will inevitably be seen as being behind others. Thus, it is best to set one's heart on this path. We have laid out the principles of service in the passages that follow.[20]

This is an expression of the author's ideal, of course, and here base concerns like wages never sully the pristine, aristocratic view of service as the completion of a woman's education. However, since wages were becoming common by the time *Kijo* was published, even in the wealthier households that constitute the text's main audience, the author is not free to ignore the situation altogether. Under the pressure of situating wages within the quasi-familial ideal of service, and thereby welding together two antithetical discourses, the text reveals fissures and cracks. In fact, while the prefatory section pointedly ignores wages, the two sections that follow are so obsessed with the phenomenon that it forms the very terms of the argument.

The section addressed to servants (it is explicitly addressed to female servants) opens by underplaying the importance of wages: "A woman's service in another household," insists the author, "is not solely for the purpose of obtaining a wage."[21] She admits that people enter service for a variety of reasons—some women do indeed become servants to obtain a wage, and some even become servants so as not to be a bother at home, while others enter service with loftier motives such as a desire to observe the daily rituals of a good household—but she insists that it is a mistake to elevate money above all else. The most important thing is that servants perform their tasks with diligence. And just in case some readers require more self-interested reasons, the author admonishes that a woman who does not effectively perform her duties as a servant will "encounter difficulties obtaining a standing in the world later in life"—a barely concealed threat that she will have trouble finding a husband without the support of her mistress.[22] Thus, the author advises that women should "be aware that performing one's duties diligently is also for one's own benefit," and in order to be even more helpful, the author offers five qualities necessary for all servants: honesty ("*Dai-ichi wa nanigoto ni yorazu shōjiki o mune to suru koto*"), stoicism ("*Dai-ni wa ukoto o shinbō suru koto*"), diligence ("*Dai-san wa kage hinata naku tachihataraku koto*"), enthusiasm ("*Dai-yon wa kiten o kikaseru koto*"), and cleanliness ("*Dai-go wa mi no mawari o seiketsu ni suru koto*").[23]

The very language used to describe the ideal servant in a passage like this matches that used to describe Omine to a remarkable degree, powerfully illustrating the common discursive space of the two texts.[24] Omine places great value on honesty (*shōjiki*). She endures harsh treatment at the hands of her mistress, thereby gaining a positive reputation for being stoic (*shinbō-mono*), and she does not burden her family with complaints of mistreatment at the hands of Mrs. Yamamura. After the initial days of uncertainty at the Yamamura house during which she makes some mistakes, Omine resolves to make every effort to be diligent in her tasks rather than take the advice of the woman at the employment agency and look for a position at another household. From the perspective of *Kijo no shiori*—especially the recalcitrant side of the text that stoically holds to traditional ideals of service in the face of the coming of the wage system—Omine would certainly be considered the perfect find for any household.

The next section of *Kijo* is addressed to the mistress of the household. It opens with an exhortation that a mistress should treat her servant "as if she were her own child," but apart from this, the admonishing, idealistic tone so evident in the previous section quickly gives way to pure pragmatism: the implicit question is, how should the mistress of the home go about handling her servants in a world in which those servants move from house to house in search of better conditions or a higher wage? The solution proposed by *Kijo* is that mistresses should tread carefully. Certainly if the servant commits some crime like theft she should be summarily dismissed. However, if the servant merely makes a mistake or breaks something, she should not be berated, but calmly and warmly instructed to exercise more care in the future. If the mistress constantly yells at her servants, they will begin to ignore her, or worse yet, they will go to another household. From an outsider's perspective, it reflects badly on the family to have servants constantly coming and going, and it is certainly inconvenient for the mistress of the house as well. At the end of the section, the author concludes that "servants who have been with the house for a long time are occasionally not so diligent, but it is more convenient to permit these little lapses and continue to retain the servant. Furthermore, the home will have a good reputation."[25]

Needless to say, Mrs. Yamamura is the exact opposite of the kind of ideal mistress portrayed in this and in the prefatory section of *Kijo no shiori*. She is not at all involved in the "education" of her servants, and this, perhaps more than anything else, underscores the lofty provenance of *Kijo*, for in wealthier circles aesthetic cultivation is held up as that which distinguishes good families from those oriented solely around the pursuit of financial well being. The Yamamuras are a merchant family, whose members are very much focused on income and expenditures. Mrs. Yamamura does not teach Omine *koto* playing, poetic composition, or flower-arranging, which we should assume are not part of her life, since such pursuits demand at least some time apart from counting money and badgering the domestic help. Because she is a harsh taskmaster who constantly berates her servants, she cannot retain them for very long ("There are many in the city who employ servants, but no house has the turnover of the Yamamuras"). When Omine slips on the ice getting water from the well one morning and loses one of the buckets, Mrs. Yamamura "acted as though the fortunes of the house had been put in jeopardy. The bulging purple vein in her temple was terrifying. During breakfast she glared at Omine, never saying a word to her." The next day "every time Omine lifted her chopsticks, her mistress lectured her, saying, 'We didn't get the things in this house for free you know. If you treat them carelessly, you'll be punished'" (140).

But perhaps more damning from the perspective of that voice in *Kijo no shiori* that holds resolutely to traditional service is the fact that Mrs. Yamamura treats Omine as a wage slave instead of "as if she were her own child." Mrs. Yamamura pays her servants a wage and demands a full day's work from them. She does not tolerate her servants stealing a few moments of warmth by the brazier in the deep of winter (139); nor can Omine pay a stealthy visit to her ailing uncle after being sent on an errand, for her mistress knows exactly how long it takes to do any task and will be counting the time until Omine gets back (140–41). For Mrs. Yamamura, the labor of the servant is not yet something measured with precision, but it has nonetheless become something bought and sold, something that has value in relation to other commodities through the mediating power of money.

If Mrs. Yamamura is a poor mistress from the standards set in *Kijo*, she is, nonetheless, a good manager of the home from a middle-class merchant's perspective, for not a single *zeni* of household income or expenditure escapes her attention. Had she been a character in Saikaku's *Nippon eitaigura* or *Seken mune zan'yō*, she would no doubt have attracted an admiring comment from the narrators, both of whom valorize hard work and savings and admonish against frivolous spending. The Yamamuras, too, operate by a similar logic of frugality, which, taken to extremes in Mrs. Yamamura, becomes mere miserliness. It is miserliness for a purpose, however. For a family like the Yamamuras, the point of saving every bit of money is to ensure the survival and healthy continuity of the family; money is earned, saved, and then passed down to one's heirs, a process repeated in every generation. Ultimately this is not so different from familial discourse in *Kijo no shiori*; it is just that the *Kijo* author would consider it vulgar to be so blunt about it. What is different, however, is that in the case of a middle class household like the Yamamuras the notion of "family" has been constricted to take in only what we would today call the nuclear family, and those falling outside the purview of this new familial circle—domestic servants, for example—are treated simply as wage labor.

Omine and her family are represented as operating by a different social logic: it turns out to be the logic espoused in *Kijo no shiori*, and this despite the fact that the massive handbook is not aimed at all at fallen merchant families. When Yasubei asks Omine to secure two yen from the Yamamuras and Omine agrees, they have every reason to believe their modest request will be met. Omine may have some personal doubts about the generosity of her mistress, but since she has worked for them diligently for nearly one year she has secured the privilege of being treated more favorably than a stranger would be (145). In fact, given that so many people still clung to the quasi-familial ideal of service at the time, Omine has the weight of tradition on her side, despite the fact that Omine comes from a vastly different class from the women who traditionally became servants. In a crisis, it is crucial to Omine's family that this time-honored practice function properly.

With Yasubei's illness, Omine's family faces such a crisis. However, Omine's request puts into open conflict the two discourses on mistress-servant relations, discourses that already coexisted in a state of tension in the mid-Meiji period, as is evident in the discursive strains in *Kijo no shiori*. The two discourses on master-servant relations also coexist in

Ichiyō's text, but, whether through a conscious act of the author or not, those discourses have been neatly distributed to the two families. Omine's family is represented as operating by an older quasi-familial logic of relations, while the Yamamuras operate by a wage-labor logic of relations. From Omine's perspective it is perfectly appropriate (though somewhat embarrassing) to ask for another advance on her wages in a crisis. From Mrs. Yamamura's perspective, Omine is wage labor and has no business making such a request, and this attitude, which is exacerbated by her miserliness and rather mean-spirited personality, leads her to refuse her maid.

iii

Omine initially broached the subject of an advance during the ellipsis between the two parts of the story, about ten days before the last day of the year. Mrs. Yamamura gave her a vague reply, but since it was not an outright refusal, Omine still retained some hope. The second part of the story opens on the last day of the year, and Omine now needs a firm commitment from Mrs. Yamamura. She has avoided pressing her mistress in the fear that Mrs. Yamamura would refuse her request in anger over being pestered; but as she is expecting Sannosuke at noon, Omine finally gathers up her courage and asks her mistress once more for an advance. In what amounts to a refusal, Mrs. Yamamura pretends that Omine never raised the issue before and claims that there is nothing to be done now. Omine is devastated, and we are given a brief but powerful inside view:

Is it such a large sum? Just two yen—and she even agreed to it herself earlier. She can't have gone senile in only ten days! Why, there's money they don't even need in that writing desk over there. One packet must have ten or twenty yen. It's not as if I'm asking for the whole thing; with just two notes uncle would be so happy, auntie would smile, and Sannosuke could have his treats for New Year. When Omine thought of this, how desperately she wished for that money! (148)

Omine's interiority here is structured around familial relations, something that is true of all inside views in the text, and
the matter of the money takes on very concrete form as she
imagines her family's reaction should she succeed. Furthermore, the relative value of two yen depending on one's position in the economic hierarchy is brutally evident here. For the
Yamamuras, two yen is almost exactly half the price of a good
seat at the kabuki theater—the price of an afternoon of relaxation and pleasure.[26] For Omine's family, two yen is a vast sum,
and obtaining it a matter of life and death. Its acquisition,
however, is so difficult that it might as well be, in Saikaku's
phrase, a thousand coins of gold. After her mistress's refusal,
the problem of the money dominates Omine's thoughts, transforming the story in the second part into a mental drama, and
the burden of representing Omine's interiority will fall heavily
on poetic tropes.

When Sannosuke finally shows up to collect the two yen,
Omine is thrown into a panic; her family is relying on that
money, and Omine promised to get it. With no other options,
she decides—very much impulsively—to steal it from the
writing desk; but by doing so she falls into a state of confusion—a conflict between the need, indeed, the promise, to
help her family and a moral injunction against theft—and
the narrator represents this dilemma with the rhetoric of the
classical *waka* discourse on dreams. This poetic language clusters around Omine's decision to steal and later around her
guilt at having done so. When Omine decides to take two
notes from the packet in the writing desk, she makes sure that
no one is watching: the master and mistress are out of the
house; the daughters are playing shuttlecock outside; one
servant has not yet returned from an errand, while another is
upstairs sewing. Finally she checks on Ishinosuke and observes that he is lying by the *kotatsu* "in the midst of his
dreams" (*yume no mattadanaka*, 149). However, no sooner does
she take the money and give it to Sannosuke than the narrator
whispers to us, "it was foolish of her to think no one was looking" (149). Since Ishinosuke is the only one who could have

seen, the reader is left to conclude that he was only pretending to be "in the midst of his dreams"; in actuality he was wide awake and saw everything. The distinction between dream and reality has become destabilized. This kind of rhetoric is prominent in this segment of the story. After taking the two one-yen bills, Omine presses them into Sannosuke's hand and sends him home, all the while being "unable to distinguish dream and reality" (*yume to mo utsutsu to mo shirazu*, 149). The narrator describes Omine's feelings of guilt and confusion later that day as "treading the path of dreams" (*yumeji o tadorite*, 151).

Ichiyō is here drawing on prominent tropes in the lyrical *waka* tradition of Japanese poetry, a tradition that Ichiyō, a *waka* poet herself, knew backward and forward. I want to demonstrate how Ichiyō takes these tropes in a new direction and expands their significance, but before doing so it is important for us to review their traditional meaning in the *waka* form. We have not even begun to map out the social significance of these tropes, but their basic meaning has been relatively stable. In the poetic tradition, the world of dreams is intimately connected to love—when longing for each other, lovers were said to appear in each other's dreams—and the most common tropes are the dichotomy of dream (*yume*) and reality (*utsutsu*), and the motif of the path of dreams (*yumeji*). The former trope characterizes love as a state of delirium or confusion so severe that dream and reality become conflated. To be in love is to be unable to make distinctions, even between seemingly transparent things. The latter trope usually signified some inability to meet in real life—in order to avoid the prying eyes and gossip of court society the two lovers could only "meet" in the world of dreams; or the love a person felt was one-sided and the only way for that person to see the object of his or her desire was to tread the path of dreams to the place where his or her beloved was.

In "Ōtsugomori," Ichiyō is gesturing toward two of the major tropes of love in the poetic tradition. This is less a direct appropriation, however, than a process of revision and renewal. Ichiyō has detached the tropes associated with dreams from their anchorage in the poetic discourse on love and substituted a concern for money in its relationship to family and social class. Here "Ōtsugomori" resonates strongly with the story "Koban wa nesugata no yume" (Dreams of Gold Coins) in Saikaku's *Seken mune zan'yō*, in which the distinction between dream and reality is also collapsed. Recall that in Saikaku's story, the desire for money invades a poor woman's sleep, and she dreams that she has woken up to wealth, when, in fact, that waking was merely part of the dream. The narrator of "Ōtsugomori" stays much closer to the actual diction of poetic language than does Saikaku's narrator, yet directly transforms the sexual desire inscribed in that poetic discourse into a desire for money. Omine falls into a confused and delirious state—not because she is in love like the poetic speakers of old, but because she has transgressed moral strictures and stolen money.

Omine is facing radical ethical uncertainty; she has lost her moral footing and is now in a state of confusion, unable to distinguish dream and reality. Omine gropes her way out of this frightening world by thinking through it, a process dramatized in the unfolding of a brief mental drama:

Omine, overwhelmed by the horror of her crime, was treading the path of dreams, unsure of whether she was even herself or not. Surely the theft would not go undiscovered. As soon as they counted the money they would notice the missing amount, even if it were just one bill from among ten thousand; they would realize it corresponded to the amount Omine herself had requested, and then suspicion would certainly fall on her. If they questioned her what would she do? What could she say? Lying would only deepen her sin, but confessing would bring shame upon her uncle. Even though it was her doing, and her crime alone, suspicion would still hang on her upright uncle like wet clothes that can't be dried. "The poor always do such things," people would surely say. How wretched!

What was she to do? The only way her uncle would be protected would be if she were to suddenly die. (151)

After a brief interruption, in which Mrs. Yamamura remembers the money in the drawer of the writing desk and tells Omine to fetch it, we return to Omine's panicked thoughts:

> This was the end! She should go to the master and tell him the whole story from the beginning. She would tell him of her mistress's heartlessness. There was nothing else she could have done. Yes, honesty would be her protection. She would confess: she wouldn't flee or try to hide her crime. She didn't steal the money for her own gain though, and she would make sure they knew that her uncle had no part in it. If they didn't believe her, she would bite her tongue and bleed to death! Then they would know she wasn't lying. (152)

Taken together, these inside views begin with Omine in a state of moral confusion and end with a resolve to do the honest thing and confess her crime. It begins with Omine "treading the path of dreams" (*yumeji o tadorite*) and ends with the resolve after waking up, so to speak, that "honesty would be her protection" (*shōjiki wa waga mi no mamori*).

Honesty is one of the central values expounded by the characters in the text, so it is worth taking a moment to unpack it. In *Kijo no shiori*, honesty is touted as the most important trait in a servant, and, as we have seen, Omine is an exemplar of this quality. For Omine it means more than simply not lying; it means forthright behavior in general. Omine's uncle Yasubei also operates by this logic—he is called "honest Yasubei" after all—and since he is a merchant, honesty contributes to his customers' trust in him. The Yamamuras also operate by the logic of honesty—Mr. Yamamura, in a futile attempt to reform Ishinosuke's ways, asserts that the family has always operated honestly—and for them, too, the quality is implicated in a whole series of socioeconomic relations. Honesty is also intimately connected to the valorization of savings and the accumulation of wealth, as well as to the disdain for frivolous spending. This attitude is tied to the fortunes of the Yamamura family as a lineage: frivolous spending endangers the family line and is thus incompatible with honesty.

When Omine moves from the moral confusion represented with the poetic discourse on dreams to a resolve to be honest and to confess her crime, she has re-interiorized and recommitted to the central value of master-servant relations that we saw in *Kijo no shiori* and to the central tenet by which the other characters in the text operate.[27] She has, in effect, been recouped into the moral order of society—or so we think. In actuality, Omine never has to confess, for when she fetches the portable writing desk and Mrs. Yamamura opens the drawer, instead of the packet of yen there is a note from Ishinosuke saying he has "borrowed" the money. He has carried the whole thing off as a loan, and the formal note is ironic; after all, he is the Yamamura heir, so the money will eventually be his anyway. He has saved Omine from the potentially devastating consequences of taking the two yen, thereby undermining the possibility of a tidy and reassuring sense of moral closure at the end of the story. Had Ishinosuke not rescued Omine, our narrative would have been very different. Having transgressed moral strictures, Omine would then have been punished in some way, moving us in the direction of the kind of narrative closure expected of the plot line of *kanzen chōaku* (encourage virtue, chastise vice), a kind of didactic fiction that still had a good deal of currency in the 1890s. Omine recommits to honesty, but she will never be punished for her temporary lapse because of Ishinosuke's intervention. Ishinosuke's actions have wrenched the narrative into an altogether different domain: that of folklore.

iv

The ethnographer Yanagita Kunio (1875–1962) collected and wrote down a number of tales from the folklore tradition in Japan, what are called *mukashibanashi*. One of the tales—a little yarn called "Ōtoshi no kyaku" (A Guest at New Year)—is of particular interest to us.[28] Unable to find work at the end of the year, a poor packhorse driver decides to head home and welcome the New Year with his wife. On his way back he comes across a beggar by the side of the road. The packhorse driver, taking pity on a man in a plight worse than his own, takes the beggar home and puts him up for the night. The driver and his wife do their best for their guest: they place a straw mat on the dirt floor and lay the beggar down on it, then light a fire to at least give him some warmth. The couple then goes to sleep. Both the night and the old year pass, and the couple wakes up the next morning and goes in to check on the guest. The driver reaches out to the straw mat now covering the beggar completely so as to wake him. He feels something cold underneath. He pulls aside the mat to uncover not the man they had put up for the night, but a large lump of gold.[29]

The beggar here is clearly nothing of the sort; he is some kind of magical figure who rewards the poor couple with material riches for their compassion. The fact that the story takes place during a transitional time is important, for the conjunction of poverty at the end of the old year and unexpected wealth in the new is especially salutary. "Ōtoshi no kyaku" is an undatable tale orally transmitted down through the centuries, and thus, as is to be expected, it exists in dozens of variations. The version Yanagita recorded represents a distillation of the common elements shared by the majority of variants.[30] Namely, a poor couple puts up an even poorer person on the last day of the old year, and when they wake up on the first day of the New Year they find gold. Sometimes the poor man — who is, of course, not always a packhorse driver — will find a beggar by the road and take him home, and sometimes the beggar will come knocking on the door of the poor man's home asking for food. Sometimes he is not a beggar, but a mendicant Buddhist priest who comes asking for lodging for the night. Sometimes the couple wakes in the morning to find the priest dead, and when they dig a hole in which to bury him they find gold.

However, as far as many of the versions are concerned, the variant Yanagita recorded gives only half the story. It tells of the reward for the poor, but does not recount the corollary story of the punishment of the rich. In many versions, the magical being disguised as a beggar or a mendicant priest first visits a rich family asking for food and lodging, only to be rebuffed. After this the being visits the poor family, and the story proceeds much as it does in Yanagita's version. When the rich man hears of the happy fortune that has visited the poor family, he makes the connection between their newfound wealth and the stranger. The next year the rich man pounces on the first stranger he finds wandering down the street and rather unceremoniously forces him to spend the night with his family and enjoy their hospitality. The rich man awakes the next morning with great expectations; he finds not gold (we knew he was not going to be rewarded after all), but, depending on the variant, feces, tile shards, or even a rotting corpse. In most versions, the rich man even becomes poor because of his insensitivity.

Yanagita's version aside, the stark dichotomy between rich and poor, crassness and compassion, that characterizes so many variants of the folk tale can be found in Ichiyō's story as the dichotomy between the Yamamura family and Omine's family. The fact that the drama of this dichotomy plays itself out during *ōmisoka* is also crucial to both texts. However, I want to suggest that "Ōtoshi no kyaku" is no mere shadow story in the background of "Ōtsugomori"; there is a much closer relationship between the two texts, which becomes apparent when we examine the actions of the Yamamura heir. In the figure of Ishinosuke, we see that Ichiyō is gesturing toward the folkloric character of the stranger who appears during *ōmisoka* to reward and punish, producing riches for the poor and poverty for the rich, or at least a gain and loss of two yen.

At first Ishinosuke may seem an unlikely character to fill the role of the magical figure in "Ōtoshi no kyaku." He is violent, boorish, lazy, and rude, to mention a few of his lesser sins, though an acerbic wit makes up for some of this. He is contemptuous of his parents. His haunts are the drinking establishments and brothels of the licensed quarters. He is extravagant with his family's money, and is even characterized as a threat to the Yamamura fortune because of it (Mrs. Yamamura memorably remarks that having Ishinosuke as heir to the Yamamura riches is like "lighting a fire in an oil storehouse" [146]). The Yamamuras considered having Ishino-suke adopted into another family or even disinheriting him, but the Meiji laws prevent this. They next tried to set up their wayward son in a separate household and to buy him off with money, but the wily Ishinosuke is too smart to fall into their trap; he knows that if he agreed he would lose his claim on the inheritance. He tells his parents provocatively, "once the inheritance is settled I'll show you all a fine New Year" (146). His plans include spending a fortune to "show the poor in the Isarago area a good time" (146). It has been suggested that this impulse to generosity, seemingly so at odds with Ishinosuke's personality, can be interpreted as an attitude of rebellion against the world of wealth represented by his parents.[31] However, it can also be read as part of a layering effect whereby the prodigal son is outfitted for multiple roles in a higher system of intertexts in order to heighten certain emotional appeals being made in the story, and I want to pursue the implications of this in light of what we might call the trope of disguise in "Ōtoshi no kyaku."

In the folk tale, the fact that the poor couple is rewarded for their compassion is meant to suggest that the stranger they encounter is actually a bodhisattva in disguise, made rather obvious in some versions by having the stranger pose as a mendicant priest. Those familiar with the religious stories in the *setsuwa* tradition in Japan (what might loosely be called cautionary tales) will not be at all surprised by this, for in story after story the bodhisattvas invariably appear in disguise to help human beings in distress. Furthermore, these deities often appear as seemingly lowly, strange, or even immoral beings, thus emphasizing the radical challenge posed by Buddhism to what passes as conventional morality and norms of behavior. In appropriating the folklore tradition, and especially the trope of disguise in that tradition, the narrator of "Ōtsugomori" is adding another layer of significance onto Ishinosuke, inviting those who know the folklore and *setsuwa* traditions to interpret him also as a Buddhist deity masquerading as the prodigal son; in this reading, Ishinosuke appears as a kind of moral alter-ego of his apparent self in order to reward Omine's decision to place compassion and filiality for her poor aunt and uncle over the miserly interests of her wealthy mistress. And the narrator makes sure we get the point by remarking at the end of the story, "it seems that Ishinosuke was Omine's protection deity" (*Saraba Ishinosuke wa Omine ga mamori-honzon narubeshi*, 152). A *mamori-honzon* (what I have translated as a "protection deity") is a Buddha or bodhisattva who protects an individual from harm, rather like a guardian angel in the Christian tradition. However, the term can also be used more generally to acknowledge someone who renders much-needed assistance. If we treat "Ōtsugomori" as a formal revision of "Ōtoshi no kyaku," we can read the double meaning of *mamori-honzon* in the text and recognize that the narrator is exploiting the ambiguity of the word; she can cloak the secular rogue Ishinosuke in the robes of a Buddhist deity in order to heighten the emotional power of the text for those familiar with the folktale — a kind of bonus of pleasure characteristic of any highly allusive text.

Ishinosuke is a master of disguise, however, and the roles assigned to him are not limited to that of the stranger in "Ōtoshi no kyaku." Consider the way he is introduced to the reader in the second half of the story:

He had begun his wicked ways when he was fifteen, and now he amused himself exactly as he pleased, bringing tears to his step-mother and ignoring his father. There was a manly ruggedness and a clever look about him, and though his complexion was rather dark, he was handsome enough. It was no wonder that one heard rumors about him and the daughters of the neighborhood. He frequented the licensed quarter in Shinagawa, often getting into fights; afterward he would spur the rickshaw over to Kuruma-machi and rouse his ne'er-do-well friends, upon which the ruckus would continue. "Hey there, some drink and food," he would shout as he emptied his wallet. His antics were the epitome of dissipation. (146)

Ishinosuke's excesses are here exaggerated to the point of being a parody of the stereotypical prodigal son. First, he is handsome in a way that defines manliness. He frequents the licensed quarters and is extravagant with money, no doubt making him as popular a figure there as he is among the respectable young ladies in the Yamamuras' part of Tokyo. It seems that he gets in fights as frequently as he visits the brothels, which is no wonder, considering his speech is unfailingly brash, insulting, and provocative. Nonetheless, in a seeming contradiction, he is insistent on supporting the cause of the less fortunate. I want to pursue what I have been calling the trope of disguise from still another angle, that of the kabuki theater.

I want to juxtapose the image of Ishinosuke described above with the masculine ideals exemplified by one of the most famous theatrical characters in the kabuki tradition: Sukeroku, the flower of Edo. When Sukeroku first swaggers onto the stage in the play that bears his name, he is quickly surrounded by courtesans of the Yoshiwara, who are infatuated with his manly good looks and stylish demeanor. He is also openly insulting to every male character appearing on stage. One of those men, however, is Sukeroku's brother in disguise, who scolds his sibling after revealing his true identity.

Every day mother and I heard stories of your fighting in the Yoshiwara. Who pushed the man in the gravel pit? Sukeroku. Who laid to rest the man before the Temple of Eternal Peace? Sukeroku. Who cut down the cut-up of Takecho? Sukeroku. The day the crows don't caw is the day Sukeroku doesn't fight in the Yoshiwara, they say. She could not believe this wastrel called Sukeroku was her son.[32]

This, of course, sounds suspiciously like Ishinosuke, who also frequents the pleasure quarters, gets in fights, and causes grief to his mother (or stepmother as the case may be). After some more scolding by his brother, Sukeroku protests that he brawls "out of filial obligation. I quarrel to find father's stolen sword, Tomokirimaru. I take the name of Sukeroku so that I can roam disguised, bickering, insulting men that throng the quarter, forcing them to draw so I can see if they are wearing Tomokirimaru."[33] The most important aspect of the Sukeroku character (at least since the early eighteenth century) is that he is a man in disguise.[34] Sukeroku is really Soga Gorō of the Soga vendetta story, which has its roots in the medieval oral tales culminating in *Soga monogatari* (The Tale of the Soga Brothers). In the kabuki play, he has styled himself up as a dandy—black kimono, purple headband, *shakuhachi* flute tucked in his *obi*, and, most important of all to his stage entrance, a snake's eye umbrella—and come to the Yoshiwara to search for his slain father's stolen sword so that he can use it to take vengeance on his father's killer. He has developed his brash, combative personality in order to provoke people into drawing their swords for his quick inspection (he does not know, after all, who actually stole the heirloom sword). Sukeroku meets Ikyū during his visit to the Yoshiwara and taunts the man into drawing his sword by hurling a barrage of insults at him. Sukeroku inspects the sword, realizes it is Tomokirimaru, and decides to attack Ikyū later that evening. After cutting down his nemesis, Sukeroku retrieves Tomo-kirimaru and escapes the constables coming to seize him.

Although it has been largely shed from the Sukeroku script that stabilized in the Meiji period, *Sukeroku yukari no Edo zakura* (Sukeroku, The Flower of Edo), it seems that in earlier versions of this play the character of Sukeroku was strongly associated with the *otokodate* figure.[35] *Otokodate* is a word that was coined sometime in the early modern period (1600–1868), and though it can still be found in dictionaries, it does not see much use nowadays. One large dictionary of early modern Japanese says that an *otokodate* is a man who topples the strong and comes to the aid of the weak and is willing to die in a righteous cause. This same dictionary quotes an Edo-period source as remarking: "In recent years there is an *otokodate* called Sukeroku."[36] Thus, it seems that historically Sukeroku was considered to be the quintessential *otokodate*. Barbara Thornbury echoes this in her excellent study of the historical transformation of the Sukeroku character and its links to the Soga theatrical tradition. She remarks that in early modern literature the *otokodate* "was a champion of the people, one who . . . evoked the model image of a man. He was a Robin Hood figure who helped the weak against the strong. He was a man of honor, chivalrous, dedicated—and he had style. He was Sukeroku."[37] The play *Sukeroku* that Meiji-period theater-goers saw featured the same trope of disguise that had been part of the Sukeroku tradition since the early eighteenth century, but it seems that the equation of Sukeroku and *otokodate* was gradually left more and more to the audience to bring as contextual information to the viewing. For Tokyoites (or the Edokko before them) the equation of Sukeroku with both the Soga vendetta story and the *otokodate* was an easy matter, since the Sukeroku character had long been a folk hero of sorts.

Ichiyō does not appropriate the Soga vendetta story as such, but just as in "Ōtoshi no kyaku," we can see that she is re-working the trope of disguise in *Sukeroku*. Sukeroku is brash and insulting; he is provocative and constantly getting into fights; he is a ladies' man who frequents the pleasure quarters. In a word, he is exactly like Ishinosuke. But on one level it is all part of a disguise for both men, for both have a higher mission. We must conclude, then, that Ishinosuke is capable of a bewildering variety of roles in our drama. He is the roguish prodigal son with an impulse to generosity in the text proper, but in a higher system of intertexts he is a Buddhist figure come in disguise in order to aid those in distress; and he is also the *otokodate* Sukeroku, who, in order to rescue Omine and her family, has tarted himself up in dandyish dress, applied the makeup of a *provocateur*, and swaggered into the pages of Ichiyō's narrative straight off the kabuki stage.

With the revelation of this final role for the prodigal son, the textual space of "Ōtsugomori" has grown complicated indeed. It incorporates Ihara Saikaku's *Seken mune zan'yō*, the folktale "Ōtoshi no kyaku," the *waka* discourse on dreams, and the kabuki theater. From Saikaku, Ichiyō appropriates a concern for the financial drama of the last day of the year, a time when the divide between rich and poor rises to the forefront of social life. The poetic discourse on dreams is utilized to represent the thoughts of a heroine caught in an agonizing ethical dilemma. Folklore and the kabuki theater are appropriated to lend emotional and symbolic weight to Ishinosuke's intervention.

Ichiyō's revisions of the tradition result in a dialogism, or intertextuality, that is a series of tropological transformations. Ichiyō's literary debt is extensive, but it is no mere imitation; each trope has been systematically oriented around the themes of family, money, and social class, a maneuver that required an appropriation and re-invention of each intertext.

Moreover, these transformations are inextricably connected to the text's thematic concerns and its preoccupation with marginal social figures. As I have tried to demonstrate, at the heart of "Ōtsugomori" is an impasse centered on the changing nature of domestic service in Ichiyō's time. There is a contradiction between the traditional quasi-familial model of master-servant relations and the newer wage-based economic logic that was rapidly coming to dominate the structure of domestic service in the late nineteenth century. The tension between these two discontinuous systems is thrown into relief when Omine asks for an advance on her wages and is refused. When Omine is forced to steal because her request is denied, Ishinosuke intervenes in order to ensure that Omine is not caught, thus foreclosing a plot line that would have seen Omine unproblematically returned to the moral order of society. In this story, Omine steals from the rich and gets away with it. In a dialogic reading, Omine's theft and Ishinosuke's intervention resonate with intertexts in which folk heroes actively topple the rich in order to help the poor; and this is where the possibility of a multifaceted social critique opens up in the story.

Certainly the text registers the gap between the rich and the poor. Surely we can also say that the text protests a situation in which those with wealth turn a deaf ear to the cries of the less fortunate. But "Ōtsugomori" goes even further than this. I have argued that the text highlights a social transformation—perhaps glimpsed only in nightmarish fragments and partially understood by Ichiyō herself, who lacked the benefit of hindsight and an extensive critical vocabulary—in which wages have come to play the central role in connections among people, a situation in which human relations take on an abstractness and a coldness that we have learned are the distinct trademarks of the commodity form. In "Ōtsugomori," then, the classical tradition is a reservoir of tropes and figures that might be drawn upon to contest the new world of commodified social relations and the callousness that arises at a particular moment in economic history. And although this is a story in which commodification is grasped in narrative terms rather than in the language of economic analysis, it is still a story about economics, one in which, as many have pointed out, the value of everything is precisely given in its equivalent in currency. Money will continue to be a central motif in Ichiyō's fictional world; as we will see in the next chapter, the coin is pitted against love.

The world of "Ōtsugomori" is one in which some have money and some do not. Those with the means can enjoy the festivities of the New Year, while those without means are haunted by debt as the last day of the year approaches; and in this text the harsh reality is that those with money are insensitive to the plight of the poor. With bold brush strokes that would be further refined in future stories, Ichiyō paints a disturbing social landscape, and the conclusion the reader seems expected to draw is that in such a world only a magical figure from folklore or a mythic stage character can help the weak; the only one who can save the poor is a stranger bearing a thousand coins of gold.

THREE

The Mind of a Prostitute

The narrative of "Nigorie" (Troubled Waters) concludes with talk of the brutal deaths of a prostitute and her long-time customer, who is called in the elegant diction of the quarter a *najimi kyaku*, or "familiar guest," a deliberate blurring of the distinction between patron and lover. Their deaths are not depicted in the text, but are instead the topic of town gossip, which centers on the unresolved question of whether or not the two committed a "love suicide." This phrase is the standard translation for the Japanese *shinjū*, in which two lovers kill themselves because of an inability to escape some insurmountable predicament. The spectacular ends of the protagonists, Oriki and Genshichi, take place at Otera no yama, a space associated with death and the otherworldly in the text; the time is the summer Obon festival, during which the souls of the dead were said to return to their ancestral homes. As Maeda Ai has taken such pains to demonstrate, the world of death always threatens to overwhelm the world of life in this text.[1]

If one fully confronts the atmosphere of grimy mortality that clings oppressively to the story, reading "Nigorie" can be a desolate experience. It is a bleaker work than *Takekurabe*, for example, which was passing the midway point of its year-long serialization in *Bungakukai* (Literary World) when "Nigorie" was published in *Bungei kurabu* (Literary Club) in

September 1895, but "Nigorie" is fully capable of standing shoulder to shoulder with Ichiyō's most celebrated story. "Nigorie" is filled with images of *dobu-ita*, the wooden boards covering the drainage gutters along the roadside, and the muddy waters flowing beneath them become symbolic of a despair that has settled in like a fog over the story. The text is haunted by the drone of the mosquitoes, and the smoke used to drive them away calls to mind a funeral pyre. Although there are scenes that occupy the daylight hours, one somehow feels while reading it that the entire story unfolds in the depth of night. No doubt the fact that "Nigorie" takes place in the gritty world of illegal prostitution rather than in the culturally sophisticated Yoshiwara also contributes to the feeling of darkness that permeates the work.

The star of this particular third-rate quarter is Oriki, who "because of some misfortune or other, had fallen into this muddy stream" (195). Oriki's hold over the male visitors to the district is such that the narrator speculates that it may be more accurate to say "Oriki's Kikunoi" rather than "Oriki of the Kikunoi" (180). She is clearly the most beautiful, the most charismatic, and the most skilled at drawing in customers and keeping them coming back for more, and that is why she is known as the "number one attraction" (*ichimai kanban*, 180). Despite her status, Oriki is haunted by a kind of melancholy or depression:

From time to time Oriki was overcome by feelings of fear and sadness. Embarrassed to be seen in such a state, she would throw herself by the *tokonoma* in one of the upstairs rooms and try to swallow her tears. This was unknown to any of the others, who thought her a strong and independent girl. No one guessed that she was as insubstantial as a spider's web — touch it, and it would tear. (195)

The cause of her condition is never made entirely clear, although the chief factor is certainly her environment, and, more particularly, her feelings of guilt over the straitened circumstances of her former customer, Genshichi.

Genshichi used to own a prosperous *futon* bedding shop, but he became so infatuated with Oriki that he spent all of his substantial capital on her over the course of only a year and now struggles to make a living as a common day-laborer. He and his family—his wife Ohatsu and son Takichirō (or Takichi for short)—have been forced to move into the dreary back alleys of the district as near-outcasts. Ohatsu, who is fully aware of her husband's visits to the Kikunoi, berates Genshichi fiercely, admonishing him to gather himself up and reclaim his old position for the sake of his family. Genshichi, however, cannot forget Oriki, and so he continually tries to meet her, though without money he is invariably turned away at the door of the Kikunoi.

It is at this point that a new figure enters the narrative, turning the triangular drama among Oriki, Genshichi, and Ohatsu into one with four parts: the new element is Yūki Tomonosuke, a man of leisure who need not pay much attention to matters of money because he has it in abundance. Tomonosuke is drawn into the Kikunoi by the enchanting Oriki one day early in the story as he strolls by, presumably in search of new diversions in the unlicensed quarter. He rapidly falls under Oriki's spell, and much of the remainder of the narrative portrays a deepening intimacy between the two. They eventually reach the point where Oriki opens up to Tomonosuke and tells him about Genshichi, her own impoverished childhood, and the failure of both her father and grandfather to make successes of their lives. In fact, the failure of her kin to amount to anything seems to weigh as heavily on Oriki's mind as does Genshichi's situation; it is one more factor contributing to her despondency.

Both a sense of guilt over Genshichi as well as sympathy for the plight of Takichi, whose childhood now mired in unrelenting poverty so resembles her own younger days, compel Oriki to buy a small cake for the boy. When Takichi returns home to a situation made extraordinarily tense by a fight between his mother and father, the cake becomes the spark that ignites a tinderbox. Ohatsu explodes, interpreting the cake as a gesture by Oriki to entice Genshichi back to the Kikunoi to spend what little remains of the family's money:

That woman is a demon! She's a demon who turned your father into a lazy good-for-nothing. She's the reason that you haven't any clothes and that our old house has been lost, child. She won't be content until she's swallowed up all of us. Just hearing you ask if you can eat the sweets you got from that monster is unbearable. (204)

Ohatsu then grabs the cake and hurls it outside, where it splits open and rolls into one of the story's ubiquitous gutters. Genshichi explodes in turn—"There's nothing wrong with the boy getting sweets from her. . . . If Oriki is a demon, you're the queen of hell" (205)—and turns both his wife and child out of the house.

The final chapter depicts two coffins leaving the district—a relatively elaborate one leaving the Kikunoi and a much more modest one coming from the back alley. This is observed by onlookers—four of whom represent what Maeda Ai once called "the voice of the town"[2]—who gossip about whether or not Oriki and Genshichi committed a love suicide. A variety of opinions are offered, all founded on hearsay, and there is no reason for the reader to believe or disbelieve any of them. The final sentence of the narrative tells of how a *hitodama*—a will-o-the-wisp object that was thought to be the spirit of the deceased—was sometimes seen thereafter over Otera no yama, where Oriki and Genshichi died. Here is an unsolved mystery, for the *hitodama* trails bitterness (*urami*); the only other occasion that *urami* is used in the text is to describe Oriki's father and grandfather as being overwhelmed with bitterness at being unable to achieve success in life.

The extraordinary ambiguity and mystery surrounding the ending of "Nigorie" reflects in part the well-documented struggle Ichiyō had in bringing her powerful story to a conclusion that was satisfactory to her. Indeed, all the evidence suggests that the composition of each chapter of "Nigorie" proved to be laborious. It has been convincingly demonstrated, for example, that a large number of the extant fragments and incomplete compositions in Ichiyō's collected works are, in fact, products of her attempt to bring to fruition the ideas that would eventually result in "Nigorie."[3] The fact that Ichiyō did not keep her diary at all from mid-June until early October 1895 also suggests that she was burning the midnight oil during the composition of the story.

Ichiyō started writing "Nigorie" sometime in mid-June and continued until the very end of July 1895. It was due to be published in *Bungei kurabu*, so on July 30 Ichiyō delivered the manuscript to the home of the editor, Ken'yūsha member Ōhashi Otowa, the same man who had helped bring out Saikaku's complete works the previous year. Strangely, Ichiyō delivered it without the final chapter. In mid-July the Higuchi women carried out the seventh-anniversary memorial services for Ichiyō's father, the deceased Noriyoshi, and the bill fell due at the end of the month. In order to pay for the services, Ichiyō was forced to deliver her manuscript as it was and to collect her honorarium, even though the story still had no conclusion. Ōhashi, unfortunately, was on holiday at the time that Ichiyō visited, so she had little choice but to leave the manuscript of the seven completed chapters there and to return home. She agonized over the ending, and when the ideas finally came, she wrote them out and sent the concluding chapter together with a letter of apology to Ōhashi on August 2, even before she received a letter from Ōhashi himself written the day before, apologizing for his earlier absence and agreeing to pay fifteen yen for the story.[4]

The narrative element that seemed to cause Ichiyō the most agony was Oriki's fate; here was a character who seemed to haunt her creator, in part, perhaps, because Ichiyō was surrounded day-in and day-out in her final years by just such women plying their trade in the illegal houses of Maruyama-Fukuyama. We know she made six different attempts to compose an ending to the penultimate draft alone, ranging from fairly lengthy passages to a few halting words, and the evidence suggests that Ichiyō at least considered having Oriki taken away from the Kikunoi by Tomonosuke, in effect rescuing her from her circumstances.[5] No doubt this struck Ichiyō as trite, so she moved toward a bleaker ending. The sixth attempt at a conclusion is by far the longest: we see Oriki leave the Kikunoi to go to the bathhouse, never to return; her body is discovered the next day with a deep knife wound in the throat. Here Ichiyō's conception of the ending approached very closely the one that was finally printed as Chapter 8. Since the draft also includes a brief section at the end of the seventh chapter describing Genshichi suddenly leaving his house after he has turned out his wife and child (a sentence that was not included in the final version), it becomes very easy for the reader to connect this to Oriki's death and thus to conclude that Genshichi killed her. Although it seems like a clear-cut case of homicide, we cannot know for sure; a knife wound to the base of the woman's throat, after all, is perfectly consistent with the classic pattern of a lover's suicide, at least in the literary representations of it, for in reality the woman rarely stabbed herself with her own hand. In addition, since the text for this draft breaks off abruptly in mid-sentence, we do not know Ichiyō's plans for Genshichi at this point in the composition process.[6]

It is, then, only in the final printed version that the possibility of a *shinjū* is explicitly invoked to explain the strange events between Oriki and Genshichi; but it is discounted and then raised again by the bystanders in the story in a spiral of vague speculation. Certainly the time pressure on Ichiyō to complete the story is a factor here in the ambiguity surrounding the possibility of a *shinjū*, but we should also keep in mind her reluctance to make crucial narrative elements too explicit. She was known to frequently make pivotal plot elements not less but *more* ambiguous when she moved from the penultimate to the final draft of many stories. She very much subscribed to the philosophy that the reader should carry out much of the work of interpretation. Nonetheless, despite the ambiguity of the final ending, and despite the fact that the short story may not have been originally conceived as a love-suicide piece, "Nigorie" puts out all the signals of being a *shinjū-mono*, even as it deviates from some of its central structural features. The ambiguity of the text's ultimate relationship to the genre has led a number of scholars to try to resolve the issue by looking solely at the representational level of the text—the wound pattern on Oriki's body or the gossip of the bystanders—in order to attempt to provide certainty where mystery is the rule.[7]

I am less interested in a crime-scene investigation than I am in uncovering how the narrative of "Nigorie" both works on and departs from the narrative codes of the *shinjū-mono*. I want to suggest that there are at least two stories told in "Nigorie" and that each is rooted in a distinct narrative paradigm or generic pattern. This approach—treating the text as an intersection of two generic lines—becomes tenable if we shift focus for a moment away from the mystery of the death scene and instead privilege the relationships between Oriki and the two men in her life, Genshichi and Tomonosuke. The stormy relationship between Oriki and Genshichi, with Tomonosuke and Ohatsu playing significant supporting roles, draws its inspiration from the love-suicide archetype, and, indeed, could have been rather easily developed as such. To be sure, it is not very persuasive to read the moment of death itself as a *shinjū*, but Genshichi certainly seems to have staged it as such for those who would discover the bodies. As my earlier summary of the plot suggested, the story of the deepening relationship between Oriki and Tomonosuke (during which Genshichi and Ohatsu are muted presences) is concerned with how a prostitute is so haunted by the failure of her kin to amount to anything in life that she becomes mired in self-doubt about her own ability to escape her environment, even though Tomonosuke all but formally extends an offer of marriage to her. As I will show, this second line in the text must be read in relation to narrative paradigms connected to the modern discourse on ambition and success. In this chapter, I want to extend the theoretical framework begun in the previous chapter and connect dialogism with genre theory, which will allow us to analyze the text as a weaving together of heterogeneous narrative paradigms.[8]

Although genre theory has often been conceived either as a system of rules to which a text more or less conforms or as a phantasmal critical imposition that is not embodied in any text, there are theories that are productive for analyzing "Nigorie" in the way I am suggesting. A good starting point is Laurent Jenny. Although he does not make his theoretical roots explicit, essentially he reexamines intertextuality and genre by drawing on the Saussurian distinction between *langue* and *parole*. The *langue* is the system of narrative archetypes that make up the literary system of a particular tradition. This is then appropriated and reformulated in a specific articulation of the codes comprising those archetypes into a new text, a *parole* as it were. The assimilation and refashioning of archetypes, each of which is the formal encoding and condensation of a number of previous literary acts, are intertextuality, without which "a literary work would simply be unintelligible, like speech in a language one has not yet learned."[9] Given this, then, the constituents of intertextuality are "not just words, but bits of the already said, the already organized, textual fragments."[10] Whereas Jenny's basic formulation is persuasive, his near-exclusive interest in literary form results in a lack of attention paid to ways in which sociopolitical elements might be inscribed in the phenomenon of genre and does not address the question implied in his own formulation: how might multiple genre threads interact in the pages of a narrative?

Fredric Jameson, on the other hand, has insistently stressed that form itself is an ideology, that all narrative paradigms and archetypes retain their socio-symbolic messages even after they have been reappropriated in a new context.[11] Drawing on Bakhtin, who had demonstrated how the ancient elements of carnival were preserved in the modern novel, and pursuing his own interests in theorizing the text as a site of class conflict, Jameson argues that the literary text consists of a host of heterogeneous genre strands and discourses, which must be functionally reckoned into the narrative: "The novel is then not so much an organic unity as a symbolic act that must reunite or harmonize heterogeneous narrative paradigms which have their own specific and contradictory ideological meaning."[12]

The views of Jenny and Jameson are useful for analyzing "Nigorie." Because textual production can be viewed as the assimilation and refashioning of archetypes, it is inherently dialogic—a dialogue, that is, between the author and the archetypes she mobilizes, as well as among the archetypes themselves. Genre provides the raw materials on which the narrative process of a text can work and be shaped. Furthermore, these views of genre give us a vantage point from which we can assess the deviations from a narrative paradigm like the *shinjū-mono* or the success story as a gesture by Ichiyō directed at the very ideologically charged narrative materials of which her text is comprised.[13] "Nigorie" exhibits Ichiyō's unwillingness to embrace fully the ideological implications of any of the major genres that constitute the fabric of her text; in the end, the dialogic interaction of heterogeneous paradigms compels her to steer the text toward its infamously ambiguous ending.

ii

The love suicide had a firm hold on Ichiyō's artistic imagination, for we know from her diary that she was an avid reader of the plays of Chikamatsu Monzaemon (1653-1724), the most celebrated creator of such dramas. In fact, when Ichiyō began her writing career in the early 1890s, Chikamatsu was at that very moment being elevated to the stature of a major figure in the Japanese theatrical tradition through the efforts of the great Meiji man of letters, Tsubouchi Shōyō (1859-1935), together with scholars at the University of Tokyo. As their pronouncement of Chikamatsu as the "Japanese Shakespeare" makes apparent, literary categories were reorganized during this time, and the popular dramatist could be remade into a leading man who exemplified a glorious national tradition in the theater. Such banner-waving resulted in the appearance of several collections of Chikamatsu's works in the 1890s—the very collections Ichiyō was reading.[14] The new celebratory collections of Japanese drama may have inspired Ichiyō to read Chikamatsu carefully, but they also led to resistance to some of the implications of the playwright's work.

Theatrical representations of *shinjū* had become common in Chikamatsu's own time in the early eighteenth century and were often based on well-publicized love suicides of the day and were staged shortly after the deaths so as to capitalize on the commotion. Chikamatsu himself was one of the main reasons that the *shinjū* stabilized into a recognizable genre, and quite a popular and long-lived one at that. The most salient aspect of Chikamatsu's love-suicide plays is the dichotomy they draw between the oppressiveness of human social mores and a powerful desire made impossible by that very social order, or more abstractly between social constraint and love.[15] The narrator of Chikamatsu's *Shinjū ten no Amijima* (Love Suicide at Amijima, 1720), for example, boldly asserts in the play's opening moments that "the love of a prostitute is deep beyond measure," and the entire drama seems written simply to prove this assertion through a kind of case-study. The dichotomy of society and love is reinforced when, at the end of the play, the prostitute Koharu exclaims to her lover Jihei, in defiance of all social constraints on them, "take me with you, to heaven or to hell!" emphatically claiming that her love trumps all other concerns.[16] The man's love for the woman is equally ardent and, despite the vicissitudes of the plot and his own wildly fluctuating emotions, it does not fail to resurface powerfully in the scene of death. The consecration of the love between the protagonists, its elevation into a transcendent bond, then, is the main business of a love-suicide drama; such theater participates in the organization of the society's collective fantasies and fears concerning the effects of commercialized desire on the social order.

To be sure, the love we are speaking of here is not modern romantic love, but rather the discourse on *koi*. *Koi* had its origins in the prostitution districts and, in its most fundamental meaning, is desire excited to a fantastic pitch by the obstacles the man has to face in order to reach the object of his longing, whether it be the accumulation of enough money to pay for the evening, the long journey to the quarter, mastering the elaborate rituals and etiquette of the demimonde, or the difficulty in obtaining an appointment with the desired lady.[17] Even as this form of love slipped past the walls of the prostitution district and became an ideal celebrated in society at large, it was subtended by the bond between a prostitute and her lover. *Koi* occurred outside social boundaries and social strictures in a world of make-believe in which the courtesan was the quintessential object of desire. Tanaka Yūko observes that a veritable mystique hovered about such women in the popular imagination: she was seen as the dispenser of all worthwhile feelings of love and compassion, a manifestation, even, of the bodhisattva Kannon; and without her *mabu*, that most reviled creature in the quarter, who stealthily tried to meet his prostitute-lover without paying the brothel for the privilege, her world was one of utter darkness.[18] The power of these illusions depended in large part on making invisible the links between love and the actual commercial world of the sex trade, and the *shinjū* dramas of Chikamatsu and others traffic in this romanticized and alluringly dangerous *koi*.

Given the implications of a mythologized *koi*, it is to be expected that the lovers must survive a journey through a metaphoric hell in order to be united at last. The lovers always pass through a series of poetically charged toponyms in a journey called a *michiyuki* (literally "going along the road"), and after they arrive at a suitable location the man kills the woman—usually by stabbing her in the throat—and then kills himself. For many, the literary and emotional center of a love-suicide play lies in its *michiyuki*. It is a journey across a poetically charged landscape, or intertextual topography, that adds a weighty aesthetic dignity to the lovers' fate and plays a substantial role in elevating their love into something transcendent and otherworldly. The *michiyuki* of *Sonezaki shinjū* (Love Suicide at Sonezaki, 1703), for example, is especially prized for its poetry, which helps make the love between the protagonists Ohatsu and Tokubei a thing of unearthly beauty before which all social concerns seem shallow and insignificant. At the same time, the *michiyuki* is also a religious journey whereby the lovers descend through a kind of Buddhist purgatory, which also functions as a summary of the perils and constraints they faced in the real world, before eventually reaching paradise after the moment of death.[19]

A love-suicide drama depends completely on this dichotomy between the wretched world of the here and now, in which the passion between the protagonists is forbidden by society, and a blissful postmortem union on a lotus flower in one of the Buddhist paradises. At the end of *Amijima*, Jihei, with tears in his eyes and with Koharu urging him on, thrusts his dagger into Koharu's throat and kills her; he then hangs himself some distance away. Their bodies are discovered the next morning by a fisherman, whose nets (*ami*) suggest that the two lovers were later reborn together in the paradise of Amida Buddha. Thus, mingled at the end of most love-suicide plays is both a sense of tragedy and a sense of celebration: tragedy because the couple, unable to escape the dilemmas and forces closing in around them, are left with no choice but to kill themselves; celebration because the reader is reassured at the end of the play that the lovers ultimately achieve a transcendental bliss in the next life that they were unable to achieve in the so-called floating world.

The plays line up a whole series of impediments and suspenseful retarding elements along the inexorable path to the next life. In *Sonezaki*, the smash hit that was Chikamatsu's first effort in the genre, the good-natured Tokubei, ignorant of the deceptive ways of the world, gets into a terrible predicament when he makes a misguided loan to a swindler. In Chikamatsu's last creation in the genre, *Shinjū yoigōshin* (Love Suicide on the Eve of the Kōshin Festival, 1722), the samurai-turned-greengrocer, Hanbei, faces parental hostility toward his wife Ochiyo. In *Shinjū mannensō* (Love Suicide in the Women's Temple, 1710), Chikamatsu pits love against money, religious duty, and homo-social (-sexual) desire. Or consider the dazzlingly convoluted dilemmas of Chikamatsu's *Amijima*: Jihei's business is threatened with insolvency because he has spent all his fortune to be with Koharu; his wife Osan has written a letter to Koharu pleading that she break with her husband so that Jihei does not kill himself; there is the threat by Tahei, "the Lone Wolf," to buy out Koharu's contract and take her as his wife, a prospect that Koharu views as a fate worse than death. Chikamatsu's plays traffic in the melo-dramatic juxtaposition of love with other elements valued highly in society: filial piety, family, money, and so on. But these are precisely the elements that prevent the couple from achieving happiness. When they are swept aside to satisfy the demands of freedom and passion, desire is transformed into transcendent love.

Such are the narrative materials that were encoded in the love-suicide plays and passed down to Ichiyō and others of her age near the end of the nineteenth century. Ichiyō's chal-lenging story has often inspired critical attempts to relate it to the corpus of early-modern *shinjū* dramas, and in looking at "Nigorie" it is easy to see why: a merchant so infatuated with a prostitute that he has spent his entire fortune on her and has plummeted down the social order; a family threatened with poverty and disintegration because of his infatuation; the entrance of another man—a potential rival—who has wealth, but is unencumbered by family, so he could potentially buy out the woman's contract and make her his wife; an ending resulting in the spectacular deaths of the merchant and the prostitute. Any of these elements could find a suitable home in a love-suicide piece. The vitality of Ichiyō's story stems in large part from its intense engagement with the genre. However, the swerving of "Nigorie" away from the *shinjū* archetype is as prominent as its similarities to it. In the end, Oriki's feelings for Genshichi are never made clear; he is obvi-ously infatuated with her, but what are her feelings toward him? Also, in many such dramas, the prostitute-heroine is in danger of having her contract bought out by a wealthy scoundrel, the very antithesis of her impoverished lover. In "Nigorie," Genshichi may see Tomonosuke as a rival, but Oriki seeks a deepening intimacy with the wealthy and charm-ing *flâneur*, not an escape from him. What "Nigorie" so obsti-nately refuses to generate is the kind of dramatic knot that would characterize a love-suicide drama, and thus it becomes difficult to uncover a suitable motive for a *shinjū*.

The biggest stumbling block in assessing the relationship between "Nigorie" and the ideology of traditional love-suicide pieces lies in the bond between Oriki and Genshichi. Genshichi's passion for Oriki is extraordinarily powerful, and even his social free fall, his lost business, and his unraveling family are not motivation enough for him to cast her from his mind. Indeed, it is as if the mystique of the prostitute is real, for Genshichi seems to be caught in a spell. The most memorable image of the *futon* merchant is of him lying on the floor of his empty home lost in reverie, enraptured by the image of Oriki, even while he berates himself for his inability to let her go.

The narrator is, however, characteristically reluctant to make Oriki's feelings toward Genshichi too explicit, and thus we have little choice but to try to guess her state of mind by interpreting the "clues" that are dropped in the text. This is complicated, as we will see shortly, by the fact that the prostitute was supposed to do and say anything that would bring the customer back to the establishment, including declaring her eternal love for him. In the opening moments of the story, when the prostitute Otaka asks her friend Oriki about her relationship with Genshichi, Oriki brushes it aside, telling Otaka that they should not talk about him where everyone can hear lest people make the mistake of thinking she has a common laborer for a *mabu* (181). Certainly this statement could be taken as Oriki's dismissal of Genshichi as an unworthy customer now that he has fallen on hard times, but it is better interpreted, I think, as Oriki trying to appear nonchalant about Genshichi in order to hide her true feelings from Otaka.

In fact, as we read the story we begin to feel little by little the strength of Oriki's feelings for Genshichi. At one point, when Oriki is with Tomonosuke, a serving woman enters the room and tells her that a man is trying to get in to talk to her. We know that this is Genshichi, of course, which is confirmed when a little later Oriki tells Tomonosuke a bit about her past with the *futon* merchant. Her tone strongly suggests that some of the old passion still lingers. But Oriki also seems to feel regret, perhaps even guilt, over Genshichi's present circumstances, and this has likely led her to maintain a stoic silence. She must feel it is best at this point not to court total disaster by meeting with her former *najimi kyaku*, who is, after all, infatuated with her to the point where he would sacrifice both his family and his position in society. Saeki Junko has argued persuasively that Oriki has come to the conclusion that the love between a prostitute and her *najimi kyaku* inevitably causes pain to third parties, here Genshichi's wife Ohatsu and their son Takichi. In this view, Oriki's despondency arises because of her realization that her relationship with Genshichi has brought about his social fall and a poverty-ridden life for his family.[20] Takichi's plight seems especially painful to Oriki, for, as we saw before, the young boy's situation resonates powerfully with her own experiences of bitter poverty as a child. When Oriki gives the cake to Takichi to take home, her gesture must be interpreted, I think, as an act of reconciliation brought about by strong feelings of guilt and remorse, though ironically the gesture ends up causing the final dissolution of Genshichi's family.

This kind of hesitation and ambivalence is a structural necessity in a love-suicide drama; it is a mandatory dramatic counterpoint to the eventual elevation of the emotional bond between a prostitute and her lover into a transcendent bond. To return to *Amijima* for a moment, Koharu recognizes the tragic effects a suicide would inevitably have on Osan and her children. In the end, though, all of this is swept away — forcefully though not without some hesitation and regret — in order to consecrate the love between Koharu and Jihei.

In contrast, "Nigorie" dwells obsessively on the problem *Amijima* displaces as secondary: the relationship between a prostitute and her *najimi kyaku* invariably causes pain to an entire circle of people. Even as Ichiyō's story relies on the dichotomy between society and love that so characterizes a *shinjū-mono*, "Nigorie" refuses to celebrate the latter. Indeed, it is worth emphasizing that the text devotes two lengthy sections, a quarter of its pages, to a sympathetic portrayal of Genshichi's family at home. We are given as many details about Ohatsu's physical appearance as we are of Oriki; we get brief inside views of Ohatsu as well. We are clearly meant to sympathize with the fallen merchant's wife—yet another woman eking out an existence on the margins of society. We are meant to sympathize with *Amijima*'s Osan, too, and the play's entire second act is centered on her, but "Nigorie" does not brush aside social concerns in its concluding pages as quickly as Chikamatsu's play does in its final act, and Ichiyō's story represents the love suicide itself as a grotesquely egotistical and selfish act.

In "Nigorie," love can never be completely divorced from a person's existence as a social being within a web of human relations. Oriki's realization of this fact contributes to her feeling of hopelessness, her feeling that there is no escape from her predicament. A careful reading of the text indicates that Ichiyō pursued the representation of Oriki's mind even further than this, however. Ichiyō forced together what the love-suicide dramas sundered and explored the connections among psychology, love, and commerce. I want to suggest that Oriki's despondency is ultimately a manifestation of the text's suspicion of the transcendent bond valorized in the love-suicide archetype; that this despondency is a result of Oriki's doubts about the possibility that the relationship between a man and a woman can ever manifest "true" feelings; and that all of this is in the end rooted squarely in the material conditions of Oriki's environment, the Kikunoi, where there is a merger of deception, desire, and fantasy.

Oriki's life centers on the establishment where she plies her trade, and the Kikunoi is described with remarkable efficiency in a few ironically telling details:

The establishment was a two-story building with an entrance twice the normal size. Below the eaves hung a festival lantern, and on the ground there was a little pile of salt meant to bring prosperity. Inside one could glimpse an area where the receipts were kept, and there were bottles of fine liquor lining the shelves, but who knows whether they were filled or not. Occasionally one heard the busy clamor of a fire being started in the stove. One might expect a light meal served up by the owner, though the sign out front would lead one to believe the place was a full-fledged restaurant. What would they do if somebody actually came in and ordered something? Surely it would be strange to claim that they had suddenly run out of everything. And it would be awkward to explain that this establishment only served men. But fortune has a way of smiling on some people, for no ignorant country folk came in expecting a full course meal. (180)

The Kikunoi is located in one of the many Shinkai-machi (a generic designation for any of the newly developing sections of the city, though the exact location is never specified).[21] Judging by its own shop sign one might think that the Kikunoi is a drinking establishment or restaurant of some kind, though the narrator's wry comment immediately puts such a presupposition in doubt. The sign hanging at the front of the Kikunoi, then, is pure fiction, a deception. The Kikunoi is a *meishuya*, one of the many fronts for an unlicensed brothel. Like any illegal establishment, the Kikunoi must operate with a certain amount of misdirection so as not to call down the wrath of the authorities; but, of course, city dwellers know the real business of a *meishuya*, for we see in the text that there is no dearth of customers at the Kikunoi, from factory workers and local shop hands to university students.

The Kikunoi does, in fact, provide food and alcohol, and it uses female servers (called *shakufu*) to this end. But these thinly disguised servers are also available for other activities, and the Kikunoi, like any *meishuya*, must simultaneously advertise and hide this fact.[22] A semiotic system congeals around these *shakufu* to indicate their real trade: their hair is done up elaborately in variations that indicate their calling; their *obi* are tied in specific ways at their waists; their gaudy kimonos are worn loosely with the front pulled scandalously wide to reveal a tantalizing amount of cleavage and to reveal the base of the neck and the upper back; white powder is applied liberally to this exposed skin and to the face; their eyebrows are shaved off and drawn in well above the original brow line with black ink. The body of each of the women on display at the Kikunoi has been eroticized by these means in keeping with their true profession, and the narrator comments humorously that "one knew without being told that these were the 'ladies' of this district" (*iwazu to shireshi kono atari no ane-sama fū nari*, 179). And, then, of course, there is the call—"*Yotte o-ide yo*" (Why not come inside?)—made countless times each day to men passing by on the street.[23] This is an utterance—another material expression of the body—discursively monopolized by the prostitute, and the narrator describes it at one point as a deceptively sweet call that was "as frightening as a snake about to eat a pheasant" (193).

The eroticization of the female body and voice is designed, of course, to draw customers into the establishment. But to prosper, the houses must exert themselves on the male consciousness even when he is away, making him constantly wish he were at the Kikunoi. In order to accomplish this, the brothels make efforts to satisfy desires of every kind, whether for food and drink, for music and song, for laughter and witty banter, or for sexual intercourse. Ideally the male wage-earner in the district will be stimulated enough that he will make it a habit to stop in every day after work in the factories and shops in the thriving district. A form of competition emerges among the men who frequent the brothels for the affections of the district's most popular prostitutes in a system of fetishization of the eroticized female body that entices them to spend more and more money.[24]

Oriki is the most proficient in creating the stimulating and erotic atmosphere that keeps men spending money, and that is why she is the "number one attraction" of the entire district. This is made apparent to us in the very first chapter. Oriki's body—the very meeting point of eros and commerce—is described in great sensual detail:

The woman called Oriki was well proportioned and of average height. Her hair, newly washed, was done up in the *ōshimada* style and tied in place with a bit of new straw. She was a real beauty. She had a naturally light complexion it seemed, and so she used only a bit of powder on her neck. The collar of her kimono was loosened revealingly, no doubt to show off the fairness of her bosom. She puffed away on a long pipe, one knee propped up. It was a good thing no one was there to scold her for her bad manners. (179)

We also learn of Oriki's powers via the contrast between her and Otaka. Otaka, one of the other prostitutes at the Kikunoi, does not seem to meet with great success in attracting customers and spends many of her evenings calling out vainly to potential clients well into the night. In contrast, near the end of the opening section, Oriki calls out easily to a pair of passing men, "Hey, Ishikawa, Muraoka, have you forgotten Oriki's place?" This works such charms over the two men that they decide to stop in at the Kikunoi, even though it clearly was not their original intention (181–82). We notice, too, in the course of the story that the ubiquitous "*yotte o-ide yo*" is rarely used by Oriki, who instead tends to improvise. Her call to Yūki Tomonosuke later in the story is also not the standard call: "I won't let you go" (*dō demo yarimasen*, 182), she brazenly declares, while tugging on his sleeve.

Her first encounter with Tomonosuke consists entirely of what Kanai Keiko has called a "psychological game."[25] However, the give and take of witty and stimulating erotic conversation—what we might call "verbal friction"—should not be underestimated in thinking about the way the desires of men are excited, so, following Wittgenstein and others, I call the initial encounter a "language game" to better highlight the centrality of erotic verbal foreplay.[26] Oriki's skill in creating this stimulating verbal friction is evident throughout her initial conversation with Tomonosuke, as we see in its opening salvos:

They started in quiet conversation in the six-mat room on the second floor, without even needing the accompaniment of the *shamisen*. The customer asked her age, then her name, and after that he tried to find out about her background.

"Are you from a samurai family?" he asked.

"Oh, I can't answer that," she replied.

"A commoner then?"

"Hmm, what do you think?"

He laughed. "Well then, I guess you must be from the nobility."

"How astute of you. If it pleases the honorable guest, please allow a royal princess to serve you a drink."

"What's this? Surely a real princess wouldn't leave the cup on the table when she poured *saké*. What school of etiquette is that? Ogasawara?"

"No, its called the Oriki school; it's a specialty of the Kikunoi. We also pour *saké* right on the *tatami*, and sometimes we even have the customer gulp it right out of the lid to a bowl. In fact, if we don't like a customer, we don't serve him at all," she said, meanwhile filling his *saké* cup right to the brim.

She wasn't shy at all, and *the customer grew more and more interested.* (182; italics added for emphasis)

Tomonosuke, who no doubt allowed himself to be drawn into the Kikunoi by Oriki's good looks, now grows more intrigued and charmed by her manner. He continues to press her to reveal her background, but Oriki always manages with the skill so evidently displayed in the beginning of their conversation to continue the erotic deception, dodge Tomonosuke's advances, and steer the conversation toward something else. Eventually Oriki turns the encounter into a search for the true identity of the new customer himself (it is only in the following chapter that we learn his name), and she calls in some of her compatriots to make a game out of it. Tomonosuke jokingly holds out his palm so that the women can try to divine his identity and occupation:

"Okay," the customer said, holding out the palm of his hand.

"Oh, I don't need that. I can guess by looking at you," claimed Otaka as she scrutinized him closely.

"All right, all right, stop looking at me like that. I won't be able to stand it if the judgments begin. I may not look it, but I'm actually just a government official," he explained.

"That's a lie. Do government types go strolling about town on any other day but Sunday? Oriki, what do you think?" Otaka asked.

"Well, I can promise you I'm not a ghost," he chuckled. "Let's see. The one who guesses gets a prize," he declared, taking out his wallet and laying it on the *futon.*

Oriki laughed. "Now you musn't say anything rude, Otaka. This gentleman is obviously a man of importance, no doubt an aristocrat. After all, he's at leisure to stroll about town whenever he wishes. He clearly has no need of a job. Isn't that so?" she asked, taking up the wallet from the *futon*.

"Now, you take this Otaka, and divide the rest up among the others," she said, handing around bills without even waiting for the customer to accede.

He just watched, leaning against a pillar, and said nothing at first. "Do as you please."

Now here was a generous man! (184)

Not only is Oriki supremely skilled at turning the direction of the conversation to her own ends, but she has also taken up Tomonosuke's initiative to make the matter of payment a part of the game itself. Thus, the fact that this is a *meishuya*, where the customer must pay for the entertainment, is made largely invisible by incorporating it into a game centered on guessing the man's identity — "The one who guesses gets a prize." After Oriki brings the fun to an end by declaring that the new customer must be a man of leisure, she takes enough money out of his wallet to pay the gentleman's bill and to give a healthy tip to Otaka and the others. Oriki, however, takes no money for herself, and when Tomonosuke asks if she wants any, she replies, "This is all I require," showing him the calling card she covertly slipped out of his wallet. "When did you?" he blurts out in astonishment, and then, recovering his composure, asks, "In return why don't you give me a photograph of yourself?" Here we see that new media technologies such as calling cards and photography have been appropriated and incorporated into the ritualistic first encounter between a prostitute and a new customer.[27] It is apparent that Tomonosuke is thoroughly enchanted by Oriki, so she needs to see that he makes another visit; Oriki uses his request for a photo as an opportunity to arrange a time for him to return: "If you come again next Saturday, we can get our picture taken together" (185).

It seems that Oriki really is the most charming and skilled woman at the Kikunoi, for Tomonosuke does indeed return, repeatedly. The erotic verbal friction between the two —

consisting of linguistic thrusts and parries, punning, even at one point oblique references to classical literature, all of a very ritualistic nature — seems to be a language game centered on the pursuit of the "truth" (*shinjitsu*), which Tomonosuke keeps pressing Oriki to reveal further with each visit. The customer is constantly trying to find the "real" or "true" person behind the prostitute's playful coyness, and she, through wit and knowledge, constantly seeks to retreat and continue the deception, but to retreat in a manner designed to entice the customer to advance further. If this erotic dance is performed skillfully, the customer can be enticed to come a second time, and then a third time, to the Kikunoi.

The third visit was supposed to make the customer a *najimi kyaku*, and the ideal is that he and the prostitute then embark on a more intimate relationship in which they open up to each other and finally, after all the verbal dodges, reveal their "true" selves. Tomonosuke's status changes significantly by the third chapter. He has become a *najimi kyaku*, and his conversations with Oriki are markedly different: gone, for the most part, is the banter and witty repartee, the language games, all of which are replaced by a more serious and intimate tone, and Tomonosuke grows more insistent on hearing about Oriki's past. By the sixth chapter, the relationship between the two has deepened even further: Tomonosuke has become not only Oriki's *najimi kyaku*, but also her confidant.[28] She feels close enough to him to reveal the story of her father and grandfather and of the bitter poverty of her childhood. At the end of her story, she invites Tomonosuke to spend the night with her, an invitation that seems to be completely outside the structure of a normal encounter between a prostitute and a customer, even a *najimi kyaku*.[29]

Nonetheless, regardless of whether Tomonosuke is visiting Oriki for the first time in an encounter consisting solely of drink and witty dialogue, or whether he encounters Oriki in a more intimate way as a *najimi kyaku*, or even in the later chapters as a confidant, currency still changes hands — from Tomonosuke to the Kikunoi — regardless of the depth of the emotional bond between him and Oriki. As long as Oriki "be-longs" to the Kikunoi (the establishment owns her contract after all), the two can never encounter each other outside the framework of prostitute-customer relations, and thus in the background of each encounter will be the exchange of money.[30] From Oriki's perspective, the circulation of money between the customer and the brothel constantly threatens to render hollow all relationships formed in such an environment.

We find this concern in the very first encounter between Oriki and Tomonosuke, during which he asks her playfully about the many men in her life: "There are too many men to count," Oriki exclaims, "but all the love letters are nothing but waste paper. If you want me to, I'll write you out a pledge of love too. Besides, even when a man and a woman exchange vows, he'll always lose his courage before she can break her promise" (183). It is unclear on a first reading exactly how seriously we are to take this passage, especially considering the nature of the witty banter that marks the contextual situa-tion. But even if Oriki's words are meant partially in jest, she nonetheless speaks to a truth of the quarter. The prostitute routinely exchanged empty promises so as to entice the cus-tomer to return, and thus there is always an air of untruth behind any of these vows. Later, after the conversations between Oriki and Tomonosuke have grown more intimate and serious, Oriki repeats this sentiment: "I can't very well be unkind to the men who come here. I have to say whatever will make them happy—to tell this one, 'how handsome,' and that one, 'how lovely,' and another, 'I've fallen in love with you'" (199). To say what will please the customer and make him continue his patronage—such is Oriki's job, even if her words ring hollow to her. The narrator chimes in and echoes Oriki at one point, representing the quarter as a world of callous indifference behind an empty facade of love:

Oriki's was a world of lies, and she spent her days in frivolous play. Love was no more substantial than a thin piece of Yoshino paper, as ephemeral as the flash of a firefly. People here could watch another shed tears for a hundred years and still not be moved to compassion. Even if a man killed himself over a woman, she might only say, 'how dreadful,' while looking away as if the matter were of no concern to her. (195)

These comments by the narrator are followed immediately by the passage, already alluded to earlier, that describes how Oriki routinely flees to a second-floor room of the Kikunoi to hide her tears from her compatriots, suggesting a direct, causal relation between the world of lies that is the Kikunoi and Oriki's depression.

In these sections of the text, we are at the heart of one face of Oriki's dilemma. In a world where words of flattery like those we have been examining, or even more weighty vows of love, are routinely tossed off at a moment's notice, how does Oriki know her own feelings for Tomonosuke are "true"? Does Tomonosuke see her words merely as expedient lies? How is Oriki supposed to take similar pledges of love from her *najimi kyaku*? After all, cannot the revelation of one's "true" self be construed as nothing but a continuation along different lines of the elaborate language games of the demimonde? Economic necessity makes the world Oriki inhabits a world of deception, just like the false shop sign that hangs under the eaves of the Kikunoi, causing her to doubt that love in the quarter can ever be genuine, divorced from the language games, or that it can ever be uncontaminated by the circulation of money. All relationships formed in this environment are overwhelmed by the material conditions that breed deception for economic gain.

The emotional bond that Oriki sees as ephemeral, even impossible, we should recall, is not that of modern romantic love, which Ichiyō explores in "Jūsan'ya," but rather the competing bond of *koi*, which was an emotion whose ideal expression was produced by literary representations of the transcendental bond between a prostitute and her lover. Furthermore, such an ideal strictly holds apart *koi* and commerce. In "Nigorie," Ichiyō refuses this dichotomy; the material conditions of the prostitution district blur the boundary between love and money, and thus throw into doubt the possibility that this transcendent *koi* can be realized or that pledges of love can be believed. There is, however, an undercurrent in many Chikamatsu dramas that echoes the suspicion toward love exhibited by "Nigorie": at one point in *Amijima*, for example, when Koharu tells Tahei, the Lone Wolf, that she does not wish to listen to his prattle anymore, Tahei responds, "you may not want to hear what I have to say, but the sound of my gold coins will make you listen."[31] Buried somewhere in the unconscious of the *shinjū-mono*, then, is a lingering suspicion that perhaps pledges of love merely follow the trail of money. Ultimately *Amijima* tries to sever the link between love and commerce and to push the emotional connection between men and women to a higher plane, but the issue does not recede quite so easily for readers or theatergoers. This repressed subtext of many a love-suicide piece is brought to the fore in "Nigorie": what the text insists on, what Oriki has come to fear, is that pledges of love in the quarter ultimately rest on nothing more substantial than the clinking of gold coins, and thus the boundary between truth and expediency in such an environment is impossible to locate.

iii

The telos of any *shinjū-mono* is a double suicide, a death scene that serves to transform the emotional bond between a prostitute and her lover into a transcendent bond. "Nigorie" also thematizes other kinds of bonds between the sexes, including marriage. Here too, however, Oriki expresses a profound suspicion of the relations between men and women. Her suspicion must be strong indeed, for the text suggests in no uncertain terms that marriage was normally a much sought-after escape from the sex trade. Even in a marriage to the wealthy and charming Tomonosuke, happiness would be elusive it seems: "But you, I've liked you from the beginning," Oriki confesses. "If even a day goes by when I don't see you, I begin to miss you. But if you were to ask me to marry you, what would happen? Would I grow to dislike being married? Perhaps only people apart are fond of each other" (199). Oriki's sentiments here, I will argue, are rooted in an altogether different narrative paradigm that exerts its own substantial force on the formal apparatus and representational world of "Nigorie." Tomonosuke, after all, could have been the villainous foil in a dramatic love-suicide narrative, but instead he plays the role of confidant in a storyline that could not be more different from a *shinjū*. We can here provisionally call this second genre element an anti-success story. The tragic tale of Oriki of the Kikunoi, then, is the locus of at least two heterogeneous genre strands, and having just followed one of those threads to its conclusion, we can now take the end of the second thread and see where it leads. The place to begin, I think, is with a reference that has puzzled Ichiyō specialists for some time now and that has been the focus of a number of critical essays: Marukibashi (literally "log bridge").[32]

One evening there is a raucous gathering of Shinkai-machi shop hands on the first floor of the Kikunoi. Some of the men ask Oriki—who is in the midst of one of her attacks of depression—to sing a song. We get only a snippet of one stanza, the full text of which is the following, according to one annotator: "My love is like the log bridge at Hosotani River; how frightening it is to cross, but cross I must, or I cannot meet the one who fills my thoughts" (*Waga koi wa Hosotani-gawa no Marukibashi, wataru ni ya kowashi wataraneba omou o-kata ni aware ya wa senu*, 195). The verse has a tone of deliberation and longing: the bridge is a metaphor for love (*koi*), which is a frightening, overpowering emotion, as frightening as crossing a valley bridge over a surging river; but not to cross is to forfeit a meeting with the object of one's desire, and, hence, never to know satisfaction. Of course, in the context of a party at the Kikunoi, the nuances of this stanza are quite different, as is indicated when Oriki attaches a flirtatious prefatory passage: "I cannot say his name, but there is someone in this room who fills my thoughts." This is playfully coy, and there is a burst of laughter and applause from the men. The pretense is that there is a man in the room who is the object of the prostitute's love, though she is too shy to reveal his name. Oriki, however, seems to be overwhelmed with emotion listening to her own words—almost as if she were suddenly overcome by the resurgence of powerful memories—and she flees the Kikunoi into the dark streets of the quarter over the protests of the men and women at the party (195–96).

Given the nature of the song's message, the reader might surmise that perhaps Oriki has just been overwhelmed by thoughts of Genshichi or Tomonosuke. However, when we turn to the inside view of Oriki as she wanders aimlessly through the streets lost in thought, we see something very different and unexpected; this is revealed in a section of a lengthy scene of interiority:

Is this life? Does my life amount to this? Oh, I hate it, I hate it! She leaned against a tree by the side of the road and paused for awhile, lost in thought. From nowhere in particular came the echo of her song, seemingly in her own voice: "How frightening it is to cross, but cross I must." There's no other choice. I'll have to cross Maruki Bridge myself. Father lost his footing and fell, and grandfather was the same. I feel the weight of generations of bitterness; I have to do what I can, whether I live or die. (196)

For Oriki, then, Marukibashi seems to have little to do with love. Through an associative leap, she has transferred the image into a different context. The bridge becomes a metaphor for success in Oriki's eyes. The near side of the bridge represents her present life as a prostitute at the Kikunoi, which she desperately wishes to escape. But to escape means she must cross Marukibashi, the far side of which represents prosperity, the fulfillment of one's ambitions, and ultimately redemption. Falling from the bridge signifies death, or more generally, failure. Both her father and grandfather tried to cross the metaphorical bridge and fell, which makes Oriki fearful of crossing herself, almost as if her bloodline makes failure inevitable. In this scene of interiority, Oriki tries to build up a resolve to "cross the bridge," come what may.

At the end of this scene, Oriki runs into Yūki Tomonosuke—she had promised to meet him that night and so he came looking for her—and she returns to the Kikunoi with him, whereupon they go up to their usual retreat on the second floor. Oriki is in tears after her flight through the darkness, and she confides to Tomonosuke that, finally after all this time, she will tell him everything about herself. The subject of her story is an incident in her poverty-stricken childhood when she was sent out to get rice, but slipped on the ice on the way home and spilled her treasure into a gutter. The other part of her story concerns her father and grandfather, who had occupied her thoughts as she wandered the streets of the Shinkai-machi. Oriki's grandfather was a man "who could read ideographs" — in other words, an intellectual — and who wrote treatises of some kind, which were largely ignored by the intellectual community and even banned by the *bakufu*, so he starved to death. "From the time he was sixteen he had decided on his path, but he was born lowly and poor, and even though he made great efforts, he died at the age of sixty without having accomplished anything, the laughing stock of everyone. No one even knows his name nowadays," Oriki explains (200). Oriki describes her father as "an artisan who worked at home because he didn't like to mix in society. He was full of pride, but lacked a merchant's charisma, so he had few customers" (200). Oriki claims her father was a skilled craftsman, who otherwise might have made a good living had he possessed a more outgoing personality. Because he had few customers, though, he and his family lived in poverty. He died an utter failure, his skill unknown, soon after his wife, Oriki's mother, died of tuberculosis (201).

Oriki is haunted by the failure of her father and grandfather to amount to anything in life, and indeed by her own failure to amount to anything more than a *shakufu*. She refers to her lineage as "three generations of failure" (200). What "Nigorie" is engaging here, albeit somewhat faintly, is the underside of the modern discourse on success (*risshin shusse*).[33] This discourse has its roots in such late-nineteenth-century texts as Fukuzawa Yukichi's (1835–1901) *Gakumon no susume* (An Encouragement of Learning, 1872–1876) and Naka-mura Masanao's (1832–1891) translation of Samuel Smiles's *Self Help* under the title *Saikoku risshi hen* (Stories of Success in the West, 1871). *Risshin shusse* is modern ambition, an energy re-leased with the collapse of the early-modern status system (*kinsei mibun seido*) after the Meiji Restoration of 1868 and di-rected, in an emergent capitalist class system, toward the tan-gible goals of education, status, and wealth. *Risshin shusse* plays a decisive role in the construction of the modern bour-geois subject under capitalism. By the 1890s it had become a powerful, even hegemonic, ideology, deeply implicated in the social distribution of power. *Risshin shusse* is also the motor that drives so many of the narratives from the late-nineteenth to the mid-twentieth century; it creates dynamic bundles of energy that coalesce into protagonists intent on marching for-ward toward the bright lights of wealth and prestige. It is re-sponsible for new genres as well. The adventure novel and military story of the Meiji period, to take just two examples from popular fiction, could not exist without the new dis-course on success. Many of the children's stories from the Meiji period were unabashedly didactic in their zeal to instill ambition in their young readers, as we will see in the final chapter of this book.

In contrast to this fiction, from at least the third decade of Meiji onward (that is, from 1888) there is also an entire line-age of anti-success stories that raise troubling questions about this powerful new discourse. Mori Ōgai's "Maihime" (The Dancing Girl, 1890) is an early example: in this story, a young man whose star is on the rise must choose between his career and his love for a poor German dancing girl; he disappoints himself by choosing the former. Later exemplars are works such as Tayama Katai's *Inaka kyōshi* (Country Teacher, 1909), which depicts a protagonist whose ambition to succeed is great, but who is fated to live as a poor country teacher and to die in obscurity; and the major works of Natsume Sōseki, many of which exhibit suspicion of *risshin shusse*: Sōseki's *Mon* (The Gate, 1910), for example, explores, among a host of other themes, the consequences of sacrificing success for a forbidden love.

"Nigorie" cannot be fully understood without reference to the corpus of fiction that deals with ambition and success as well as to the line of fiction that developed alongside it and placed it in question. Indeed, this second narrative thread in "Nigorie" would have been impossible without *risshin shusse*. After all, the new discourse on success would have been anachronistic in Oriki's grandfather's time and even to a large extent in her father's time, yet she has still translated their bitter experiences into this new social category, probably as a way of making sense of their failure in terms she can understand.[34] "Nigorie," then, is one of many contributions to the construction of a new narrative paradigm that was in the early stages of formation during the 1890s.

Ambition and success had an impact on many social practices, and Oriki's negative attitude toward marriage can be connected to *risshin shusse*. We must start with the recognition that *risshin shusse* was a distinctly gendered discourse. The path of success involving ambition and education that leads to rewards of material wealth and social status was gendered male. Success for women was cast in terms of marriage to a successful man, that is, a marriage into wealth and social standing. This is reflected in much of the literature of the period. For example, Ozaki Kōyō's explosively popular *Konjiki yasha* (The Demon Gold, 1897–1903), which began serialization the year after Ichiyō died, stages a drama of ambition and regret that challenges the entrenched ideology of the extended family, but that nonetheless breaks clearly along gender lines. The protagonist, Hazama Kan'ichi, gives up his respectable inheritance of status and wealth in order to pursue a far less reputable path—that of moneylending. His reasons for turning his back on his heritage lie in the rejection of his own love by his cousin and fiancée, Miya. Miya has been offered a marriage proposal by the wealthy and charming Tomiyama Tadatsugu, and she decides to accept it. But while everyone around her is celebrating her "success," Miya deeply regrets sacrificing her love for Kan'ichi to social ambition and spends the rest of the sprawling, unfinished narrative unsuccessfully trying to win him back.

What is so unusual about "Nigorie" is that Oriki can be situated not in relation to her mother or to countless literary characters earlier or later, like Miya, but rather in relation to the male lineage of her family, in which "three generations of failure" include first her grandfather, then her father, and finally herself, the only woman in this group. This is even more astonishing if we consider that social conditions in Meiji would have made her desire for success and redemption largely impossible. It is as if Ichiyō had discovered a contradiction in the emergent ideology of success—a contradiction between success as a universal promise theoretically open to all with ambition, and success in relation to distinctly gendered spheres of activity. This contradiction is the structuring principle of Oriki's interiority. The reason for Oriki's patrilineal orientation is never made clear, although it is quite apparent that she never seriously entertains the idea of an ambitious marriage that would free her from her environment. Female success, it seems, is not for her. Oriki is bending the gender roles of the period and orienting herself toward her male forebears, and success for her becomes indissolubly joined to the redemption of her family as the last in a line.

Oriki's refusal of the gender roles that link marriage and success is perhaps at its most transparent during her conversation with Tomonosuke after her flight through the Shinkaimachi darkness. "You want to succeed [*shusse*], don't you?" Tomonosuke bluntly asks Oriki after she has finished her story about her childhood, and it is unclear at first what exactly the connotations are here. Oriki is very much caught off guard by Tomonosuke's question. Perhaps she is shocked that Tomonosuke has caught a glimpse of her ambition; or perhaps she just interprets it as a recommendation for social advancement through marriage. She answers, "With my lot in life, all I could hope for in marriage is a *miso* strainer. There's no jeweled carriage waiting for me" (201). Her reference to a *miso* strainer (*miso-koshi*) suggests that only marriage to a poor man awaits her were she to choose the path of matrimony as an escape from the Kikunoi. The image also links us to the scene from her childhood in which she goes to collect rice in a *miso* strainer, but accidentally drops it all in the gutter, thereby forcing her family to fast for a day. For Oriki, then, the *miso* strainer is a bitter symbol of the poverty she wishes to escape, but fears she cannot. Her reference to a jeweled palanquin (*tama no koshi*, which is also a pun on *miso-koshi*) suggests marriage into fantastic wealth, which Oriki sees as absurd, even though Tomonosuke essentially offers his hand in matrimony during their conversation. This is significant because a "jeweled palanquin marriage" was the locus of female fantasies of success in the period, as is so evident in the popular fiction of the era (as we will see, too, in the chapter on "Wakaremichi"). There is a demimonde variation of this dream as well. Judging from "Nigorie," it seems that the prostitute's ultimate fantasy is to have her *najimi kyaku*, a veritable knight in shining armor, rescue her from her tawdry world and whisk her away in a jeweled carriage to a life of aristocratic comforts—hence the cheerleading by the women at the Kikunoi when it seems that Tomonosuke is attracted to Oriki, opening up the distinct possibility of her marriage to a wealthy man (185).

Oriki's response to Tomonosuke's sudden question about ambition implies that in a third-rate prostitution district such as the Shinkai-machi the best she could hope for is a humble marriage of the *miso*-strainer variety. Tomonosuke claims that her talk is a ruse and that he sees right through her: "You don't need to lie to me. I've understood you from the beginning. There's no need to hide your ambition. You've got to reach for it" (201). Oriki responds to this encouragement with apathy, though. If Tomonosuke is right, and Oriki is being purposefully misleading here, then it suggests that Oriki does indeed have the ambition to achieve some kind of success, with whatever specific meaning that connotes to her. Success through marriage would have been perfectly acceptable in the social terms of the day (and literary narratives of the era are overflowing with this trope), but Oriki's own desires are quite different. Vague and amorphous her longings may be, but she is resolutely oriented toward a success very different from the normal fantasy in order to redeem the failure of her male ancestors and break out of the cycle of degradation and poverty.

At the same time, Oriki feels doomed to fail and to remain where she is, unable to make the break from her environment that she so desires. Near the end of the lengthy scene of interiority in which Oriki is wandering through the dark streets, terrorized by the word "Marukibashi," this sense of hopelessness is most strongly expressed:

What will become of me? There's no way to know, so I may as well go on as Oriki of the Kikunoi. Maybe I have no sense of compassion or obligation. That can't be true, though. No, it won't do me any good to think such things. But with my station in life, with my occupation and my fate, I'm not really like other people. To think that I am just adds to the pain. (196)

The way Oriki asserts something only to deny it, then circles back around to assert something else only to deny that, too, is characteristic of the representation of her interiority. Oriki makes great associative leaps in her thinking. Her mind spirals through patterns of self-pity, resignation, and a longing to escape, unable to find a solution to her dilemma or liberation from her tortured thoughts. Time and again, she desperately longs to escape the Kikunoi only to immediately doubt the possibility of doing so. These constant pendulum swings between despair and hopeful ambition make her tremendously fearful that she suffers from some mental instability (*kichigai*) that has been inherited from her father and grandfather (201). If her entire bloodline is tainted with a tendency toward insanity, she wonders, would it not be an explanation for her family's inability to make anything of themselves?[35] Moreover, each generation's failure to realize its ambitions leads inexorably to feelings of resentment toward the world; Oriki laments, "I feel the weight of generations of bitterness [*urami*]; I have to do what I can, whether I live or die" (196). Interestingly, the word *urami* appears again at the end of the text, where it is filtered through a supernatural register; the narrator, gesturing toward the ghost stories and macabre tales of an earlier era, describes a *hitodama* flying over the skies of Otera no yama trailing *urami*, thereby suggesting that the weight of three generations of bitterness is not relieved with death. The narrator seems to suggest here that Oriki's resentful spirit stayed on in the world, her longing for success and redemption unfulfilled.

The complexity of the dilemmas Oriki faces inevitably turns the thrust of our story inward, into Oriki's own mind. Extended passages of interiority are rare in "Nigorie," but the narrative is nonetheless a story about the overwhelming dilemmas afflicting one person's mind, about a woman's despair and hopelessness as she tries to make her way in the shadowy world of illegal prostitution, trying in vain to maintain some semblance of human connection to people, even to her customers. An intense psychological focus is, of course, not new to late-nineteenth-century Japanese fiction, but the interiority represented in "Nigorie" is of a strikingly modern variety, linking Oriki's psychology to modern structures of class, hierarchy, and ambition, while also, as we analyzed earlier, suggesting Oriki's profound distrust of representations of love in the quarter. There was certainly a renewed emphasis on psychological portraiture in Meiji, and it was daring, perhaps even revolutionary, of Ichiyō to contribute to this trend by delving so deeply into the mind of a marginal figure like the prostitute and laying bare her tragic complexity and essential humanity. The *kibyōshi*, *ninjōbon*, and didactic tales of an earlier age had certainly featured many marginal figures, but they never attempted a psychological portrait of such impressive depth; nor had any of Ichiyō's contemporaries ever fixed their gaze quite so intently on the mind of a social pariah.

The text certainly cannot rescue Oriki from her situation and shower her with an offer of marriage and the material comforts and respectability of a life in the upper reaches of society, since this would have entailed bowing before the illusory fantasies of the success story, which is a narrative pattern that "Nigorie" forcefully resists at every turn. Instead, "Nigorie" must be understood in relation to the line of anti-success stories of the period, a kind of paradigm that exerts a good deal of force over Ichiyō's narrative. The conclusion of an anti-success story is never bright and, as might be expected, frequently ends in a scene of death. Tragically, the "three generations of failure" does indeed come to an end with Oriki's murder.

"Nigorie" is a split text, however, for the love-suicide archetype exerts its own substantial power over the narrative. Ichiyō, after all, was infatuated with Chikamatsu's dramas and with Edo-era literature in general. Nonetheless, she could not accept all the implications of the love-suicide genre. Such a narrative draws a line between love and society and demands a series of impasses that threaten to separate the lovers in the story, thereby compelling them to choose death, the endpoint of any *shinjū* drama. As I have argued, a crucial feature of this genre is the way that death functions to elevate love (*koi*) into a transcendent bond. The love-suicide archetype is fully inscribed in "Nigorie," but Ichiyō's text exhibits a profound suspicion of the obfuscation of the ties between love and commerce and of the way such theater sweeps away every other concern. Furthermore, the text remorselessly tracks the roots of Oriki's own suspicions about love back to the material conditions and deceptions of the quarter. "Nigorie" may be a split text, then, but it is also a ruthlessly demystifying text, which lays bare the ideological presuppositions of its own foundational materials.

These two paradigms interfere with each other sometimes, but they are also brought together and dialogically interact at other times, especially in the final chapter. As I suggested before, excessive focus on the scene of death involves us in potentially intractable problems, but critics who have performed a kind of literary autopsy on Oriki are ultimately onto something important. The pattern of wounds suggests that

Oriki put up a fierce struggle when faced with the homicidal intentions of Genshichi. In the moment when she was faced with the threat of death, perhaps even with Genshichi's insistence that a love suicide was the only option for them, did Oriki's desire to escape the muddy stream of the Shinkaimachi suddenly surface powerfully and make her wish for life after all? Ichiyō's ambiguous stories invite just such speculation, making interpretation the construction of alternative narratives. Maybe as Oriki exhaled her last breath, in that fleeting, absolutely decisive moment between life and death, she was overwhelmed with a desire for continued existence, perhaps so as to finally cross Maruki Bridge and get hold of some form of redemption. Read in this way, "Nigorie" becomes a terrifyingly pessimistic and profoundly tragic vision of one woman's life.

It also suggests that the image of Maruki Bridge could stand a little more scrutiny. Nakanishi Susumu points to the importance of the image of the bridge in many depictions of *michiyuki* as a transitional point hovering between life and death, able to lead either way.[36] In *Amijima*, for example, the lovers Jihei and Koharu pass over a multitude of bridges on their way to the spot where they will kill themselves, thereby emphasizing their movement between life and death. Marukibashi is the only bridge name that appears in "Nigorie." It may well be that the *michiyuki* and *shinjū* that Ichiyō could not stage because of her resistance to the ideological implications of such a maneuver may have been displaced onto the image of Marukibashi, which would then function as a surrogate for that which could not be depicted—a surrogate that avoids any representation that would serve to elevate the feelings between Oriki and Genshichi into a transcendent bond.

Maruki Bridge becomes a metaphor for the divide between success and failure, life and death, in Oriki's thoughts about her male kin. Read against *risshin shusse* as a gendered discourse, we can also interpret Maruki Bridge as representing marriage as a way out of the Kikunoi, and Oriki is highly ambivalent about this course of action. In addition, the bridge is strongly associated with love in the classical literary tradition.[37] A reference to the Hosotani River and Maruki Bridge (sometimes pronounced Marokibashi) can be found, for example, in the fourteenth-century *Heike monogatari* (The Tale of the Heike). In an analepsis in one section, the lady Kozaishō is being wooed by the warrior Michimori. She is at first reluctant to agree to a meeting with him until she receives a poem from him one day that changes her mind:

> *Waga koi wa / Hosotanigawa no / Marokibashi*
> *fumikaesarete / nururu sode kana*
> My love is like a log bridge at Hosotani River—
>   trodden beneath so many feet, my sleeves are soaked
>   with tears.[38]

There is a pun in this verse: the phrase "*fumikaesarete*" can mean "trodden beneath many feet," but it can also mean "my letters are ignored." Michimori is thus wittily referring to the many times his letters to Kozaishō have been left unanswered, and he urges her once more to meet with him. His wit must be attractive, for the lady sends a reply that indicates her consent. Nonetheless, the romance between Kozaishō and Michimori is cast in a tragic register overall, for Michimori dies in battle, and Kozaishō kills herself in the aftermath. As we saw, the fragment of the song about Maruki Bridge that Oriki sings is also about love, but it simultaneously refers to danger: while the speaker in the song may want to cross the bridge in order to rendezvous with her lover, she also exhibits fear of doing so, a fear represented by the surging river below the bridge.

Given the rich implications and multiple meanings associated with the bridge and the river in "Nigorie"—love, death, danger, escape, success, marriage, failure—Marukibashi threatens to dislodge itself from any firm anchorage in the text, to float across the chain of signification, and to become a symbol of anything and everything. It seems to be a focal point for the multiple generic strands, themes, and discourses in the text, the meanings of which cannot be decisively pinned down by the reader nor fully contained by the author. In rhetorical terms, we might consider the bridge the very trope of dialogism, or intertextuality. If it is true that Maruki Bridge is also a surrogate for the absent scenes of *michiyuki* and *shinjū*, then it is emblematic of the conflicts and contradictions that Ichiyō could not resolve in her negotiations with the intertexts for her story.

FOUR

Happiness Foreclosed

The suffering heroine must surely be the closest thing to a constant in Higuchi Ichiyō's stories. Omine and Oriki are not exceptional figures; there is an entire population in Ichiyō's fiction—almost all women—who live and breathe the air of sorrow and suffering and whose desperate situations stir the reader's capacity for knowing commiseration. These women are daughters, wives, and mothers caught in matrices of gender and class domination that lead to lives of subordination, misery, and even tragic ends. In the most general terms, the structure of domination thematized in Ichiyō's later fiction goes by the name of patriarchy, whether in the broad sense of a socioeconomic system that makes women trophies of male prowess or in the more specific sense of a family system centered on male prerogatives and desires. Furthermore, Ichiyō's heroines never seem to have the power to fight back; they invariably resign themselves in one story after another to a life of profound sorrow. The question is: how do we interpret this aspect of her fiction within the problematic posed by this book?

Such portraits of suffering and resignation have brought out the ire in some readers. Hiratsuka Raichō (1886–1971), a progressive feminist and a co-founder of the group Seitō, or Blue Stockings, wanted to see strong female protagonists and a forceful critique of patriarchy rather than to read about women who tearfully and meekly submit to male authority. In an essay penned in 1912, Hiratsuka suggests that Ichiyō's works are really only attractive to a male readership, for the portrayal of the "sad fates" of "weak women" allows men to bask in their own superiority.[1] She harshly adds that Ichiyō's fiction is largely devoid of creativity and ideas. Hiratsuka was not a sympathetic reader of Ichiyō, and there was little chance that she would consider interpreting the tears in Ichiyō's works as part of a strategy of social critique.

In this chapter, I want to try reading the tears and suffering in Ichiyō's "Jūsan'ya" (Thirteenth Night), which appeared in December 1895 as part of a special edition of *Bungei kurabu* (Literary Club) devoted to women writers, precisely as a concerted social critique; and I use as a point of leverage on this problematic the mode of literary imagination known as sentimentalism. "Jūsan'ya," after all, works overwhelmingly by affect and sensibility, like most of her early stories and completely unlike *Takekurabe*, "Nigorie," and "Wakaremichi." We as readers are not meant to reflect dispassionately on the abstract issues raised by the plot—the impossibility of love, the baleful influence of money, or the intolerable situation of many women in Meiji society—but to have an emotional, even visceral, reaction by encountering a fictional situation that deeply offends our sense of justice and that thus leads us out of fiction to ask critical questions of the real world.[2] I find support for such a reading in the response of Hasegawa Shigure (1879–1941), an early admirer of Ichiyō's stories and a contemporary of Hiratsuka Raichō, who, in her commentary on the work, asked of her society, "how many hundreds or even thousands of Osekis are out there in the shadows, making their ways through life barely noticed?"[3] This feeling has been shared by many readers, both Ichiyō's contemporaries and those in later generations, who have reacted strongly to the plight of a woman all too well acquainted with anguish.[4] Whether sentimentalism can be linked to social intervention in every text is doubtful but remains a problem for future research.

The work of sentimentalism is carried out at both the thematic and rhetorical levels, and another facet of "Jūsan'ya" I emphasize is that its critical message is mediated by, even fused to, the formal and literary qualities of the text in a way that ultimately makes it impossible to separate the literary from the social, the artistic from the ethical. Classical rhetoric carries much of the burden of drawing out the tears of the reader. Ichiyō's particular brand of sentimentalism had always been dramatically amplified with gestures toward the lyrical, tearful stream in classical literature, especially *waka* poetry. The pitiable figures of the early stories are, in their moments of greatest suffering, often graced with the poignant lines of a classical verse. The sentimental mode has an affinity with classical rhetoric in Ichiyō's oeuvre, as if Ichiyō knew that such rhetoric still had nerve endings in the minds and bodies of actual readers at the turn of the century, despite the many contemporary calls for a new vernacular literary language that supposedly spoke more directly to people. The technique in "Jūsan'ya," however, does not involve draping the heroine in *waka* poetry, as in the early stories, but in utilizing another well-worn device from traditional literature: at several points, the natural world is represented as coming to life and commiserating with the dejected heroine. Ichiyō mobilizes this device at times of heightened emotional intensity (typically, as characters have their tear-drenched faces pressed into their sleeves, another tried-and-true motif, incidentally, from classical literature). These moments, I will argue, always implicate the issues of family, class, success, and love in their modern guises. There is in "Jūsan'ya" a conjoining of these very modern concerns and a classical rhetoric pressed into the service of sentimentality and social critique.

In the first of the two parts of "Jūsan'ya," we find the suffering heroine, Oseki, alighting from a rickshaw at the doorstep of her natal home. She has come in secret, leaving behind her only child to beg her parents for permission to divorce her husband, the wealthy and powerful Harada Isamu. Isamu's courtship of Oseki had been a fairy tale of sorts, with many assertions on his part that differences in social station were immaterial. Yet, seven years of marriage have proven to be a kind of hell for Oseki, who has been continuously tormented and ridiculed by her husband despite his assurances before the marriage. Now Oseki wants a divorce; but this would jeopardize her family's tenuous security, for it relies on Harada a great deal. No safe solution is found but for the heroine simply to resign herself to a cruel and loveless marriage. In the second part, Oseki hires a rickshaw for the trip back to her husband and discovers, much to her surprise, that the rickshawman is Kōsaka Rokunosuke, the very man she was hoping to marry before Harada appeared in her life so suddenly. As the two walk through the dark streets exchanging their sad stories, Oseki discovers that Rokunosuke ruined himself in dissipation after he learned of her marriage to Harada; Rokunosuke, it seems, had once been in love with Oseki, and she recalls her own longing for a life with him as well. There is nothing to be done now, however, so the two part beneath the moonlight, their lonely footfalls echoing their forlorn destinies.

Tears flow in a steady stream throughout the narrative, and the power of this story line is typically — and quite sensibly — viewed as turning on a particular emotional dynamic or double bind, which can be found in its most fully articulated form in the opening of the story as Oseki stands at the door of her parents' home and overhears them congratulating themselves on their daughter's good fortune:

Oh, listen to them, so happy for me — they don't even suspect! How can I hang my head and beg them for a divorce? They're sure to lecture me. I'm a mother myself, but I've left little Tarō behind and fled here. I've turned this over in my mind again and again. After all this time, they'll be stunned; all their happiness will vanish, just bubbles on the water. I should just go back without telling them any of it. If I do, I'll be Tarō's mother again — and Isamu's wife forever. My parents can be proud to have a stepson with an imperial appointment, and I can still give them the treats they like and some spending money from time to time. If my wishes come true and I'm divorced, my boy will be so sad with a stepmother, and my parents won't be able to hold their heads up any more. What will other people think? And what about my brother? Because of my selfishness, all his chances for success would come to an end. I should go back! Just go back! But go back to that man, that demon, that demon of a husband? Oh, it's just too awful! (209)

What are given weight here are the *relations* between family members and the *consequences* of particular actions on those who are dear. If Oseki is granted a divorce, she can throw off the chains that bind her, but the happiness of her parents will be destroyed, her brother's future may very well be jeopardized, and she herself will be forever separated from her son, who by law would remain with his father. Also, in the daughter's mind, the hopes and security of her parents have been yoked to filial piety so that it seems to her a decidedly selfish, unfilial impulse to worry about her own happiness at the expense of her family's security. On the other hand, if Oseki returns to Harada, she is giving up her own happiness, but she will at least have the comfort of being with her child, of seeing her parents beaming with pride at her "successful" match, and of seeing her brother achieve some degree of success himself. The introduction of Rokunosuke in the second part has sometimes been viewed as an immodestly tearful contrivance. Yet even detractors generally admit the emotional power of the ending. Oseki's chance encounter with the man she wanted to marry as she returns to the man who detests her gives the story a moving atmosphere of pathos in its final pages and emphatically underscores the theme of happiness foreclosed; and foreclosed happiness is one of the most frequently recurring themes in Ichiyō's fiction.

My own plan is not to debunk an interpretation that is, as I said, quite sensible, but to broaden our understanding of the complexity of Oseki's double bind and the tears it evokes by situating the text in a historically specific matrix of class and gender. Ichiyō's cautionary tale can be pressed into revealing a fuller engagement with the surrounding social world through certain historicist reading strategies geared toward evoking the complex milieu of Ichiyō's story, especially in relation to the rise of the bourgeois nuclear family in the late nineteenth century and the position of women within this new domestic space. By reading "Jūsan'ya" in this way, I hope to reanimate its intertextual connections with modern discourses on class, gender, and the family, which will, I hope, produce a different view of the thematics of this story and help us come to terms with a text that devotes so much of its energy to the solicitation of tears.

Sentimentalism is a literary mode that places affect at the forefront of a text centered on trials and suffering. Tears are copiously shed inside the pages of such a text, and a variety of rhetorical and representational strategies are employed to draw out the sympathy of the text's readers over the plight of the protagonist. It is only fairly recently that scholars have begun to devote serious, sustained attention to literary sentimentalism, and this chapter seeks to contribute to this scholarly current. Before the rise of feminism and cultural studies in the academy, sentimentalism was more often than not a pejorative term for what was seen as an immodest and base kind of writing, which slyly went for the reader's heartstrings rather than for the reader's head. In some national literatures, it became nearly synonymous with women's writing between the late-eighteenth and early-nineteenth centuries, and recent studies have shown how this literature was gendered negatively as feminine.[5]

It is tempting to want to find a similar gendering of sentimentalism in Japanese literature, but the historical record for the Meiji period is ambiguous at best, and we must inevitably speculate until more work is done in this area. First, we do not yet have a very clear sense of just how many women were writing in nineteenth-century Japan. Rebecca Copeland has done a tremendous job rescuing several Meiji-era women writers from obscurity. She rightly celebrates the courage needed on the part of the Meiji woman writer to take up the pen or brush and to write and publish a *shōsetsu*, or prose narrative; but we are still left with the feeling that the number of women who accomplished this was relatively small, a fact that seems to be even more true for the preceding Edo period.[6]

The widespread participation of women in the modern literary world really dates from the 1920s, even as many later writers drew their inspiration from the pioneering Meiji women writers. Second, although the tearjerker had a fairly distinct generic status in the nineteenth century, Meiji women writers were viewed less as participants in the competing literary currents of the day than as occupying a category unto themselves, a category contemporaries called *keishū sakka*, or "talented lady of the inner chamber." If there is a gendering of sentimentalism in Japan, it must be a twentieth-century phenomenon, but as yet not enough work has been done on the topic to even be confident of such a hypothesis. Given what we know about the gendering of the readers of *katei shōsetsu* (the "home novels" that were so prominent in the early years of the twentieth century), we might recklessly speculate that the writers of sentimental novels in the twentieth century also presumed their audience to be primarily women. Perhaps it was not the writers of such fiction who were feminized, but the readers.[7]

The issue of sentimentalism in Japanese literature may turn less on the problem of gender (at least in the nineteenth century) and more on the distinction between art and lowbrow fiction, or, if one prefers, on the distinction between Literature and literature. Jonathan Zwicker's recent work on sentimentalism and the nineteenth-century Japanese novel bears this out. As Zwicker compellingly demonstrates, tears are the cornerstone of a momentous literary shift in the 1780s and 1790s, and sentimentalism dominated the nineteenth-century aesthetic. Yet despite its pervasive influence, even around 1800 sentimentalism was castigated by the proponents of wit as a lowbrow, profit-seeking form of fiction that pandered to the masses. In the 1890s, writers like Ozaki Kōyō and Tokutomi Roka (1868–1927) tried to harmonize commercialism and art, but the subsequent fall of each into the ignoble category of "popular writer" tellingly reveals the fate of sentimentalism (and melodrama, for that matter) after the novel's new mission of serious cultural analysis became an important aesthetic beginning in the 1880s.[8]

The fateful separation of serious and popular fiction—
which can be dated at around 1906 or 1907 with the rise of
Naturalism—was still in the future when Higuchi Ichiyō was
active, and Ichiyō herself maintains a prominent place in the
modern canon even though she relied on sentimentalism in
more than a few stories. A sentimental work like "Jūsan'ya"
participates in a line of fiction that is dominated by male writers in Japan, from Tamenaga Shunsui (1790–1843), probably the
most commercially successful writer in the 1820s and 1830s,
to Ozaki Kōyō, who was the most popular and commercially
successful writer of the 1890s. When Ichiyō began her career
in the early 1890s, sentimentalism was a major stream in the
literary currents of the day. By using "Jūsan'ya" as my text,
I investigate the possibility that Ichiyō fruitfully combines a
male-dominated literary mode with a long tradition and the
shōsetsu's new seriousness of purpose, its new power of inter-
vening in the social world (and open social engagement is to
my mind one of the things that makes the Meiji-era *shōsetsu*
different from Edo-period fiction) in order to lodge a critique
of the social structures that oppress late-nineteenth-century
Japanese women and thus to compel her readers to become
indignant over the fate of the suffering heroine and perhaps
even to change those structures of oppression.[9] The most fruitful entry point is the representation of marriage in the text.

ii

Incomprehensible as his proposal is, given the families' vastly
different social stations, a match with Harada Isamu promises
rewards that cannot be passed up by Oseki's family. He is,
after all, a *sōninkan*, an aide to the Prime Minister, and his
position is of sufficiently high rank as to warrant appointment
by the emperor himself.[10] Harada Isamu is a man held in high
esteem by society, a man of immense social influence. Furthermore, it does not appear that he was born into wealth and
power, but rose to it by acquiring the necessary educational
credentials.[11] Our information about Harada is rather slim, as

he never actually appears in the story itself, but consider, for example, the comments of Oseki's father, who mentions that his prestigious son-in-law is "clever" (*rihatsu*), "an intellectual man" (*gakusha*), and a "hard worker who is widely admired" (*seken ni homemono no hatarakite*, 218). In the Meiji-period cult of success, or *risshin shusse*, these are the telltale signs of the man climbing the social ladder by converting educational credentials into social advancement.[12] It suggests that Harada occupies a lofty position in what David Ambaras has called a "new middle class" in Meiji Japan:

The new middle class that emerged at the turn of the century incorporated civil servants, professionals, educators, journalists, managers, and office workers. Their educational backgrounds and occupational careers distinguished this group from the 'old middle class' of small-scale business owners and manufacturers, who remained a significant presence in both urban and rural areas. While stratified in terms of income and status, the new middle class comprised, in Desley Deacon's formulation, "workers who depend[ed] on the sale of educational, technical, and social skills, or 'cultural capital.' As intellectual workers, they were 'the chief interpreters, creators, and disseminators of knowledge.'" The key to the influence of the new middle class lay not in their numbers, but in their use of this cultural capital and knowledge.[13]

If Harada does indeed occupy a high rung in an economically stratified new middle class, he is certainly not in a state of happy stability, but is an ambitious man who is moving steadily upward through the government bureaucracy and will likely make even more gains in the coming years. He is the quintessential self-made man and an established literary type, joining the ranks of such fictional foils as Honda Noboru in Futabatei Shimei's *Ukigumo* (Drifting Clouds, 1887–1889) and Tomiyama Tadatsugu in Ozaki Kōyō's *Konjiki yasha* (The Demon Gold, 1897–1903).

Marriage to the wealthy and respected civil servant has, of course, completely changed his bride's material life, and wherever we turn our attention in the story, the narrator of "Jūsan'ya" never lets us lose sight of this fact. Oseki lives with her husband in his mansion, a dwelling perfectly in keeping with his lofty position. Our heroine is usually surrounded by servants throughout the day (216). Although in the beginning of the story Oseki makes her way to her parents' home in a simple hired rickshaw, the narrator comments that she normally rides about in the splendid, black-painted Harada family rickshaw (209). She wears luxurious kimonos (210) and the kind of expensive lacquered clogs known as *nuri-geta* (226) and routinely carries large amounts of money (220, 225). Thus, Oseki is enveloped in the material possessions and luxuries indicative of her recently acquired status.[14]

The luxury and leisure in which Oseki is now swathed stands in marked contrast to the shabby conditions in which her parents and brother live, which we glimpse at several revealing moments in the narrative. The Saitō house is cramped and dirty, and Oseki's father worries that his daughter's sumptuous kimono will be soiled by the grimy, worn-out *tatami* matting (210). The atmosphere in their home seems even more oppressive because the father is ill, and his sickbed has been laid out in the living room, presumably for lack of any space in which to prepare a proper sickroom. Naturally, the poverty of Oseki's family extends right down to everyday articles: Oseki's mother, for example, frets over the fact that she wears plain kimonos and carries a cheap umbrella (212). The treats for the moon-viewing celebration and the pampas grass in the vase, which are the only decorative objects to be found in their home, clash violently with the surrounding poverty. The decorations and the mother's worries over fashion do, however, suggest a family used to better things; they hint that the Saitōs had been more prosperous previously, when it seems that they were several rungs higher on the social ladder, perhaps even middling-level townsfolk. Anything beyond this is mere speculation, but the point about a social fall over the years is echoed by Seki Reiko, who has observed that the Saitō family now lives in a lowly area of Tokyo called Shinzaka in present-day Ueno; only five years earlier the family had lived in a better area of the city, a place called Sarugaku-chō in present-day Chiyoda Ward, a move that suggests the family's situation has deteriorated badly over the years.[15]

There could be no greater contrast between Oseki's current material situation as the wife of Harada Isamu and her former life as the daughter of the Saitō family. What we have in Oseki, then, is a character who has taken a gigantic leap up the social ladder by means of the institution of marriage, a point that is valid whether we look at the situation of the Saitōs at the time they gave away their daughter or at their much deteriorated position in the narrative present. By contracting so far above her family's station, Oseki has escaped a fate that would have eventually consigned her to the life of an impoverished *shita-machi* (low city) girl residing in a cramped home in Tokyo's backwater, and has snared a husband whose star is on the rise to become the regal matron of a splendid *yamanote* (high city) mansion.

That the Saitō family itself benefits materially from the match is perfectly apparent: Oseki's father admits as much in his lengthy speech to her (219); and her brother Inosuke's new position and higher salary at his place of employment seem to be the direct result of Harada's intervention (210). That is, Oseki's marriage to Harada creates a kinship bond, which can then be exploited by Oseki's family for material gain in quite socially legitimate ways. The family will continue to make use of it to stave off the worst effects of a social free fall. Although such familial welfare should not be dismissed lightly, of equal weight in the minds of Oseki's parents is the new status the marriage confers on Oseki herself; this is exactly the self-congratulatory praise Oseki overhears in the beginning of the story. Her unexpected and impressive leap up the social ladder makes her a veritable emblem of female success, a status obtained through marriage to a self-made man.

The world of "Jūsan'ya" is thus one with a fluid class structure, as is the case with most of Ichiyō's later stories; it is a world of extraordinary social mobility, with some people rising gloriously to dizzying heights and others tumbling ignominiously to the bottom rungs of society. All the players in "Jūsan'ya" are either moving upward or downward. What the text represents in its pages, then, is not just class difference (social class, after all, is a highly unstable category in the Meiji period), but the dynamic of social mobility in a world in which everything is shifting underfoot and the meaning and price of female success in such an uncertain, floating world.

Oseki's successful match has brought her not only a stately coiffure, luxurious clothes, and a good amount of spending money, but a great deal of suffering and trouble as well. The promise of marital bliss vanished after a few months of wedlock. After enduring her husband's torment for seven years, Oseki has fled in order to plead with her father to grant her a "letter of divorce" (*rien no jō*), which Meiji law required a woman to obtain from her father or male guardian.[16] With her eyes clouded by tears, Oseki relates the circumstances of her unhappy union: she speaks of how Isamu is a "demon" (*oni*) who abuses her psychologically; of how he never has a kind word to say to her; of how embarrassed he is to have her as a wife; of his probable dalliances with other women. This is a far cry from the fairy tale that Oseki's parents have treasured up until their daughter relates the shocking truth.

Oseki herself admits that during the first six months of her marriage she was indeed put on a pedestal by Isamu just as he said he would do. When she muses on the cause of the sudden change in Isamu's attitude toward her, she concludes that it was due to the birth of their son: "After Tarō was born, Isamu became a completely different person. It's fearful even to recall. It was as if I had been pushed into a dark valley, unable even to glimpse the warm light of the sun" (214). The impending birth of his son seems to have caused a radical change in Harada's feelings toward his wife.

A close analysis of Oseki's account of Harada's abuses reveals the absolute centrality of education, and especially of what we might call polite accomplishments and refined graces, to the domestic discord. Isamu complains that Oseki is "untalented and unmannered." He claims that she is "a person without education." From his point of view, she is "tiresome, dull, and ignorant." Isamu "can't talk with her about anything." Isamu claims that their house lacks liveliness and charm and that "when a household is uninteresting, it's the fault of the wife" (214–15). Such are Harada's complaints, as related by Oseki to her parents. Oseki herself seems to concur to a large extent, reminding her mother and father that she "wasn't brought up having gone to the Peeress's School." She adds, "I never learned flower arranging, the tea ceremony, poetry, or painting like other wives, and so I can't make a good conversationalist" (214).

If Oseki's account of Harada's dissatisfaction is accurate (and the text gives us no reason to be suspicious), it seems that Oseki's lack of education and polite accomplishments are central to the marital strife.[17] Given Oseki's class position, it is impossible to expect that she could have received an education in any way similar to that acquired by the kind of women who normally married men like Harada Isamu, women who had schooling and who were accomplished in the tea ceremony and flower arranging. Our first exegetical moves here suggest that women's education is an important theme in "Jūsan'ya" and that the emotional center of the story might be found as much in the anxieties of class difference as in issues of gender.

I want to forge ahead with this line of inquiry and explore what at first appears to be a minor part of Ichiyō's well-known story by drawing into the same orbit "Jūsan'ya" and a group of polemic essays by Iwamoto Yoshiharu (1863–1942) published the following year, essays that will open a window onto an emergent discourse on the nuclear family in the mid-Meiji period. A fuller understanding of this new discourse will allow us to situate "Jūsan'ya" in a new context and to see Oseki's double bind and the sentimentalism of the text in a new light.

iii

The essays I want to discuss appeared in the "Home" column (*Kateiran*) of *Taiyō* (The Sun), which was a staple of the magazine from its founding in 1895 until 1902 (the magazine itself survived until 1928). The fact that the column ran for so many years suggests the importance of the family in public discourse at the turn of the century. It is true that no one text or group of essays decisively dominates this discourse, but Iwamoto was one of the most influential male theorizers of the female, and his essays allow us to glimpse with unusual clarity the links between the ideals of domesticity, child-rearing, and female education, ideas that are at the heart of "Jūsan'ya."

Iwamoto was a magazine editor, essayist, and schoolteacher. He was a cosmopolitan thinker steeped both in the religious and social ideals of Christianity and the ideas of the Japanese Enlightenment thinkers of the 1870s. No facet of life seemed beyond his interest, whether it be gender roles in contemporary society, the place of religion in Japan's modernization, or even the techniques of modern agriculture. Women's education, however, was first on his agenda. He helped found the journal *Jogaku zasshi* (Journal of Women's Learning), which was devoted to raising the standards of women's education, and participated in the establishment of the Meiji Women's School. He was even its principal for a time.[18] This institution, whose alumnae included many prominent women activists and writers, was the laboratory in which he put his theories about women's education into practice.

A new discourse emphasizing women's education and domesticity arrived in Japan in the 1870s as the translated ideal of Victorian womanhood in England and the United States. Japanese Enlightenment thinkers of the period were smitten by Anglo-American images like the "angel of the hearth," the woman who was graceful and educated, a loving mother and a caring wife.[19] While these ideas were influential among intellectuals (especially Japanese Christian intellectuals), they had limited social penetration in the first few decades of the Meiji period, during which competing ideals of womanhood and family had the upper hand. The Meiji state, after all, was trying to universalize the old *ie seido* (family system), which offered a model of a lineal, extended family in which the position of patriarch was passed down from father to son. Under this kind of familial roof, women's education was not paramount; the system was interested primarily in the woman's womb, not her head. While the state continued to push its version of the *ie*, a number of competing visions of the family and women's roles were proffered: chief among these was the *katei*.[20] This ideal, which depended on the earlier Victorian image of femininity, de-emphasized the sprawling structure of the *ie* and instead placed at its center a loving couple caring for their children; it was less concerned with the father-son relationship, or inheritance, and more concerned with the mother-child relationship.[21] This model was honed and modified, and by the mid-1890s proponents of the *katei* could offer a compelling image of the new nuclear family. They accomplished this by reinforcing existing ideas about the male sphere of work and the female sphere of domesticity, by marketing the nuclear family as an economic unit, and by proffering a new view that this unit was the foundation of the nation.[22] Interestingly, the new emphasis on the link between nation and hearth made it easy for the state to eventually incorporate the *katei* into an uneasy dual structure of the family around the turn of the century—the sprawling, patrilineal *ie* was maintained as an overarching kinship system, but it was made up of collateral *katei* centered on its married sons.[23]

It was in the climate of the mid-1890s, a period of heightened ideological conflict over the family, that Iwamoto and others began emphatically to reassert the Victorian ideals of womanhood and domesticity. The essays Iwamoto penned in 1896 elaborate a systematic ideology of feminine roles in society, and at the core of Iwamoto's doctrine is the gendered division of labor. Nowhere is this given greater attention and rhetorical flourish than in his May essay entitled "Kazoku no danran" (Family Harmony): the domestic sphere is explicitly gendered as a female preserve, while the sphere of public life outside the home—the world of "wind and waves," as Iwamoto is prone to call it—is coded as a male space. This public, outer world is where men sally forth in order to do the work of the nation and secure a livelihood for their family.

It is a world of honor and duty, but also one of tension and stress. Men who venture into this hostile and dangerous environment have their family as protection and shield, a notion predicated on a view of the inside of the home — the woman's sphere, in Iwamoto's doctrine — as a realm of tranquility, harmony, and pleasure, the very antithesis of the modernizing world raging outside its protective walls.[24]

At the same time, Iwamoto strives to elevate the status of the housewife in Meiji society. He wants to create a climate in which women, too, feel that they are important contributors to a modernizing Japan, and thus he sets out to glorify the domestic realm to that end. In "Katei wa kokka nari" (The Home Is a Nation), which appeared in March, Iwamoto boldly asserts that "[t]he home is a nation. Overseeing the home is a kind of politics, and thus each of you [housewives] is its prime minister" and also that women have "made use of nineteenth-century civilization" and thus "achieved a revolution inside the home in perfect accord with political changes rooted in the establishment of the new constitution."[25] This rhetoric elevates the status of the housewife — indeed, here she is at the forefront of reform and technological progress and thus indispensable to a modernizing Japan — even as it more firmly shackles women to the *inside* of the home and to two respectable roles, wife and mother.

The domestic sphere may be the realm of women's activities, separate and distinct from the sphere of masculine endeavors, but for Iwamoto and many others the state has a clear interest in what goes on inside the walls of the nation's homes. The modern nation-state is especially interested in its youth, for they are, after all, its future; and no aspect of the domestic sphere is more important to Iwamoto than the health and early education of the country's children. Iwamoto emphatically declares, "mothers who are not healthy will be unable to deliver a healthy baby."[26] This statement is the heart of an essay called "Joshi no taiiku" (Physical Education for Women), which attempts to demonstrate that the state has a legitimate, abiding interest in the physical well-being of all the female bodies within its borders, as the nation's children are at risk when the bodies of Japanese women are not strong and fit.

Just as an unhealthy female body can endanger the children of the country, so too can an uneducated mother, a point upon which Iwamoto places enormous emphasis in the opening essay of the 1896 series, "Haha no mugaku" (Ignorant Mothers). Here Iwamoto suggests that mothers who, because of sheer ignorance, do not know how to properly raise and educate their children will end up inadvertently harming, even killing, them.[27] Iwamoto's cures for "ignorance" are not just "sewing" and "cooking"—for him, the traditional, backward, unenlightened roles for women—but include more aggressive treatments, such as a knowledge of "biological science," "psychology," and "pedagogy."[28] The cure, in other words, is education for women. After all, since children spend nearly the entirety of their early years in the home, in the company of their mothers, then the influence exerted by such women is powerful; if the nation were to have any hope of having an educated citizenry who could protect its borders and interests, it had to have educated women.

In the February "Tsuma no mujō" (Hardhearted Wives), Iwamoto had already made his first tentative connections between the gendered division of labor and women's education. In it, he argues that when the husband returns home at the end of the day, exhausted and troubled by the affairs of the world, he seeks consolation from his wife. Part of being able to lend emotional support to him is the ability to handle conversation about his world, so she must know something about the way society works; she must be an educated person, familiar, at least in outline form, with a great variety of fields of endeavor and intellectual inquiry.[29] This view caught on among progressive households, but Iwamoto never pursued it further in the 1896 series, for in the themes of child-rearing and nation-building he had discovered a far more powerful justification for women's education than the role of conversation partner, and all of his later views on women's education focus on the interests of the state.

Iwamoto emphatically asserts that women's education is crucial to all levels of the child's development. Early learning among children often takes the form of persistent questions directed at the mother. Wise and knowledgeable mothers recognize these questions as being crucial to the child's education and development and answer them patiently. Ignorant mothers—those same women who understand only sewing and cooking, rather than biology, psychology, and pedagogy—misunderstand their importance and ignore their children's queries. This is extraordinarily damaging to the child's education and development, Iwamoto suggests, for it kills off the child's "enthusiasm for study" (what he calls *benkyōshin* or *benkyō no kokoro*).[30]

It is worth taking a moment to unpack the significance of this phrase. *Benkyō*, or study, is inseparably connected to success in the Meiji period, as we see in such common expressions of the day like "study is the capital for wealth and honor" and "study is the foundation for success." The historical sociologist Takeuchi Yō has traced the history of the word in the context of larger social transformations, beginning with the maxims I just mentioned, continuing through the crystallization of the school system as the place in which the educational credentials that would lead to success were acquired, and concluding with the onset of the age of testing, in which study and success essentially meant passing crucial exams and entering the most prestigious schools.[31] From the 1880s on, the route to success through study was highly circumscribed, and the diligent few who were able faithfully to follow this course constituted the new middle class of Meiji; these were men who found themselves in the enviable position of steady promotion and advancement in the government bureaucracy or in industry by trading on their educational capital. Such ideas were yoked to Social Darwinism, and society was imagined as a competitive struggle in which only the most studious and diligent survived and achieved success. As study (*benkyō*), testing (*shiken*), and success (*shusse*) became firmly and indissolubly linked, life itself was viewed as being analogous to an exam, and children needed to be prepared for it early.[32]

The influence of the home was thus instrumental in inspiring enthusiasm for study in a child, and this was the surest defense against failure later in life. In the essay "Katei no kankaryoku" (The Influence of the Home), Iwamoto explicitly links home education to success: "Parents [read "mothers"] who sincerely wish success [*shusse*] for their children, must do more than have them read books and enter school. They must recognize the importance of a good disposition."[33] Thus, it is not just book learning that is at issue here, but the inculcation of certain dispositions, skills, and attitudes that are prerequisites for future education and success, and a woman's primary responsibility in her capacity as mother was to see to this business. But consider, too, that in the course of this essay Iwamoto expands the idea of the influence of the home to include its "beauty," or level of cultural refinement, and argues that this also exerts a powerful influence on childhood dispositions and the formation of character as the child matures. The "influence of the home" is thus a pivotal concept in Iwamoto's doctrine, for, among other things, it allows him to link gender roles, women's education, the cultural atmosphere in the home, and child-rearing practices.

In the July piece, entitled "Katei no yūraku" (The Pleasure of the Home), Iwamoto begins to move from child-rearing to the broader contours of family life. He situates the location of cultured, civilized pleasure—rest, relaxation, enjoyment, play—firmly within the contours of home and family, yoking the pleasure of the home (*katei no yūraku*) to family harmony (*kazoku no danran*), an important idea that was rapidly coming to be the central preoccupation of the modern bourgeois nuclear family, as Muta Kazue has demonstrated.[34] In his final essay in the series, the November piece "Katei no fūga" (The Elegance of the Home), Iwamoto's discussion of family pleasures shades over to the loftier matters of elegance, refinement, and culture in the home, what he variously calls *fūga* or *fūryū*: "Whatever we pronounce enjoyable is due to our taking pleasure in its beautiful features. In other words, it is to satisfy one's sense of elegance [*fūga*]." The class implications of this seemingly innocuous pronouncement begin to take shape within a few paragraphs with a thinly veiled diatribe against the laboring classes: "Those who do not enjoy elegance [*fūga*]," Iwamoto asserts, "are typically people mired in the animal passions."[35] Elegance and refinement seem to be all that stands in the way of the rude and unsavory pleasures. Iwamoto also decries bourgeois pretenders who cannot live up to his standards: "It is said that our world has advanced to the state of civilization, yet while there are many who praise the lady and the gentleman, it is truly astonishing how practices degenerate into lowly pleasures."[36] At the opposite end, Iwamoto insists that people not mistake expensive tastes and luxuries for elegance and refinement: "When one speaks of elegance, perhaps some immediately think of luxury or view it as reckless profligacy, but this is a mistake. Spending a great deal of money is prodigality, not elegance [*fūryū*]. Likewise, being idle is laziness, not elegance [*fūryū*]," rants Iwamoto, strongly suggesting that his target here is the aristocratic class.[37] In Iwamoto's hands, then, civilized pleasure, elegance, and cultural refinement seem decidedly middle-of-the-road and middle-class experiences. But Iwamoto is also able to universalize bourgeois tastes by removing them completely from the material world; he accomplishes this by asserting, "[e]legance is to be found in the midst of shabbiness, in the midst of poverty, and even in the midst of the hustle of daily routine. In other words, elegance is a matter of the heart."[38] Iwamoto's maneuvers here are not without a degree of skill: the lower orders and middle-class pretenders do not know elegance; the upper class has confused luxury with refinement. Bourgeois gentlemen like Iwamoto, however, have discovered that true elegance is a matter of cultivating the spirit or heart.

It is worth noting, by way of conclusion to this part of the discussion, the links between Iwamoto's bourgeois elegance of the heart and the matter of enjoying Japanese traditions with the family: "One should make every effort to determine the days when the moon is full, when it will snow, or when the blossoms will be in bloom, make preparations to gather the whole family together, and partake fully of these elegant pastimes."[39] Since Iwamoto assigns the domestic sphere to women, it seems that in his scheme women become the keepers of what was then being coded as Japanese tradition. As wives, women create a consoling preserve of the old ways to which husbands return after struggling in the wave-battered, wind-smitten world of a modernizing Japan; in the role of mother, women cultivate a learned, cultured nest for their children. Muta Kazue has pointed out that in the patriotic fervor following the Japanese victory in the Sino-Japanese War, the proponents of the *katei* began to conceptualize the home as the site of Japanese tradition, and women were to play a crucial role in keeping the ancient customs alive.[40] Iwamoto, too, participates in this project. Interestingly, an argument that began by emphasizing that Japanese housewives are the potentates of modest, four-walled kingdoms and at the cutting edge of modernization has ended by emphatically declaring these same women to be the guardians of traditional culture. What Iwamoto has accomplished is a skillful manipulation of the domains of tradition and modernity by appealing to gender roles. Japanese women have a foot firmly and reassuringly planted on each side of the divide between tradition and modernity: they preserve the best of the old ways, but they are also open to new ideas and new technologies.

In the logic of Iwamoto's argument, spun out over the course of these eight essays, culture, women's education, and child-rearing are brought into the same locus—a particular class ideal of family and hearth. The gender roles Iwamoto has defined necessitate an educated woman in the house; this is a cultured woman with refined graces, who can create an elegant atmosphere in the home and raise children who will be cultured, ambitious, and successful national subjects. This woman is the Victorian "angel of the hearth" transplanted with new attire into the emergent Japanese *katei*.

iv

As I hope to have demonstrated, Iwamoto's ruminations are by no means haphazard gesticulations, but instead elaborate over the course of nearly a year an organized, coherent, and influential view of gender roles in the family, women's education in modern society, and child-rearing practices in the bourgeois home, all of which are concerns he shared with other prominent ideologues of the *katei* in his day. In "Jūsan'ya," Ichiyō finds in these discourses a potent, emotionally charged terrain for literary exploration.

Consider how the major themes in Iwamoto's essays surface in "Jūsan'ya," thus indicating the dialogic relationship between Ichiyō's story and *katei* discourse. The marital tension between Oseki and her husband centers on what Harada perceives as a lack of education and cultural refinement in his wife, which, having worked through the ideas behind the cultured home, we can now view in a new light. Harada's major complaints about Oseki, we might recall, are that she lacks polite graces, that their home is dull and unrefined, and that she does not make a good conversation partner because she is not properly educated. Oseki herself admits that she cannot make a good conversationalist (and thus cannot be a consoling presence for her husband after he returns from the stressful, workaday world of the government bureaucracy) because she did not receive the kind of training that would prepare her for such an unfamiliar wifely role. Oseki confesses, too, that she feels anxious in the presence of the wives of Harada's colleagues, for she does not know flower arranging, the tea ceremony, poetic composition, painting, or any of the other polite accomplishments indicative of a privileged female education. In other words, Oseki lacks precisely those talents that are held up as ideals of womanhood in discourse on the *katei*. Cultural refinement—with an emphasis on the cultivation of a sense of beauty and elegance, an appreciation for nature and native traditions, and, for women, the acquisition of the polite accomplishments and refined tastes associated with these native traditions—was elevated into a new ideal, what we can call "cultured wife, educated mother," and placed at the very heart of the new *katei*. In this vision, a home without refinement overseen by an uneducated and uncultured woman was an intolerable embarrassment.

The ideal of the *katei* as a progressive vision of the family from the 1870s into the twentieth century is most strongly associated with the bureaucrats, educators, and salaried workers who constituted the new middle class in Meiji Japan.[41] Recall that I speculated before on Harada's class affiliation; the way he is represented in the text as an adherent of the ideals of domesticity and education associated with *katei* discourse lends further support to the hypothesis that he is a member of the new middle class, albeit a person now occupying its upper reaches. Nowhere is Harada connected more firmly to this class and its ideals than in his exasperation over Oseki's lack of refinement.

Recall, too, that Oseki's lack of education did not become a serious issue for the powerful government official until his son Tarō was born. It was only then that Harada became disappointed with his wife's perceived lack of cultural achievements. Of course, this marriage was perhaps doomed from the start because of the severe differences in social rank (and thus marital expectations) involved, and so one could well imagine a variety of reasons in Ichiyō's mind why Harada would suddenly begin to complain loudly about Oseki. Perhaps the marital friction arises as Harada's own bourgeois leanings begin to outweigh his earlier infatuation with Oseki; or perhaps he is no longer enraptured by the fantasy of courting a marginal social figure and then remaking her into a proper bourgeois wife.[42] Nonetheless, the birth of Tarō is unequivocally represented in the text as being the chief factor behind the fighting, so it behooves us to offer at least a hypothesis about it in terms of class ideals of the family. As we witnessed, since elegance and refinement were linked to the inculcation in children of a certain disposition toward success, it was thought by proponents of the *katei* that a home without culture was actually a serious hindrance to a child's ability to make something of himself. This is an especially important consideration for the elder son and heir (*chōnan*). Once the *chōnan* is born, the matter of a cultured home becomes crucial. After all, in the Meiji world of *risshin shusse*, with its relatively fluid class structure, families compete with others for prestige and wealth; and a family's status is determined in large measure by the status of its head, and later of its *chōnan*. In such a world, cultural refinement and educational credentials become cultural capital, which helps secure a prestigious place in the social order for a particular family and its members. In the bourgeois view of the home, Tarō's chances of success, and beyond that, the status and position of the Harada family, would be seen as being in some jeopardy because of Oseki's alarming lack of education and because their home is devoid of beauty and elegance.

When read against other textual traces in other culturally demarcated zones, then, we discover that Oseki's marriage to Harada founders on the rocks of culture, polite accomplishments, and refined graces, which were distinct class ideals of femininity and domesticity that were taking final shape precisely during the decade in which Ichiyō was writing and that were being propagated by exactly the kind of men whom the fictional Harada represents. This reading of "Jūsan'ya" places the text squarely in modernity and is opposed to many earlier interpretations, which view Oseki as being caught in a traditional, premodern, feudal family structure. Seki Ryōichi's reading has been enormously influential in this regard, casting a long shadow from the 1970s to the present day. His conclusion is that "this story is, put simply, a fateful premodern tragedy" (*Kono shōsetsu wa, iwaba, zenkindai teki na unmei higeki de aru*).[43] It is, of course, easy to poke holes in 30-year-old essays. I mention Seki's conclusion because it underscores how new conceptions of the family in Meiji Japan can provide new tools for analyzing literary texts. Seki was working within a framework that saw all oppression in the modern family as an unfortunate holdover from premodern times, something that had not yet been fully ironed out by modernization. In a post-Foucauldian world, in which modernity itself is suspiciously seen as spawning many new forms of oppression, we can view the institution of the modern nuclear family within the context of a reconstituted patriarchy and an emergent bourgeois ideology of the cultured home—precisely the problems Ichiyō confronts in "Jūsan'ya" and shows to be sites of tyranny of their own.

Put in more concrete terms, at issue in this modern tragedy of the *katei* is whether Oseki should remain in a marriage steeped in a tension rooted in class ideals of the family or obtain her coveted letter of divorce and return to her natal home. As we saw, neither option is satisfactory, so the heroine faces an intolerable double bind, which is both the heart of the social critique lodged by the text and the engine of its affective machinery. Marriage to Harada has made Oseki an exemplar of female success, but the fact that the two do not share the same ideals has created such strain in the marriage that Oseki can no longer bear it. She is willing to make the ultimate sacrifice—abandoning her son—in order to be free of the cage that confines her. However, if Oseki returns to her natal home, she will be forever separated from her child, and both the security of her parents and her brother's chances of success will be seriously threatened. In this reading, the supreme irony of the story is that female success rests squarely upon certain class differences between husband and wife that ultimately lead to an intolerable married life. Furthermore, the material security of the Saitō family depends upon that very difference in social rank and upon their daughter's ability to weather the storm that such difference generates in her marriage.

Oseki's mother is sympathetic toward her daughter's plight, but her father is ultimately unwilling to pay the price that would accompany a divorce. Their reactions thus break clearly along gender lines. Oseki's mother explodes with rage over Harada's treatment of her daughter: "How stupid of us! How arrogant he is, treating you like some urchin he picked up off the streets! What business does he have telling anyone you

aren't educated?" (216). She indignantly declares that the family did not go fishing for a wealthy son-in-law; it was Harada,
she reminds everyone, who claimed to have fallen for their
daughter and wished to wed her. Given the circumstances of
the marriage, Oseki's mother sees it as shameless that Harada
should treat Oseki the way he does, even if his social position
is intimidatingly lofty. The thing that really seems to infuriate
Oseki's mother is that Harada scolds Oseki in front of the
maids; regardless of her social station before her marriage,
Oseki is now Harada's wife, and thus he has no business
ridiculing her in front of the household help for her lack of
education and polite graces. The mother concludes her diatribe with a threat: "I'd like to see Isamu just now and give
him a piece of my mind" (217).

Next is the father's speech, which Ichiyō has pointedly cho-
reographed as the voice of patriarchy overriding the maternal
voice. Reacting to his wife's anger, the father warns, "Now
mother, don't say anything rash" (217). He represents his own
discourse as the calm voice of reason, and even while expressing great sympathy for his daughter's situation, the father's
speech essentially consists of laying down the reasons why
Oseki must not divorce: 1) Differences in social station often
cause misunderstanding, so it is unlikely Harada is being cruel
on purpose; 2) As an important figure in society, Harada is
under enormous pressure of a kind that is difficult for anyone
in the Saitō family to appreciate, and he unwittingly takes his
stress out on Oseki; 3) A wife's role is to do her best for her
husband, regardless of his mood, and thus Oseki should not
expect sunny tranquility all the time; 4) Inosuke's new position
and salary are the direct result of Harada's intervention on
behalf of the Saitō family, and furthermore, the material situation of the family is directly dependent on keeping in Harada's
good graces; 5) If Oseki divorces Isamu, she will never see her
son again, for she will cease to have any legal claim to her boy.
The father's conclusion is essentially a plea to his daughter to
put her family before herself: "Oseki, I know it's hard, but for
the sake of your parents and brother, for the sake of little

Tarō—if you've been able to hold out this long, surely you can do so from here on out" (219).

Oseki collapses into tears and loses her resolve to get a divorce, a reversal that has proved immensely troublesome for those wishing to find a subversive feminist streak in "Jūsan'ya."[44] Many scholars have interpreted her capitulation exclusively as a personal issue involving a handful of family members, but it seems more fruitful to view the matter as one in which Oseki is pressed in by a variety of very powerful social ideologies—filial piety, wifely duties, motherhood—and is unable to find a position from which to lodge a protest that would be socially legitimate in this period, and thus credible in the eyes of her father. Oseki is caught in the shifting sands of class, ambition, love for her child, trepidation over her family's security, and feminine ideals. The network of expectations is too dense, and so by the end of the first part of the story Oseki's options have been reduced from one to none: she must return to Harada.

With this sacrifice of individual freedom for the welfare of the collective, we are at the emotional center of the story, and the advantage of a model that sees Oseki as being unable to lodge a credible protest, as opposed to the perspective of capitulation, is that it allows us to situate the affective levers of the text in relation to the social critique enacted by the story. After all, one way to reveal the injustice of a particular social institution is to have the heroine tragically succumb to its power, and we must react emotionally to this, because we as readers can see that there should be other options. In my view, this is the heart of Ichiyō's socially engaged sentimentalism. The text relies heavily on the sentimental mode throughout its pages as the scope of Oseki's dilemma is made clear, but in these final moments of the first part of the story, as all alternatives to a hateful marriage are taken from Oseki, the dominant emblem of sentimentality, the tear, becomes especially prominent. We see Oseki shed a veritable river of tears over the injustice of her situation, and her mother, too, seems to have her face perpetually buried in her sleeves. Even Oseki's father

appears on the verge of tears at one moment over his inability
to extract his daughter from her shackles. The text's typical
representation of weeping—the face pressed into the sleeve—
is a familiar motif from traditional Japanese literature; indeed,
it occurs so frequently in classical and medieval fiction that
we tend to take it for granted. This motif is designed to draw
out the sympathy, even the very tears, of the tale's readers.
It is an appeal to the reader's capacity for sensitivity and sympathy when confronted with a scene of intense emotion.

Tears do even more work in the text: they also create a
bridge between the human and the natural worlds. Consider
the mother's reaction to the fate of her daughter near the close
of the first part: "Oseki's mother burst out, 'Oh, how unlucky
the girl is,' and wept a deluge of rain. On this sad night, the
unclouded moon suddenly looked disconsolate, and the wild
pampas grass in the vase, which her brother Inosuke had
picked from the thickets along the bank in the back of the
house, beckoned as if to offer its sympathy" (220). Here the
mother's tears are likened to rain, which provides an associative transition to the preoccupation with the natural world in
the second part of the passage; tears give way to rain, which
in turn gives way to an image of the clear moon and the pampas grass. Following the lead of traditional literature, Ichiyō
brings the two worlds of nature and humanity into even closer
alignment, for nature is represented here as something very
like a living creature offering its sympathy to the suffering
heroine. Once the decision is made to send Oseki back to
Harada, the moon suddenly appears "disconsolate," and the
leaves of the pampas grass beckon in a gesture of commiseration, which is at the same time an embodiment of Oseki's
absent brother Inosuke.

Ichiyō does not go so far as to conclude emotional passages
by decorating the weeping heroine with a classical *waka*,
which she might very well have been inclined to do were this
story written earlier in her career, but she does avail herself
fully of classical poetic diction. The pampas grass, which
seems to sway in sympathy for Oseki, is a seasonal word (*kigo*)

for autumn. Seasonal words, such as references to plants, animals, and celestial and meteorological phenomena, were the poetic vocabulary of the natural world, which were grouped around particular seasons and were meant to be evocative of the essence of each season. The moon, which puts in several appearances in the story, was also a seasonal word for autumn. The story takes place on an evening of a clear moon, the thirteenth night of the eighth month of the lunar calendar, which is autumn in that way of reckoning time; and autumn is the season of ends, death, parting, and grief, an evocation perfectly in keeping with the mood and temporal setting of Ichiyō's story. Indeed, from the perspective of someone like Ichiyō, who had internalized the rich vocabulary from Heian and medieval literature through her training at the Haginoya, how could the story not be set in autumn? To avoid the association would be to lose the entire repertoire of classical poetic language and imagery, a vocabulary that was still vitally connected to the tear ducts in the Meiji period and that could open up vistas of a vast intertextual field populated by other dejected heroes and heroines from the past. At the same time, classical rhetorical devices are revised and situated within a new context, thus providing new layers of meaning that are available to later writers. Ichiyō has used classical language for different ends; she has drawn from its storehouse that which will arouse in the reader sympathy and compassion for a heroine who is caught in a particular double bind, the contours of which are specific to the ideological reconfiguration of the family in modern times.

In a slightly later passage, Ichiyō repeats this gesture and continues her reliance on autumnal seasonal words. At the end of the first section, Oseki "put her sleeve to her face to hide her tears," and her father coughs so as to conceal the fact that he too is crying (220–21). The opening lines of the second half, which immediately follow this moment of pronounced weeping, offer another portrait of a living, feeling nature offering its sympathy to the heroine, who is at that very moment on her way back to a husband who despises her:

"To the bright moon was added the sound of the wind, and the cry of the insects was mournful" (*Sayakeki tsuki ni kaze no oto soite, mushi no ne taedae ni monoganashiki,* 221). There are three autumnal seasonal words in this passage—the moon, the wind, and the crying of the insects—all packed tightly and efficiently into a phrasing that, for the most part, follows an alternating pattern of seven and five syllables, a poetic effort in prose that would have made Ichiyō's literary forebears proud.

V

Still another representation of nature using classical personification can be found in the closing moments of the narrative as Oseki walks in the direction of her husband's mansion: "The branches of the willows along the main road trailed languidly beside her under the light of the moon" (226). Once again nature is not only seemingly alive, but appears to bend and move in sympathy with the heroine. However, Oseki's anguish and the text's sentimental bent are colored by a rather different hue at the end of the narrative, for here she and Rokunosuke meet and part company within the space of a few pages. Now our interpretive efforts must shift somewhat, and we as readers are forced to reassess some of the assumptions we may have had while reading the first part, in which the presence of a childhood sweetheart is never mentioned. The second part casts Oseki's marriage in a new light by showing us what could have been, what had to be cast aside in a family's scramble for social advancement and material security.

After Rokunosuke appears on stage, Oseki, in an inside view, characterizes him as a "friend of old" (*mukashi no tomo*) and as "a person with whom I was connected," or *yukari no aru hito* (224). The term *yukari*, while written with characters that may imply a banal form of relationship, is actually an erotically charged word with an ancient pedigree. It is made to bear an enormous amount of weight in the eleventh-century *Genji monogatari,* for example, where it is used to indicate women who can function as erotic substitutes for Genji's displaced desire for his stepmother Fujitsubo. Ichiyō fully exploits the erotic charge of these words: "friend" and "connection" are used together in order to suggest that Oseki and Rokunosuke were "childhood sweethearts," or *osananajimi*, a gesture that is greatly strengthened when the narrator presents us with Oseki's memories, which mention in the same breath the daily encounters during adolescence and Oseki's fantasies about marrying the tobacconist's boy (225).

Osananajimi was a common motif of the day and one that Ichiyō frequently appropriated throughout her writing career, perhaps most recognizably in her first published work, "Yami-zakura" (Flowers at Dusk, 1892), and in *Takekurabe*. The trope of *osananajimi* has its roots in the well-curb episode of *Ise monogatari* (Tales of Ise, tenth c., sec. 23), in which a boy and a girl who begin as childhood playmates grow increasingly intimate as they mature; they eventually decide to marry — against the initial misgivings of their parents.[45] In the Meiji period, this familiar trope or motif from classical literature was pressed into rather different service. It became one of the dominant metaphors for modern romantic love. Modern love (variously called *ai*, *ren'ai*, or *rabu* in the Meiji period), which initially was the vehicle by which Christian ideals of platonic love entered Japan, emphasized a spiritual connection between a man and a woman and de-emphasized any physical or carnal relationship. The ideal was one of closeness, familiarity, and intimacy, with sexuality either bracketed or pushed far into the background. This is why the image of *childhood sweethearts* could figure so perfectly as a trope for modern love as it expanded from its platonic roots in the 1880s and 1890s.[46] By drawing on the trope of *osananajimi*, then, Ichiyō has cast the relationship between Oseki and Rokunosuke in terms of modern love.

The trope of *osananajimi* was obsessively yoked to the ideal of a marriage freely entered into (*jiyū kekkon*) in the literature of the period, as Saeki Junko has observed.[47] The free choice of a loving union suggests its own antithesis, the coerced marriage, or *kyōhaku kekkon*, which was generally represented as being the result of vested familial interests rather than of feelings of love and intimacy. That is, if the notion of a coerced marriage referred to selfish negotiations between families, which turned women into exchangeable objects in an economy that Gayle Rubin, in a widely read essay indebted to Lévi-Strauss, has termed "the traffic in women," a free marriage implied a radically different ideal—a man and a woman fall in love and decide of their own accord, without the intrusive and interest-ridden familial negotiations that characterize the other form of marriage, to live out their lives in each other's company.[48] Indeed, the tension and interplay between a "free" and "coerced" marriage constitute one of the most common story lines in Meiji-era fiction, and thus Ichiyō is in the company of many others here.[49]

These two antithetical forms of marriage are present in "Jūsan'ya" in the form of conflicting accounts of Harada's courtship of Oseki. This is the mother's story:

It was during the New Year when you were seventeen, on the morning of the seventh, before the pine boughs had even been taken down from the front gate. You were playing shuttlecock with the neighbor girl in front of our old house in Sarugakuchō. She hit that white shuttle, and it flew straight into Mr. Harada's carriage as it was passing by along the street. You were the one who went over to fetch it. Oh, he fancied you from the moment he first saw you, and right after that the go-betweens began hurrying to our door. I don't know how many times we refused. There was such a difference in your stations, we said. You were still such a child. You hadn't received a proper education. We didn't have the means to arrange a proper ceremony, and so on. He wouldn't hear any of it. He didn't have any meddlesome in-laws to worry about, he said. It was his choice and it was you he wanted. There was no need to worry about status. As for education, there was no need to worry about that either; he would see to your training after the ceremony. If only we would agree to the match, he would put you on a pedestal. He pressed his suit, countering with this and that. And even though we never suggested it, he went ahead and saw to all the arrangements for the ceremony. It was a match of love. (216)

In the streets of Tokyo, where men and women of different classes are visible to each other and rub shoulders together, an encounter between people from backgrounds as different as those of Isamu and Oseki floats into the realm of possibility, even if the odds are slight. Yet the very possibility, however remote, of a chance encounter between an ordinary woman and a successful man that then leads to matrimony has been transmuted in the mother's telling into a wish fulfillment that looks rather like a matter of destiny. All the linked elements of a fairy-tale pairing are brought into play here in the mother's speech: the stroke of fate that brought the two together; infatuation at first sight (at least at the man's first sight); ardent statements on the gentleman's part that his feelings are strong and true; a strenuous insistence that matters of class birth, culture, and money are trivial concerns where matters of the heart are involved. In a passage such as this, one has the discomforting sense that Harada's courtship of Oseki is a matter of destiny and at the same time that it is almost too fantastic to be believed.

In fact, the mother's story is not the only version of Oseki's fateful chance encounter with Harada Isamu. When, in the second half of the story, Oseki is walking along the street with Rokunosuke, her mind on the past, on missed chances and missed happiness, her mind races back to youthful fantasies of the tobacconist's boy:

He must have been in love with me all this time. Oh, from the time I was twelve until my seventeenth birthday, I dreamt of sitting in that store, minding the business while reading the newspaper, seeing each other day in and day out. But then I was married to a man met unexpectedly. I didn't say anything, just following my parents' wishes. I thought I would be the wife of Roku, the tobacconist, but I guess that was just a childish fantasy. (225)

This is a completely different perspective on the pivotal moment of Oseki's life. Oseki's ruminations here are given to the reader as her direct, unmediated thought. Her mother's version of the story is given as a direct, verbal utterance. Thus we have not one objective account of Harada's courtship of

Oseki, but two subjective versions, and the narrator makes no attempt to harmonize the disparate accounts. Oseki's recollections stand in direct competition with her mother's version. While both stories are highly subjective and colored by the situational context, the order is important: by placing Oseki's version after that of her mother, the narrator casts a great deal of suspicion over the latter; the sentimental mode has made Oseki the more believable and by far the more sympathetic character, after all.

At the end of the narrative, we as readers are forced to reevaluate any assumptions we might have gleaned from the mother's speech in the first part regarding the circumstances of the marriage between Oseki and Harada. It was not a marriage freely entered into, at least not from Oseki's perspective; nor was it simply a bad choice on Oseki's part. Rather, it was a marriage coerced by the wishes of a suitor who could not brook refusal and by parents who saw the prospect of material gain and a social boost for their daughter. The specter of coercion is actually present in the mother's narrative of the courtship in the form of go-betweens and negotiations between families, but it has been shunted off to the margins and thus barely impinges on the reader's consciousness until we retroactively look at it with Oseki's version of the courtship in our mind.

In "Jūsan'ya," then, Ichiyō constructs and literarily explores a certain dichotomy, which only comes into full focus in the second part. On one side is the impressive figure of Harada Isamu, a "rich man met unexpectedly." The powerful government official represents material gain, the possible forestalling of a social fall among the members of the Saitō family, and the burning desire for social advancement; but he also represents class ideals of home and family life that are impossible for Oseki to fulfill. Given the material rewards that lead Oseki's parents to pressure their daughter and Harada's own obstinacy once he has his heart set on Oseki, we must also view him as representing a coerced marriage, or something very like it. On the other side is Kōsaka Rokunosuke, who represents the possibility of love and a marriage entered into freely. The negotiations and go-betweens that ornamented Harada's courtship play no role in Oseki's dreams about a life with Rokunosuke. Indeed such a union would have been—at least in her fantasies—a marriage free of the kinds of vested family interests that ultimately make it impossible for her to free herself from Harada. Love or success, a marriage freely entered into or a union compelled by the dictates of others—these are common dilemmas in Meiji fiction, ones that are ripe for a sentimental treatment. Oseki's tragedy stems from the realization that there was never really a choice in the first place. Nor is there any choice in the narrative present of the text: by the end of the story, Oseki's ability to choose disappears. The prospects of material gain and social advancement have won out over a woman's freedom and happiness, and female success is cynically, ruthlessly represented as resulting in abuse and emotional isolation.

Seven years earlier advancement and material gain came between Oseki and happiness. Seven years later Oseki tries to free herself from her unhappy chains, but finds they are still too strongly connected to the family and its interests. Rokunosuke appears unexpectedly in the second part to suggest alternative possibilities and a missed chance for happiness. Yet Oseki cannot break with Harada, and so the man who occupied her dreams for so long when she was young becomes a horizon figure who recedes more and more into an impossible utopian vision of a happy marriage. Yet even this utopian dimension is quietly tempered in the narrative, for we are told that Rokunosuke himself married another woman after receiving news of Oseki's betrothal to Harada and ended up treating his new wife as cruelly and callously as Isamu treated Oseki (223–24). Perhaps Ichiyō is saying that patriarchy corrupts everyone or that suffering would have befallen Oseki no matter which path she pursued. In any case, Ichiyō's treatment of Oseki's tragedy is not elusive and understated, but openly sentimental, even drenched in tears. Furthermore, Ichiyō does not utilize classical rhetoric in order to lend a sense of elegant repose to the story, but to help generate strong, overpowering emotions among her readers. In the end, the suffering heroine does not achieve the freedom for which she yearns, and yet the text gives Oseki a voice and dramatizes her plight with an appeal to the reader's capacity to shed sympathetic tears for her. In staging such an emotional scene, Ichiyō must have hoped that our capacity to react viscerally to injustice via the mediation of classical rhetoric would ultimately lead us out of the fictional world of "Jūsan'ya" to unflinchingly ask hard questions of the world around us, perhaps the same one posed by Hasegawa Shigure when she closed the pages of Ichiyō's story many decades ago: "How many hundreds or even thousands of Osekis are out there in the shadows, making their ways through life barely noticed?"

FIVE

Subjection in the Yoshiwara

Given the stature of Ichiyō's *Takekurabe* (Child's Play, 1895–1896) — one of the treasures of Japanese literature and the one story in her oeuvre that is read by every specialist in Japanese literature and by many a non-specialist as well — it should come as no surprise to encounter a wealth of interpretations. For some, the story is a nostalgic portrayal of childhood innocence on the verge of disappearance as the young characters grow up. Others see a story of children's cliques and conflicts that mimics the interest-ridden world of adults. For others, *Takekurabe* is the story of foreclosed adolescent love between the priest-to-be Nobuyuki and the young Midori, who is violently torn from a world of youthful, carefree play and forced into the adult world of prostitution.

Each of these readings finds something of vital importance in the text. Yet it is remarkable how the major thematic concerns that critics have located join at certain pivotal moments in the tale: the fight in front of the sundries shop between the two cliques is one example. In this scene, Chōkichi and his Back Street Gang (the *yokochō-gumi*), on the prowl for Shōta, head of the Main Street Gang (the *omotemachi-gumi*), find instead the turncoat Sangorō and proceed to pummel him mercilessly. Midori, also of the Main Street Gang, tries to intervene, but Chōkichi calls her a "whore" (*jorōme*) — "What are you talking for, whore? You're just a beggar like your sister! This is all the opponent you need!" (237) — and throws a dirty sandal at her, striking Midori on the forehead. Midori's budding love for Nobu is colored by this incident, for, although Nobu has ostensibly joined Chōkichi's group, Midori mistakenly believes that Nobu instigated the fight; in actuality, he knew nothing about it and had even warned the arrogant Chōkichi to avoid such altercations. In this way, the tale of adolescent love becomes intertwined with a story of children's conflicts and rivalries. In addition, the word "whore," which is associated with the world of the adult sex trade, violently intrudes into the world of childhood play here — even as this play turns momentarily to violence itself — thus foreshadowing Midori's fate.

In the second half of the novella, the word "whore" burrows into every corner of Midori's mind, darkens her outlook on the world around her, makes her confused and embarrassed, colors her relations with the other children, and compels her to seek a measure of isolation. This suggests that we might fruitfully reread *Takekurabe* as thematizing the workings of subjectivity. Midori's humiliation stems from being struck on the forehead with an object that belongs on the foot, making it both a physical and psychological scar. The force of the incident is amplified since the word *jorō* (a relatively neutral term for prostitute at that time) has the derogatory suffix *me* attached to it and since the sandal that strikes Midori is covered with dirt. The dirty mark on the surface of the body is coupled with a derogatory term that etches itself into her mind, suggesting continuity between the physical, corporeal body and the mind. *Takekurabe* thus seems to demand a model of subjectivity that does not make strict distinctions between mind and body; Ichiyō's text calls out for a model of what has been called by feminist critics "embodied subjectivity."[1]

The details of a theoretical framework can be postponed for a little while, at least until we immerse ourselves more in the world of the novella, but it is worth emphasizing at the outset a couple of points that can orient the discussion. The focus of this chapter will be on Ichiyō's representation of the psychological implications of the fight in front of the sundries shop and Midori's violent transformation at the end of the novella. I want to frame the discussion of this thread with the concept of subjection. The text shows us the subjection of one girl to the imperatives of the libidinal economy in Japan's most prominent prostitution district, the Yoshiwara. The erotic gaze playing across the body is a crucial agent of subjection and has the power to violently alter the lived experience of the subject. Ichiyō also dwells on the discursive effects of subjection, representing it as the loss of the ability or willingness to articulate one's own subjective desires, even one's own resistance to the process of subjection. Subjection is, in part, a mechanism of internal censorship. Ultimately, I connect these thematic issues to Ichiyō's literary method in *Takekurabe*.

ii

Yoshiwara. A single word calls up a host of images: the five-square-block walled compound of brothels nestled in the flat-lands north of central Tokyo, not far from the famed Sensōji Temple complex in Asakusa, on the west bank of the Sumida River; the wall itself encircled by the Ohaguro *dobu*, the moat named after the black dye used to darken the teeth of the quarter's beauties; the famous Mikaeri *yanagi* or "looking back" willow tree, at the main gate (*ōmon*) of the Yoshiwara, so called because the customer returning home from a festive night was said to look back longingly at the tree, whose languid branches almost seemed to bid a sad farewell to him. There were clusters of teahouses near the main gate, where a well-off gentleman might arrange a rendezvous with one of the famous courtesans. There would be scores of men strolling along the grand central avenue or in some of the back alleys, looking into the slatted street-side rooms seating many a lady to see if one of the painted faces caught his fancy. Onto these sights were layered the sounds of the quarter: the laughter, the plaintive tunes from the *shamisen*, the clip-clop of the little serving girls rushing about the streets, but above all the clatter of rickshaw wheels. Ichiyō described the racket in her diary after her first night in her new home in Ryūsenji at the back side of the quarter:

The new house is on the only road leading from Shitaya to the Yoshi-wara. After dusk, the rickshaws come roaring by, their lanterns swinging in all directions. The racket is beyond the power of words to convey. This doesn't let up until after 1 A.M., and at 3:00 the clatter of wheels ferrying customers home begins. This is the first time I've ever experienced such a restless, sleepless night since we moved from our house in quiet Hongō.[2]

A week and a half later, Ichiyō, again unable to sleep for the insistent clatter of the rickshaws, tried quantifying the noise: at a high point, she counted 75 vehicles in the span of only ten minutes![3]

By the time Ichiyō recorded this little bit of trivia, for generations various forms of transport had been carrying men to and from the Yoshiwara. The Yoshiwara was an *institution* in all senses of that word, and, with its 300-plus-year history stretching from its establishment in the early seventeenth century to the abolition of prostitution as a legal activity in the late 1950s, it was an ancient one at that. Thus, we must not make the mistake of thinking about the Yoshiwara of *Take-kurabe* as *merely* a compound of brothels, for any representation of the (in)famous prostitution district at the end of the nineteenth century carries quite a lot of historical and representational baggage with it, and it is worth giving this some attention at the outset.[4]

In an effort to control prostitution in the country, the Tokugawa authorities agreed to the establishment of a system of licensed prostitution districts in Edo and other cities in the early seventeenth century. Licensed prostitutes could work without fear of reprisal provided they did so in one of the legally designated areas. The Yoshiwara, which in time would become the most famous of Japan's licensed quarters, was originally established by government decree (at the urging of

local entrepreneurs) in 1617 on a plot of land in Nihonbashi
in the very shadow of the castle headquarters of the Tokugawa
shoguns, but was moved after a fire in 1657 that destroyed
a huge swath of the city to an area of rice paddies beyond
the outskirts of the old city in present-day Taitō ward. The
bakufu was ever concerned to set the district apart symbolically
from the city proper and from the normal rhythms of life and
to thus convey its view that the Yoshiwara was, like the theater, an *akusho*, a tawdry place of wickedness; like some medieval fortress, the Yoshiwara was situated behind its wall and
surrounded by its moat. But in a dramatic example of the return of the repressed, these protective measures only served
to intensify desire, for in a kind of ritual foreplay men now
had to go to considerable trouble and expense to make their
way to the quarter, an activity that always carried the faint
glow of transgression, a feeling that could only be heightened
where walls and moats were involved.

From early on, this venerable institution was deeply imbricated in metropolitan life in Edo and then Tokyo, for there was
a rich and vibrant culture that circulated between the Yoshiwara and the larger social order. The wall and moat that
prevented the prostitutes from mixing with the respectable
citizens of the city were hardly an obstacle to the circulation
of representations of the courtesan in urban life. The fashions
and hairstyles of the quarter swept through the city at regular
intervals, spurred on by portraits of the prostitute in the visual
arts. Indeed, the high-ranking courtesans who captured the
imagination of the people of Edo were depicted with loving
care by the masters of the woodblock print in numbers compa-
rable to prints of the famous kabuki actors. There were also
guidebooks to the quarter and its beauties, often with lists of
prices and assessments of particular courtesans included, and
new literary genres centered on the demimonde and its inhabitants and connoisseurs.

Though the Yoshiwara's days of greatest glory were during
the eighteenth century, the lights had by no means completely
dimmed after the Meiji Restoration of 1868; and this despite

the fact that in the 1870s the prostitute was the target of a flurry
of legal activity that abjected her. Perhaps the most important
factor was the establishment of examination centers (*kensaba*)
to which the prostitute was forced to go three times each
month to be checked for sexually transmitted diseases, especially syphilis. Thereafter, the body of the prostitute would
be subject to the disciplinary technology of the Meiji state,
and even as the government took every opportunity to loudly
vilify the quarter as a threat to the family and to public health,
it also discovered that additional tax revenues could be quietly
drawn from the demimonde and that the Yoshiwara might
also be a suitable place for sexually servicing the state's new
conscript army.[5] Mention of the *kensaba* two times in our text
situates the Yoshiwara of *Takekurabe* squarely in modernity,
and the new disreputableness of the quarter is apparent in
the novella in its representation as sordid and corrupting;
but then again, also quite apparent are the lingering glitter
and wealth.

Takekurabe is actually set just outside the Yoshiwara in
Daionji-mae, the same area where the Higuchi women operated their sundries shop from the summer of 1893 to the spring
of 1894 and where Ichiyō recorded her calculation of passing
rickshaws. We are introduced to this Yoshiwara satellite
community in the opening lines of the novella by a narrator
who must surely be counted among the most fascinating and
flamboyant figures in Meiji literature. This is a narrator who
somehow manages to be both detached and judgmental. She
postures as the consummate insider, our guide to the world
of the narrative, but she somehow stands apart from its milieu
at the same time. Her style is a masterful display of the pyro-
technics of classical rhetoric combined with the most fashion-
able street slang of the demimonde.[6] She is a paradoxical
figure, and fittingly it is with a paradox that she opens the
narrative:

It's a long way around to the great gate at the front of the quarter
and the willow tree there with its long, trailing branches; and yet
the revelry from the third-floor rooms of the great houses, whose

lights reflect off the moat, dark as teeth-blackening dye, seems so near as to be almost tangible. The establishments of the quarter must be quite prosperous judging from the incessant coming and going of the rickshaws, which let up neither night nor day. The streets here behind the quarter are called "Daionji-mae"; the name, "In front of Daion Temple," might call to mind the Buddha himself, but the people who live here will tell you it's actually quite a lively place. (227)[7]

This is our introduction to Daionji-mae and the Yoshiwara. The name Yoshiwara is nowhere spoken here, but we none-theless know that this is the venerable prostitution district because there is an oblique reference to its two major symbols: the Mikaeri *yanagi* and the Ohaguro *dobu*, that is, the willow and the moat, respectively. The paradox here has two aspects. First, though the name of the area connotes a quiet, religious atmosphere, it is not at all a serene place, for the clatter of the rickshaws is persistent; and it certainly cannot be considered a sacred place, because these rickshaws are ferrying customers to and from the brothels. There is a second paradox: Daionji-mae is somehow both near to and far from the Yoshiwara.[8] Since the Yoshiwara is a walled compound, the famous willow tree at the main gate (normally the only gate open) can be reached from Daionji-mae only by a long walk around the wall, suggesting that Daionji-mae is far from the pleasure quarters, or at least psychologically distant. In addition, both the wall and the moat serve to mark a boundary between the Yoshiwara and the surrounding communities, intensifying the sense of psychological distance, one might think. However, Daionji-mae is adjacent to the back side of the Yoshiwara, and thus the revelry from the brothels near that end of the district spills over the wall and can be heard in the surrounding areas. Furthermore, the lights from the upper floors of the brothels reflect off the moat, which is, for the inhabitants of Daionji-mae, right at their feet. Thus, the lights and the revelry pene-trate the wall and skip across the moat, making the boundary rather permeable between the Yoshiwara and a satellite com-munity such as Daionji-mae.

However, the boundary never becomes completely transparent, for in one sense it is strictly maintained by the narrator; we are teased with the music and revelry that emanates
from the establishments inside the wall and with rumors of
their beautiful denizens, but the narrator never crosses the
boundary to take us inside the quarter.[9] *Takekurabe* is the story
of Daionji-mae and its *relationship* to the Yoshiwara, not a story
about the Yoshiwara itself. In terms of genre, *Takekurabe* stands
at an angle to the literature centered on the Yoshiwara, such
as the demimonde fiction from the Edo period in the various
gesaku genres like the *sharebon* (books of wit and fashion),
the *kibyōshi* (pictorial fiction), and the *ninjōbon* (sentimental
fiction).

There is, nonetheless, an inescapable connection between
Daionji-mae and the venerable prostitution district, as we
learn in the lines that immediately follow the introductory
passage:

Once you turn the corner at Mishima Shrine, you won't find any
grand, imposing houses. Here there are only ten- and twenty-unit
tenement rows, all with sagging eaves. Business, it is said, does not
flourish in these parts. Outside the half-opened shutters of each
house are hung strangely shaped objects, cut from paper, painted in
a variety of colors, and stuck on a spit. It's all very strange. And it
isn't just one or two houses either; the entire neighborhood is caught
up in the business, hanging them out to dry in the morning and
bringing them in at night. "What are those?" you might ask. "You
don't know?" someone will reply in astonishment. "They're *kumade*
charms. On *ōtori* festival days the pilgrims really buy them up." For
nearly the whole year from the time the pine boughs are taken down
from the front doors everyone becomes a true merchant, and by
summer their arms and legs are splattered with paint. They need
the sales in order to buy fresh clothes at New Year. If the gods and
buddhas are said to bestow good fortune on those who purchase
the charms, how much more will come to those who make them. So
everyone says, at least, but it's funny, you don't find any wealthy
people in these parts. (227)

The narrator's characteristic irony is on magnificent display
in this passage, but the point is serious: the relationship be-

tween Daionji-mae and the Yoshiwara is one of economic dependence. The fame of the Yoshiwara draws a great crowd during the festivals in November at the nearby Ōtori Shrine — so much so that they really must be considered Yoshiwara festivals, as Maeda Ai long ago observed[10] — and the economic activity of Daionji-mae as represented in this passage seems to center more or less exclusively on making goods to be hawked to the "pilgrims" and revelers who venture to the area during the festivals. Indeed, Yoshiwara and the satellite community are yoked together in such a way that the very livelihood of the residents of Daionji-mae and the economic viability of the satellite community depend enormously on the continued existence and fame of the Yoshiwara, on its ability, in short, to draw a crowd.

The nature of this economic dependency goes far beyond the matter of annual festivals and the making of trinkets: "Most of the people who live in these parts are connected with the quarter," the narrator explains to us (227). Throughout the text, we are given numerous examples of such connections: husbands might be manservants for the great houses of the quarter, while wives might do sewing for the prostitutes. The majority of the daughters of Daionji-mae seems to be servants or errand girls for the brothels; the beautiful among them might be selected to become prostitutes themselves. The circulatory system whereby the Yoshiwara draws crowds that provide the economic sustenance for the people of Daionji-mae and the prostitution district draws on the surrounding communities for its labor pool shows that a concept such as economic dependence must be nuanced enough to account for a relationship that is partially symbiotic. Daionji-mae could not exist without the Yoshiwara, but the quarter gets something from its satellite community as well.

To be sure, even with this qualification we must admit that the relationship is still rather lopsided, for the famed prostitution district clearly casts a very long shadow over the surrounding areas. The point here is that, despite the wall cordoning the Yoshiwara off from Daionji-mae and other

satellite communities, *Takekurabe* is set in a locale that ultimately must be considered a somewhat autonomous socioeconomic dyad that nonetheless relies on a very peculiar kind
of tourist from the city; all of this has important implications
for thinking about the way subjectivity is represented in the
novella. The material condition of economic dependency, together with the Yoshiwara's own fame and lengthy traditions,
are shown to be powerful forces acting on the psychology and
sensibilities of the people of Daionji-mae.

Perhaps the most fundamental impact is that the material
conditions of the quarter reverse traditional gender hierarchies:
"Success was limited to women," the narrator proclaims, mimicking the discourse of the locals: "A man here is worthless,
not even amounting to the tail of a mutt rooting about in
a dust heap" (245). It should, of course, be unsurprising to
find that the chief interest of the prostitution district lies in
women, and the Yoshiwara is shown to construct specific
forms of subjectivity, a specific lived relation to the world,
among the girls of Daionji-mae. Again with characteristic
irony, the narrator thematizes this in another passage from
the introductory chapter:

The daughters are either serving girls of the great establishments
or escorts for the famous tea houses; they hurry about their duties,
always carrying a lantern with the house insignia. What will become
of them when they graduate from their present positions? Isn't it
strange? They act as though they were performing on a grand
wooden stage. But before long each one has passed the age of thirty,
so smart in her matching kimono, skirt, and dark blue socks. Clomp,
clomp she hurriedly goes in her wooden clogs with a package tucked
under her arm—we certainly don't need to ask what she's carrying.
She stomps on the bridge to the back of the teahouse to announce
herself: "It's too far around to the front; I'll drop the package off
here." Apparently she's a needlewoman now. Customs here are a
little different. There aren't many girls who snugly tie their *obi* in the
back in the proper way; they like bright colors and *obi* cut wide. It's
one thing to see such fashions on an older woman, but these saucy
girls are just fifteen or sixteen, blowing on the very same ground

cherries that are used as contraceptives around here. There must be many who look askance at the goings on in these parts. (228)

There is perhaps no fuller description in the text of how the Yoshiwara pulls girls into its orbit. The girls of Daionji-mae are completely immersed in the culture of the quarter, which shapes not only their sense of fashion, but their very psychology and outlook on the world: the narrator comments that the girls of the demimonde see their lives as being akin to the glamour of the stage. Even their speech is infected with *kuruwa-kotoba*, the language of the quarter: "Maware-dōya, koko kara agemasuru" (It's too far around to the front; I'll drop the package off here). In a passage like this, we can see that there is a long process of initiation, and that the lives of these girls are dyed in the colors of the erotic long before they reach adulthood. They exemplify the eroticized female subject in the dyad of Daionji-mae/Yoshiwara, and the quarter needs to construct precisely these kinds of willing subjects to thrive.

The Yoshiwara is a powerful presence, but it is certainly not the only institution portrayed in the novella. The Buddhist church, in the form of the Ryūgeji, is another institutional presence, but it is largely written off by the narrator herself in a barrage of magnificent, withering irony that reduces the temple's bronzed, heavy-set priest, who happens to be Nobu's father, to yet another merchant selling shoddy trinkets to the demimonde's visitors and hawking dubious prayers to a skeptical congregation (247–49).

On the other hand, the narrator exhibits enormous interest in the area's school: "Near Iriya was the Ikueisha, which had nearly a thousand students even though it was a private school. In its cramped classrooms, with children jostling each other, the popular teachers quickly become known. The very word 'school' was enough to indicate the Ikueisha among the people who live in these parts" (228). The Ikueisha is home to Midori, Nobu, Chōkichi, and Sangorō; Shōta attends the more prestigious public school, which goes unnamed. The Ikueisha, though private and less prestigious than the public school, is still embarked on the same project as is the newly established national public school system, and, in fact, is not at all as independent of the state as its status may at first suggest. Its overt aim is to educate its pupils as best it can in a variety of subjects in the newly constituted, Western-influenced fields of knowledge, but it has a much more subtle mission as well: to contribute to the construction of national subjects loyal to country and emperor, and thus subjects capable of functioning successfully in the new imagined community of the nation-state. Like some foreign body in its host, one job of any school in Meiji Japan is to pull people away from their limited identification with the small community of which they are a part (Daionji-mae, for example), to encourage them to identify with the larger national body, and to make respectable national citizens of them.

Among the many tools it uses to accomplish this ulterior goal are *gakkō no shōka*, or school songs. More often than not, school songs consisted of lyrics praising nation and emperor and thus worked in tandem with the obligatory recitation of the Imperial Rescript on Education on certain regular occasions, such as the athletic events that are mentioned in *Take-kurabe*, in order to help construct national identity.[11] The school songs were part of the massive, long-term reprogramming process that turned local inhabitants with local sensibilities into national subjects who imagined themselves part of a larger social body. The Yoshiwara also had a great number of songs associated with it, though the topics were naturally bawdier in content than the ones dutifully sung in the schools each day. In fact, the songs of the demimonde tended to be on the lips of everyone, children included, at almost any time, even when they were supposed to be singing their school songs (228). In the words of the narrator, the songs of the Yoshiwara "steal the melody of the school songs, so popular they were. A proper tune couldn't be held at the school athletic meets without lapsing suddenly into the modish rhythms of the quarter" (228). This is not the harmonious combination of melodic lines, but tense discordance with strong institutional implications: the Yoshiwara's tunes invade the melody and words of the school songs and blasphemously subvert them.

Considered within the light of a Bakhtinian concern with the conflict inherent in all signifying practices, the skirmish here between two antithetical genres of song can be viewed more paradigmatically as a battle between institutions over the hearts and minds of the children of Daionji-mae. Stated another way, discourses and material practices associated with specific institutions are represented in the text as dialogically competing over children's subjectivity; and it seems that the school is always in danger of being reduced to impotence before the color and might of the quarter: "One can well imagine," the narrator notes, "how difficult education is here and how frustrated the teachers must be" (228). The ability of the Yoshiwara to construct subjects useful for its own ends (and errand girls and apprentice courtesans are only the most prominent examples) seems almost unsurpassed, at least within the socioeconomic dyad itself. Some children may indeed be influenced enough by the school to approximate model citizens, but no child from Daionji-mae remains completely free of the Yoshiwara; as the narrator laments, "there is no child untainted by this [milieu]" (228).

Takekurabe thus seems to offer its own theory of subjectivity with which it can be read, even if Ichiyō would have lacked the theoretical vocabulary to articulate it in analytical or clinical terms. The text consistently represents the subject as being split or decentered because it is always being pulled in multiple, often conflicting directions by institutions with radically different aims for the individual. The individual is a site of competition between institutions and discourses, each of which is trying to make her conform to a normative ideal conducive to its own ends. The body is centrally involved here, for wearing the fashions associated with the quarter and articulating its songs through one's own vocal chords pull the subject even more decisively into the orbit of the Yoshiwara, while an analogous situation holds for the Ikueisha.

The competition here between school and demimonde (and this could, of course, be multiplied further by accounting for other institutions) is played out in shifting patterns of advantage and disadvantage, and some institutions are capable of overpowering their competitors and radically altering the lived experience of the subject. Indeed, the text ultimately shows us that the Yoshiwara has the power to beat back all other claims on a young woman, thus closing alternative life paths. The available historical evidence indicates that the state's power was growing exponentially in the 1890s, so the Yoshiwara can be convincingly portrayed as winning this competition perhaps only in a place like Daionji-mae, where the relationship of economic dependency is the central material factor.

This incipient theory of subjectivity is not incompatible with a Foucauldian perspective, a perspective that may, in fact, help us read more deeply into Ichiyō's novella. For Foucault, the constitution of the subject is inseparable from the subjection of individuals to power, and so we are witness to a process of, to use Foucault's neologism, subjectivation. Subjectivation takes place primarily through the body, which is constituted within force fields of power and regimes of discipline; this process forms the subject into an approximation of a discursively constituted norm or ideal.[12] In my reading of *Takekurabe*, such a regime will take the form primarily of the erotic gaze playing on the body of the prostitute-to-be, which acts as an overlooked agent of subjection in the Yoshiwara. We will also need to consider the continuity between mind and body—that is, embodied subjectivity—since subjection causes the flight of certain thoughts and feelings deep into the interior of the psyche. Of use in this area is Judith Butler's work, which extends the paradigm of subjectivation by bringing together Foucault and Freud in an analysis of the psychic effects of subjection.[13] The narrator of *Takekurabe* frequently takes us into the mind of the heroine to show that such psychological effects primarily manifest as the loss of the power of speech. Foucault has often been accused of proffering a hegemonic view of power, which allows no room for resistance; Butler brings a Freudian critique to her discussion of Foucault in order to show where we can locate sites of resistance. *Takekurabe*, with its thematization of yet one more instance of happiness foreclosed, offers no such hope; it pessimistically represents a situation in which a resistance that cannot be verbalized has no force.

Before moving to the specifics of Midori's situation, which will occupy the remainder of this chapter, I want to inscribe a dialogic perspective or critique within the basic Foucauldian framework that we are using to draw out the latent theory of subjectivity in *Takekurabe*. Foucault and Butler certainly allow us to read institutional competition over the subject along the lines *Takekurabe* itself suggests. Their conception of power as a complex field of force emanating from hetero-geneous sites perfectly captures the complex interplay at work in subject formation in our novella. However, there is a great tendency in Foucault, and especially in Butler, for power to become a unitary, totalizing force that, while often un-named, often comes rather close to being synonymous with the state. A Bakhtinian injunction to always multiply is a useful corrective that prevents us from totalizing power in the hands of a single institution, a formulation that Ichiyō's text belies in any case. Subjection or subjectivation (in both senses of the formation of the subject and its subjection to power) in *Takekurabe* is represented as a dialogic tug-of-war in which one institution with its own unique discourses and material practices wins out, rather decisively, though never completely, over its competitors.

iii

The text's preoccupation with subjection centers on its heroine, Midori of the Daikokuya, and on the budding love she feels for Nobu of the Ryūgeji. Like the other children of Daionji-mae, Midori is pulled in different directions; at times, though, the Ikueisha seems to have only a modest impact on Midori's sensibilities, for what truly captivates her are the customs and culture of the quarter (246). In part, this is because she ideal-izes her older sister who is already a courtesan, but it is also more fundamentally due to the prestige and economic might of the Yoshiwara. The weight the two institutions have on her life will eventually swing completely in one direction as Midori is thrust once and for all inside the wall among the other painted faces, making her situation entirely unique among the youthful protagonists. At the end of this narrative arc, the Yoshiwara also demands that Midori make a major sacrifice, love.

A prominent thread in *Takekurabe* is the burgeoning attrac-tion between Midori and Nobu. At first this seems a wholly one-sided infatuation. Midori has taken a fancy to Nobu even before the narrative opens, but he grows embarrassed and self-conscious at her attentions and spurns all her advances. When he leaves for the seminary at the end of the story, how-ever, he leaves a paper flower at the gate of Midori's home, thereby indicating that he may have been equally attracted to Midori, but was simply too flustered by her attentions to respond in any way but to retreat with her every advance. The fact that Midori is destined for prostitution—a fact that seems obvious to everyone but her—is one reason why Nobu, who is ever concerned with social face, always shies away from her; and it is also the embarrassment and awkwardness of first love. In one sense, then, *Takekurabe* is about a potential love that is foreclosed by the quarter, and this is indeed how the novella is usually read.

This narrative of desire plays itself out on the representa-tional level of the text and also on an intertextual level. It has long been recognized, for example, that Ichiyō has incor-porated the trope of the well-curb in *Takekurabe*. The term "well-curb" (*izutsu*) operates as a metaphor for a boy and a girl who begin as childhood playmates and who fall in love with each other upon growing up. As we uncovered in the previous chapter, the roots of this trope can be found in the tenth-century *Ise monogatari* (Tales of Ise), and it is worth tracing the details of this narrative paradigm a little more fully in the context of a discussion of *Takekurabe*. The *Ise* story tells of a boy and a girl in the countryside who went out to play by a well every day as children, but after they grew up they became embarrassed about continuing their relationship, even though the young man certainly desired the woman for a wife, and the young lady wished to marry the man. The young woman, after refusing her parents' own candidate, one day receives the following poem from her childhood playmate:

> Tsutsuitsu no / izutsu ni kakeshi / maro ga *take*
> Suginikerashi na / imo mizaru ma ni
>> My *height*, which we measured at the well-curb,
>> seems to have passed the old mark since last I saw you.

The woman sends the following poem in reply:

> *Kurabe*koshi / furiwake-gami no / kata suginu
> Kimi narazu shite / tare ka agubeki
>> My parted hair, whose length we once *compared*,
>> hangs below my shoulders.
>> If not for you, for whom shall it be put up?

If not for you, for whom shall it be put up? She is speaking, in other words, of a bridal coiffure. They continue their poetic exchanges and then become man and wife.[14]

It has long been thought that Ichiyō was gesturing toward this narrative paradigm when she chose her title.[15] Critics note that she has taken one word from each poem in the exchange (indicated in italics in both the original and the translation above) and joined them together to make a neologism, "takekurabe," which literally means "comparing heights." In a kind of bonus of pleasure, those familiar with the trope of the well-curb are invited to read *Takekurabe* against the backdrop of one of the archetypical stories of young love, with Midori and Nobu filling the roles of the two childhood friends who become attracted to each other.

The trope of the well-curb is prominent in Meiji literature, especially in Meiji women's writings, and is the most common way of evoking the motif of childhood sweethearts in Ichiyō's fiction. Furthermore, as we saw in the last chapter, Ichiyō and her contemporaries often used "childhood sweethearts," or *osananajimi*, itself as a metaphor for modern romantic love, a pairing that was well established in narrative fiction by the 1890s. The desire Midori feels for Nobu, the desire he feels for her, is precisely this modern form of desire framed here as budding adolescent love.

There is an understandable tendency in *Takekurabe* criticism to idealize this adolescent love and elegize the harm that is wreaked on it by the Yoshiwara, which has the effect of re- ifying love and removing it from all connections to history. The text itself is partly responsible for this, since the appro- priation of the classical trope of young love within the text's economy of pathos can certainly have the effect of idealizing the burgeoning desire between Midori and Nobu. However, if we resist the temptation (or perhaps the invitation) to idealize and instead read against the grain of the text, we can locate adolescent love within a certain historically specific institu- tional site, which then allows us to view Midori's situation as an example, a case study as it were, of the more general phe- nomenon of institutional competition over the subject. What is crucial here for such a reading is the fact that this modern form of desire is located primarily in the school, the same Ikueisha we examined a moment ago with its jostling students and overworked teachers. We are given the origins of this un- consummated desire in an analepsis in the seventh chapter: "Nobu of the Ryūgeji and Midori of the Daikokuya were both students at the Ikueisha," it begins. On his way home from the school athletic meet one fine spring day, Nobu is so dis- tracted by something he trips over some tree roots. "I wonder what's the matter with Nobu?" the narrator coyly asks. As if to answer her own question, the narrator brings Midori on stage, who offers her help (242).

The Meiji-era school in which this burgeoning desire is an- chored was heavily involved in shaping normative subjects on whom the new nation-state could rely, and this extends to the construction of normative sexual subjects, whose desires are oriented in the right way toward the right objects and who find fulfillment in a proper marriage between respectable citizens. Such normative desire is part of the long-term reorganization of sexuality in modern Japan. It is a very different kind of desire from that which animates the Yoshiwara, which, from the point of view of the Meiji state, created distressingly dilettantish and aberrant subjects who frittered away family wealth and could not be counted on to contribute to national projects.

Modern desire can also be linked to the emergence of new discourses on childhood and adolescence in the late nineteenth century, especially adolescent sexuality. *Takekurabe* puts on stage characters who are at exactly that moment of maturation that witnesses the onset of sexuality. Recognition of the historicity of maturation, adolescence, and the experience of sexuality allows us to immensely complicate and enrich our reading of foreclosed adolescent love before we turn our attention back to the Yoshiwara. Although it is not yet especially well documented in historical studies, it is at least now widely accepted that childhood was "discovered," to use Karatani Kōjin's well-known phrase, in the 1890s in Japan.[16] Children, of course, have always existed, but their social significance, the discourses about them, and the social practices centered on them, shifted markedly in late-nineteenth-century Japan. We can discern in *Takekurabe* a marbled structure in which older notions of childhood coexist in a state of tension with modern conceptualizations. For example, most of the boys in the novella will follow their fathers in their occupations: Chōkichi will become a fireman like his father; Nobu will enter the priesthood and take over the family temple; Shōta will inherit the family business of moneylending. Sangorō is something of an exception; he will not necessarily become a rickshaw puller like his father, and ironically his family's poverty allows him more flexibility in his choice of occupation, which will nonetheless be some pursuit on rungs near the bottom of society. Thus, Daionji-mae exists in part in an older apprentice-style socioeconomic system, and an additional long-term function of the modern school was to pull children out of that system and program them for life and work in the new world of state-nurtured industrial capitalism. This was accomplished using tools such as the cult of personal advancement, or *risshin shusse*, which opened possibilities for career and life ambitions beyond those of one's parents. In Europe, ideas such as child-hood, adolescence, and youth—all those minute distinctions we now make between birth and adulthood in order to cap-ture the intricacies of human development—were a long time in the making, as Philippe Ariès has demonstrated in his path-breaking book.[17] This aspect of European modernity, like so many others, was rapidly translated into Japan in the mid-Meiji period and was firmly in place by the end of the first decade of the twentieth century.

We can mobilize the term "translated" here in two ways. We can use it in the narrower and quite literal sense: words in Japanese were invented so as to correspond with concepts in a European textual archive about "children," an archive that was then rendered into the Japanese language. The pref-ace to Iwaya Sazanami's *Kogane maru* (1892), a vendetta tale set in the world of animals that is regarded by many as the origin of children's literature in Japan, is indicative of the early process of translating "childhood" between Europe and Japan: "The word '*shōnen bungaku*' in the present work's subtitle is meant in the sense of literature for *shōnen* and comes from the German word *Jugendschrift* (*juvenile literature*). Since we did not have an appropriate word in our country, it was necessary to temporarily give it this name."[18]

We can also use translation as a trope of cross-cultural ex-change to indicate how certain Euro-American material prac-tices were adopted in the Japanese context, thus producing modern children as such. Often this occurred via household manuals, advice columns in journals, and similar materials, as well as in the modern school system, all of which sought to shape the raising of children. In the Meiji period, we see a be-wildering variety of magazines directed at children or mothers or both—shorter-lived ones include *Shōkokumin* (Little Citizens, 1889–1895), *Shōnen'en* (Youth Garden, 1888–1895), *Kodomo* (Child, 1889–1892), *Nihon no shōnen* (Japanese Youth, 1889–1894); longer-lived ones include *Shōnen sekai* (Boy's World, 1895–1934) and its sister magazine *Shōjo sekai* (Girl's World, 1906–1931) — which serve to translate (in the narrow sense) categories and concepts associated with childhood in Europe into the Japanese context, which contributed to the transformation of material practices (translation in the broad sense).

The emergent ideas embodied in such texts are key concepts in modern notions of childhood, once children cease being viewed as small adults and are seen instead as adults-in-the-making. An idea such as maturation describes a period of gradual development of the human subject, from birth to adulthood, while at the same time the idea insists on the continuity of the human subject as it moves along this time line. As Karatani describes it, in the modern notion of childhood, in distinct contrast to older ideas such as rites of passage, "we have a 'self' that develops and matures gradually," a division that thus "creates continuity between child and adult."[19] Maturation is a process that takes time, and thus the modern conception of childhood carries within itself the idea of an elongated temporality quite distinct from older notions of the child.

Takekurabe thematizes the point along this new time line that witnesses the onset of sexuality. At the time the novella was written, a discourse on what we now call puberty was just beginning, but which would become quite noisy by the end of the first decade of the twentieth century. In order to acquire surer footing navigating through the marbled world of Ichiyō's text, I want to turn briefly to a work published a decade after *Takekurabe* was completed and discover where the vectors that are only faintly visible in the 1890s are pointing. This will help us acquire the tools we need to locate the signs of newer conceptions of adolescence and the institutions and discursive regimes in which they are anchored.

The text I want to briefly take up is a quasi-medical treatise by Hara Masao called *Shikijō to seinen* (Sexuality and Youth), published in 1906. This work purports to be a scientific explanation of the onset of sexuality in boys and girls, though it is actually a highly didactic work, which utilizes a great deal of figurative language to grapple with its shadowy topic, and its main concern lies in instituting regimes of discipline over sexuality. Here is its thesis:

Boys and girls, once they reach a certain age, witness the onset of sexuality, which is a process beckoned by nature. The time for this varies considerably with individual circumstances such as race, climate, occupation, health, and environment, but, although it is not always the same, it normally appears between the ages of fourteen and eighteen. We can call this time "the period of the onset of spring feelings" [*shunjō hatsudō ki*].[20]

There are a couple of things worth noting from this early passage. First, the onset of sexuality is represented as a process that occurs in a subject and that creates continuity in the subject. Sexuality is thus being written into the modern narrative of maturation, which sees both development and continuity in an individual human subject. Second is that the process Hara describes is represented as entirely natural, that is, brought on solely by the imperatives of biology, while material social practices surrounding sexuality are radically de-emphasized, at best causing a slight variation in the biological time clock.

Hara relies especially on biological tropes such as dormancy and awakening:

When people are born, they are infants incapable of anything. This is because when one is born, there is no need for any kind of special ability. For example, a newborn does not have a single tooth, but between the first and second years teeth that were dormant in the gums begin to appear. In the same way, until a child reaches a certain age, the sexual organs are in a state of being dormant and thus do not exhibit any functioning, but eventually after the child has reached the age of fifteen or sixteen, they exhibit special organization and function and thus gradually awaken and develop.[21]

Hara goes on to describe both the physical and psychological changes that accompany puberty. During the period of "the awakening of spring feelings," the bodies of boys enter their most rapid period of development: their voices deepen, whiskers sprout on the chin and cheeks, their bodies become firm, and the sexual organs develop. Girls develop body fat, their cheeks become rosy, their hair takes on its characteristic luster, and they become, in general, quite radiant (interestingly, Hara chooses not to discuss the development of the female sexual organs here).[22] These physical changes are accompanied by psychological ones—"An unusual type of feeling" (*isshu fukashigi naru kanjō*), "unsettled, passionate thoughts" (*bonnō fuan no nen*), and so on—that get rather vague and metaphorical treatment in Hara's discussion, and which he lumps together by invoking a single, electrically charged word: *seiyoku*, or sexual desire, which by 1910 became one of the keywords in the modern discourse on sexuality.[23]

For Hara, this is a crucial, pivotal development in the process of maturation; it is a moment of violent upheaval in the otherwise gradual, continuous development of the subject, and one that carries enormous risk: "Will one turn left from this point or right? Will one become a good individual or tumble into a degenerate life? Will one cross safely to the other shore or sink on the way? With this period as a border, their [*karera*] fates will be decided one way or the other."[24] This statement will be the axis on which the rest of Hara's slim book will turn, for the remainder of the treatise is preoccupied not with laying bare the psychological changes he metaphorically invokes before a scientific or medical gaze, but rather with strategies for containing this potentially very dangerous energy called *seiyoku*. Hara has, in fact, reduced the experience of adolescence to a period of coming to terms with sexuality, a kind of reductionism into which *Takekurabe* does not fall. Hara's little book, then, stresses danger, supervision, and discipline in its account of adolescent sexuality.

It does not require much reflection to understand why the onset of sexuality should be of such concern to Hara. After all, the sons of good households cannot be allowed to turn into young rakes prowling about the Yoshiwara (or worse, one of the unlicensed districts), dipping into all the varied sexual pleasures of the world and thus threatening the standing, wealth, and lineage of the family. For Hara, the sexual energy of boys (notice the *karera* in the previous quotation) needs to be contained until they can take an appropriate woman as a wife and get on with the business of producing an heir. Female pleasure and sexuality, while acknowledged by Hara, are radically marginalized and traits like "purity" are emphasized instead. Hara's text participates in the construction of the normative gendered, sexual subject of modernity. Nor was this concern over sexual desire limited to men like Hara; educators of all stripes were also deeply concerned about the onset of sexuality in young people because it occurred while boys and girls were in school and were thus charges of the state.

Ichiyō does not exhibit as much awareness of the institutional location of the discourse on adolescent desire as she does of the socioeconomic entanglement of the demimonde and its satellite community or of the effects of the Yoshiwara's practices on the psyches of the daughters of Daionji-mae. Indeed, as I suggested, it is possible to interpret the mobilization of the trope of the well-curb as a reification by Ichiyō of love itself in telling of her two star-crossed protagonists. Nonetheless, by delving into the historical archive and reading against the grain of the text rather than idealizing or reifying love, we can draw out some of the implications of the narrative. My goal in this has been to argue that modern adolescent love is anchored in a particular, historically specific site. The foreclosed love idealized in the novella is itself part of modern regimes of power, which create normative sexual subjects. And this discursively constructed ideal is a competitor of the sexual subject constructed by the Yoshiwara. Thus, there can be no space untouched by power, no pristine childhood innocence. By reading in this way, we discover that it is not just happiness that is foreclosed, but the possibility of experiencing desire and sexuality in ways that were at that time being gradually codified as "normal" and "acceptable" in the larger social body. It is, then, this possibility of normative subjectivity and sexuality that is made unattainable by subjection in the Yoshiwara.

iv

The text suggests that subjection is closely bound to visuality and the body and that the gaze is a crucial agent of subjection in the quarter; we witness the way a gaze that is tied to both eros and commerce plays across the body of the prostitute-to-be, and how the future courtesan becomes aware of and transformed by the gaze. In some ways, these issues should perhaps be unsurprising given that the prostitution district was an area crisscrossed with gazes, desires, and fantasies, which are in turn implicated in the circulation of money, the appropriation of female sexuality, and its subordination to the imperatives of this economy. Despite its centrality to the whole narrative, however, visuality is a feature of *Takekurabe* that has not yet received due attention in criticism.

When Midori makes her first appearance in the third chapter of *Takekurabe*, she is immediately situated within a field of vision. As she walks down the street near the Yoshiwara returning home from the public bath, she becomes the object of a number of admiring male gazes. Her admirers are young men returning home from a night spent in the quarter, and they remark about Midori, "I sure would like to see her three years from now" (232). We might be tempted to attribute this simply to her beauty, and this, of course, would not be wrong. However, there is much more at work here, so we must gather together a number of facts about Midori scattered far and wide throughout the text in order to understand why she becomes the object of the gaze, here and at later times.

Immediately upon Midori's introduction the very first thing the narrator draws our attention to is her long, beautiful hair: "Were you to undo it, her hair would surely reach all the way to her feet. She wore it drawn up tightly into a bun with the forelocks showing. This style was called the *shaguma*, or 'red bear,' style—certainly a rather fearsome name, but it was now all the rage, even among daughters of respectable families" (232). Clearly there was something a little disreputable about the *shaguma* style, as the reference to "respectable families" makes apparent. This particular coiffure had its roots in the demimonde and then spread out to the general population; it became very popular in the 1890s, starting with school girls.[25] We also learn that Midori is wearing high, lacquered clogs (*nuribokuri*) that are also associated with the quarter.[26] Thus her hairstyle and dress form a semiotic system that suggests her connections to the Yoshiwara—and her eventual fate of becoming a prostitute—at the very moment she is introduced to the reader. The feminist critic Seki Reiko has argued that Midori is always revealing her affiliations with the Yoshiwara, whether it be through her hairstyle and clothes or through the personal articles and accessories she carries with her. Furthermore, Seki emphasizes that while the Meiji-era reader and most of the characters in the novella are well aware of Midori's fate, Midori herself is not conscious of the symbolic nature of her hair, clothes, and accessories.[27]

There is another example of this: among the many items Midori carries is a red silk handkerchief, which we see when, at one point in the analepsis we looked at earlier, she offers it to the fallen Nobu, who has tripped over some tree roots on his way home from the school athletic festival. We are not given Nobu's reactions directly; instead the narrator shifts the point of view to Nobu's friends, who are all green with envy over Midori's ministrations: "Fujimoto's [Nobu] a priest, but look how he flirts with her and says his thanks with that grin. That's pretty strange, don't you think? Maybe Midori will become his wife. A priest's wife—hey, then she'll be the god Daikoku of the kitchen instead of Midori of the Daikokuya" (242). Nobu becomes upset at these remarks and thereafter makes every effort to avoid Midori. The narrator makes much of this scene, and there seems to be a significance attached to the handkerchief that is not made explicit. A little snooping reveals a very interesting fact: respectable young ladies at

the turn of the century did not carry things like red silk handkerchiefs; red was an erotic color, and the red handkerchief,
specifically, was a major emblem of the prostitute.[28] At the
age of fourteen, Midori is as unaware of the social symbolism
of her handkerchief as she is unaware of the social resonance
of her other accessories.

So why should Midori have begun carrying things like red
silk handkerchiefs in the first place? Partly, she carries such
articles because she imitates the women she sees around her,
and those women happen to be prostitutes. The cultural prestige of the high-ranking courtesans of the Yoshiwara (among
whom we must count Midori's sister, Ōmaki) and the Yoshiwara's power in Daionji-mae no doubt contribute to Midori's
desire to emulate these women. But this does not fully convey
the situation, so we need to elaborate by connecting these
issues to other things we learn about Midori. When she first
arrived with her parents in Daionji-mae, she wore distinctly
unfashionable clothes, being unfamiliar with the ways of the
city: "She was laughed at by the girls of the neighborhood,
who called her 'country bumpkin.' It was very vexing to her.
She cried for three days and three nights on that occasion"
(233). She "cures" her faulty fashion sense by copying the
stylish women of the quarter. Now, we are told, it is Midori
who casts contemptuous glances on those wearing yesterday's
styles, and no one is brave enough to send her scorn back
at her (233). In addition, Midori spoke the Kishū dialect of her
native place and was laughed at for this too when she arrived
in Tokyo. She "cures" her dialect by quickly mastering the
special language of the quarter, or *kuruwa-kotoba* (246).[29] Thus,
Midori self-consciously copies the women of the quarter without understanding the social significance of the modes of fashion and speech she adopts; the main impetus is to overcome
derogatory slurs from the other children.

These observations can give us an effective purchase on that
moment when Midori becomes the object of the male gaze as
she is introduced to the reader. Again, the men whose eyes
she catches remark, "I sure would like to see her three years

from now." We should be clear about what exactly is meant by this comment: cutting a beautiful figure as she returns home from the public bath, Midori's body has been eroticized and situated within the Yoshiwara's world of sexual commerce, for "see" here carries distinct connotations of purchasing sexual services, a point underscored by the fact that the men are returning home from one of the brothels. Although Midori is as yet sexually unavailable, she attracts the male gaze not just because she is pretty, but, more importantly, because she has acquired the speech patterns, fashions, and body language that characterize the women of the quarter; ironically, these elements function as signs to almost everyone but herself of her position and destiny.

The scene I have been analyzing is by no means an isolated occurrence. Midori's body is frequently found in a field of vision, and the gaze plays an immensely important role in *Take-kurabe*. What draws the gaze is less Midori's physical body, which is never substantially detailed in the text, but rather her hair, the adornments in her hair, her *obi*, clogs, and other accessories. These articles are commodities that command enormous erotic power, drawing attention because they circulate as fetishes within the sexual economy of the Yoshiwara. As Peter Brooks has observed of Emma Bovary, Midori's body is fragmented, and the eye of the observer is arrested by those commodified, metonymic details of her hair, dress, and accessories that are invested with erotic significance.[30] In the beginning of the narrative, Midori, at age fourteen, hovers uncertainly between childhood innocence and the adult world of prostitution, and thus her body, clothes, and accessories partake simultaneously of two worlds. By the end of the narrative, her body is manipulated to conform to that of a full-fledged prostitute, and Midori becomes aware that this signifies her preordained relation to the demimonde.

The brothels of the Yoshiwara were expert at manipulating the female body so as to arouse male desire, a desire that could be satisfied with an outlay of cash. Indeed, if it were not so adept at this, the institution itself would never have survived for as long as it did. The prostitute was very much on display in the larger social order, and the circulation of representations of the prostitute in popular culture mirrors the exhibition of the prostitute within the Yoshiwara itself.[31] The methods used to put the wares of these women on display depended a great deal on her rank; there was, after all, a complex and rigid system of distinctions and hierarchies among the women of the Yoshiwara, from a handful of the highest-ranking courtesans, who had great flexibility in choosing their customers and arranging their schedules, to the lowest-ranking prostitutes, who had no such rights. The fronts of the brothels typically consisted of a large room with widely spaced slats. The lower-ranking prostitutes sat in groups in these slatted rooms facing the street, from which they could be scrutinized by prospective customers passing by. The elegant and accomplished courtesans at the opposite end of the hierarchy were also on display, but in a far more flamboyant way. Since the courtesan typically met her customer at a teahouse, she had to walk from the brothel, which gave her the opportunity for theatrics. This was known as the *oiran dōchū*, or the procession of the courtesan, and a famous woman might draw a large crowd of spectators as she made her way to the teahouse. She was elaborately decked out and walked with an entourage of apprentices and assistants. In addition, there were fashion parades and annual events, such as the display of bedding and kimonos, which punctuated the calendar of the Yoshiwara and intensified the erotic appeal of the prostitute, an appeal that centered on visuality.[32]

Given the cultural practices in the Yoshiwara of displaying the female body, is it any wonder that Midori's body becomes the object of exhibitionism? Near the end of *Takekurabe*, we are witness to one of the Ōtori festivals, preparations for which the people of Daionji-mae were busily engaged in by making *kumade* charms at the beginning of the novella. Unlike the Senzoku festival, which is a communal affair unassociated with the pleasure quarters, the Ōtori festival is entirely about money and the Yoshiwara. As we saw, the *kumade* are commodities to be hawked to the sightseers who flock to the area. The crowd is enormous and the noise spectacular: "The revelry at the Ōtori Shrine was astounding. The roar of the young men rushing from the shrine into the Yoshiwara through the *kensaba* gate was enough to make one think the Pillars of Heaven were about to burst asunder" (261). Midori appears among this crowd a changed person. She is dressed in festive attire looking very much like a doll, we are told. Her hair is done up elaborately in the *ōshimada* style, and, when her friend Shōta asks, Midori says that she got her hair done in her sister's room that very morning (262–63). The *ōshimada* hairstyle often functioned as a visual indicator of a girl's transition into an adult woman. For Midori, however, this is not a simple right of passage, but is instead symbolic of the fact that she will soon be (or more likely already is) a prostitute.[33] Midori has been paraded around the streets of the Yoshiwara to make sure she is seen, and whether or not she has taken her first customer at this point, the clothes and hair now mark her unmistakably as a woman of the quarter. Seen she is: in fact, she cannot raise her head to meet the gazes of the passersby (263). It is almost as if her subjectivity has been taken from her as the "doll" is trapped in a web of crisscrossing gazes, which is only to say that she is now fully subjected to the designs of the Yoshiwara.

When she walks through the streets and people turn to admire her hairdo, Midori feels they are looking down on her. When she hears their praise she thinks they are making fun of her (263). Midori's body, which is once again fragmented into metonymic details of dress, accessories, and hairstyle that are invested with erotic significance, is blatantly juxtaposed by the narrator with the commodities being hawked on the streets. On this festival day centered on money and commodities, in this place devoted to the exchange of money for physical pleasure, Midori has become completely, violently, the object of the gaze. Men now look on her, and will continue to do so, as a commodity to be purchased. Unable to endure their gazes for long, Midori flees home, with Shōta trailing behind,

trying to comfort her, but unable to understand the significance of her transformation. Midori can only cry alone on
her bed: "She hated, just hated this growing up. Why did
people have to get older? She wanted to go back to before,
a year ago, or seven months even" (264). For Midori, growing
up means a growing awareness of how her own body is exhibited as an erotic object before the gaze, or what Laura Mulvey
has called "to-be-looked-at-ness."[34] Growing up means being
caught in a tightening spiral of eros and commerce and being
unable to do anything about it. Growing up is synonymous
with subjection.

V

None of Midori's feelings are verbalized at the end of the
novella; everything is given as an inside view. Confusion,
resentment, humiliation, despair, and desire—Midori feels
all these emotions and more, but they remain unarticulated.
What is thematized in the second half of *Takekurabe* is the
discrepancy between what is felt or thought and what can
be spoken. Subjection, the text ultimately suggests, is precisely
what creates this gap, this internal censorship. A poignant
example of this is when Midori cries alone near the end of
the novella, unable to convey her feelings to Shōta. However,
the most intricate example of the text's model of the psychic
effects of subjection, as well as the way the theme of foreclosed
love is bound up with subjection, can be found in the rainy
morning encounter between Midori and Nobu in front of the
Daikokuya.

One rainy morning, Nobu is asked by his father to drop
off a package at his sister's house in Tamachi before going
to school, and, as is his habit, he takes a shortcut along
the moat that leads in front of the house of the master of the
Daikokuya. This time, unfortunately, his sandal strap breaks
as he passes by, and he struggles vainly in the rain to mend it.
Nobu's bad luck is the reader's good fortune, however, for the
stage is now set for what must surely be one of the great

moments in Japanese literature. Midori sees someone wrestling with his sandal through the gate and takes a strip of cloth out to help; when she gets close enough, she sees that it is Nobu and stops, unable to go forward or to retreat, unable to utter a single word. It is a powerfully suggestive moment of silence, which takes some time and effort to unpack.

This entire scene plays itself out against the backdrop of *Genji monogatari* (The Tale of Genji, early eleventh c.), to which the narrator refers in no uncertain terms:

Whenever Nobu went to his sister's house in Tamachi, he took a shortcut along the ditch. If only he had taken another route today. As usual, he saw the simple lattice gate, and behind it the stone lantern and the thatched fence stretching to the garden, all very elegant. The bamboo summer blinds were rolled up on the veranda. It brought back memories. One might even think that inside, behind the sliding doors with their glass insets, might be a present-day Azechi at her rosary; there might even appear a young Murasaki with her hair done up. This was the house of the master of the Dai-kokuya. (255–56)

Specifically, the narrator is gesturing toward the "Waka-murasaki" (Young Murasaki) chapter of *Genji*, which tells the story of Genji's fateful first glimpse of the central heroine of the tale, Murasaki, when he is in the hills north of the capital. While there seeking relief from an ailment, Genji discovers a mansion in the valley. He goes down and spies on the inhabitants by looking through a gap in the fence, a classic example of the topos of erotic gazing, or *kaimami*. He sees an old nun (this is Azechi) and a number of children; then, a pretty girl about ten years old with "waving hair spread out like a fan" comes out to tell the nun that her sparrows were let out. Genji is astonished at the likeness between this girl and his stepmother Fujitsubo, with whom he is in love. The likeness is not coincidental; the girl is the young Murasaki, who is, in fact, the niece of Fujitsubo, and the nun is Murasaki's grandmother. Genji brazenly asks Azechi that he be entrusted with Murasaki's care and upbringing; he will treat her, he says, as his own daughter and make certain she lacks for nothing. Murasaki's guardians, assuming that Genji is interested in the girl in a romantic way (and they are not incorrect), decline his offer, saying she is still much too young. To their dismay, Genji presses his suit over the following days and then, overcome by the girl's resemblance to Fujitsubo, abducts the young Murasaki in the night, spiriting her away to his own mansion in the capital where he proceeds to transform her into his ideal of femininity.[35]

Ichiyō is not at all concerned with the matter of resemblance in this allusion; instead, by explicitly gesturing toward a specific scene of *kaimami* in Murasaki Shikibu's masterpiece, she has invited the reader to interpret the rainy morning encounter between Midori and Nobu as a moment implicating desire. One of the earliest extant examples of *kaimami* can be found in *Ise monogatari* (Tales of Ise, tenth c.), a section of which features a certain man, whom the reader is likely meant to identify with the poet and lover Ariwara no Narihira (825–880), coming across two beautiful sisters in the old capital of Nara. His heart is aroused after spying on them through a gap in the fence (*kaimamitekeri*), and he tears off a piece of cloth from the hem of his robe, dashes off an allusive and elegant verse, and sends it to the two beauties.[36] In the classic pattern, the necessary ingredients for any scene of *kaimami* are a boundary or border of some kind—usually a fence—and a gaze that penetrates it. Typically, as in both *Ise* and *Genji*, it is the gaze of a male hidden from view that fixes on a female who does not know she is on display. If the man's desire is aroused by this act of transgressive voyeurism, he will send a poem, to which the woman may send a reply, thereby initiating a romantic relationship. The anecdote in *Ise* does not recount the woman's reply, but I hope my rehearsal of the "Wakamurasaki" chapter from *Genji* makes clear that an entire machinery of romantic entanglement is set in motion with any staging of *kaimami* in classical tales from the late-Heian era onward. *Kaimami* is no static event of voyeurism; rather, it is merely the beginning of a forward dynamic, for the stolen look generates desire, which, in turn, generates more plot and more complications, in short, more narrative. The erotic gaze here is like a spinning wheel, churning out narrative threads that wind their way into the tapestry of the story.

Ichiyō did not merely appropriate the *kaimami* topos, but transformed it in order to meet her own narrative requirements. First, the gender roles are reversed, and it is the female who gazes silently upon the male through a barrier. Second, unlike the typical scene of *kaimami*, in which the person being observed is totally oblivious of the gaze, Nobu is painfully aware of Midori's gaze on him, but cannot bring himself to return her look. More than either of these, however, I would emphasize the following: in this electric scene, desire is achingly evoked with the classical topos of erotic gazing and is reinforced throughout the narrative with the trope of the well-curb, which we examined earlier, but it leads nowhere in *Takekurabe*. The forward dynamic of the topos, in which desire generates plot, does not occur, for all action grinds to a halt in a scene that essentially becomes a mental drama without spoken words. Action is short-circuited in *Takekurabe*, and the question the reader must wrestle with is, why has desire been strongly suggested, while the expression of desire has been made impossible?

We would not be very attentive readers if we did not at least intuit that the answer is somehow connected to Midori's destiny to follow her sister behind the walls of the Yoshiwara. This suspicion is actually reinforced by continuing to read on an intertextual level because Murasaki Shikibu's eleventh-century masterpiece is not the only tale evoked here. There is actually a double palimpsest, the second being Ryūtei Tanehiko's best-selling parody of *Genji*, *Nise Murasaki inaka Genji* (A False Murasaki and a Rustic Genji, 1829–1842). Tanehiko (1783–1842) transformed the Heian classic into a kabuki-inspired tale of shogunal intrigue and the demimonde set in the late fifteenth century during the rule of the Muromachi shoguns. In the sixth book of his burlesque parody, Tanehiko's hero Mitsu'uji (Genji) peers through a gap in the fence and spies an older woman (Azechi here goes by the name Kodama), several younger women, and a twelve-year-old girl called Murasaki, crying that her sparrows have been let out. The great difference here is that the scene of *kaimami* in Tanehiko's text takes place in a brothel, and the young Murasaki has been sold to the master of the establishment as an apprentice courtesan. Money troubles forced Kodama into prostitution, and the same fate has visited her granddaughter Murasaki because money was needed to buy medicine for Murasaki's ailing mother Sawagiku, who died despite their ministrations.[37] The forward dynamic or narrative principle of *kaimami* is preserved, for Mitsu'uji, like his predecessor Genji, eventually abducts Murasaki. However, the rambunctious eroticism of Tanehiko's wildly popular text is contained (barely), for Mitsu'uji's flagrantly rakish behavior is shown to be a master strategy for saving the government; he spirits away Murasaki as a hostage in order to prevent her father from allying himself with enemies of the shogun.

The double palimpsest, while complicating interpretation a great deal, is also enriching and suggestive. Midori, like Tanehiko's Murasaki, has been sold as an apprentice courtesan. The idea of mapping characters across texts encourages us to look for the figure of Azechi and Kodama in *Takekurabe*, which we find in Midori's mother. Even while Midori gazes on Nobu, she is also acutely, painfully aware of her mother's presence nearby and repeatedly looks back over her shoulder.[38] It is the mother who eventually ends this freeze-frame when she tells Midori to come back inside before she catches a cold. The narrator explicitly states that Midori's mother is oblivious of the specifics of the situation (259). Nonetheless, the gaze of the mother can be read, I think, more creatively than has usually been done. On one level, Midori is apprehensive about her mother's presence nearby because she has internalized the fact that her mother represents a restrictive force. Midori's mother can be equated with the figure of Azechi in Genji's encounter with the young Murasaki, but the mother in *Takekurabe* is an ominous being who has decided to sell her daughter into prostitution. She is more like Kodama in this respect, though the guiltless Kodama is motivated by a painful financial dilemma. Azechi and Kodama, then, have been transformed: the benign, even protective figure has become a disciplinary figure, and the gaze of Midori's mother can be read metaphorically as an ever vigilant gaze that interferes with the potential play of desire between Midori and Nobu.

This is not the first time we have encountered the mother's gaze. When Midori is before her mirror at her toilette at an early point in the story, the eyes of her mother fall upon her, or more specifically, on the details of her hair and clothes:

The summer evening was made pleasant by a cool breeze. Midori had washed the heat of the day away in the bath and was preparing her makeup and dress to go out. Her mother had set Midori's hair herself. "She's my own child, but what a beauty she is," she thought *as she scrutinized her daughter from every angle.* "The makeup on the neck is just a little thin," she added. They chose a cool, light blue single layer kimono and an *obi* that was cut to Midori's own waist. It would be some time before they could choose a pair of sandals from amongst those lined up at the front gate. (236; italics added for emphasis)

Though we are given less detail about Midori's accoutrements here than usual, the mother's eye is arrested by a set of metonymic details similar to those we examined earlier: *kimono, obi,* fair skin, and such. The satisfaction that the mother feels here is no innocent pride, but arises because Midori is a valuable commodity in the sexual economy of the Yoshiwara. It is, in other words, a gaze of appraisal. Indeed, by helping to dress her daughter in this way, the mother is actively involved in *producing* Midori as an erotic object for the male gaze. The appraising gaze of the mother early in the story has turned into a disciplinary gaze in the later scene because Midori is rapidly approaching the moment when she will be transformed into a courtesan. The master of the Daikokuya no doubt feels a similar sense of satisfaction as he watches Midori blossom into womanhood over the years, and thus the mother's gaze must ultimately be read as a substitute for the *proprietary* gaze of the master of the Daikokuya, and by extension, of the Yoshiwara itself. In the conspiracy between Midori's parents and the master of the Daikokuya, Midori is an investment (the characters used to write her name mean "beauty and rising profits"); moreover, she is an investment on the verge of womanhood, and, thus, will soon be producing returns. No threats to that investment will be tolerated by the beneficiaries. Midori's expression of desire for Nobu might have been possible when she was a schoolgirl, but her own subjective longings and wishes will soon be curtailed. In the rainy morning scene, Midori has already internalized the policeman, a psychological dynamic that works together with the earlier sandal incident to erect an impassable wall—no less powerful for being immaterial—between Midori and Nobu.

In addition to implicating desire, the play of gazes also evokes intense anxiety for both Midori and Nobu, and the result is paralysis. The narrator moves masterfully back and forth from one character to the other in the scene, giving us alternating inside views. Nobu is petrified: "When he heard footfalls on the stones, he felt as if someone had poured ice water down his back. Even without turning around he knew it was she. His body shook and his face turned pale. He turned his back on her and pretended to concentrate on his sandal strap" (258). Nobu's paralysis stems from many things: the awkwardness of first love, the transgression of propriety, the fact of being a priest-to-be confronted by an object of desire who is simultaneously feared for her connections to the quarter. Midori, too, faces anxiety and paralysis, but it stems from something different.

Since Midori, her heart fluttering in confusion, is unable to speak, the narrator takes us into her soul and reveals what its contents might have been on another, more normal, occasion. In effect, she speaks for the silent, brooding Midori.

Had Midori been her usual self, she would have pointed at the struggling Nobu and scoffed. You're hopeless, she might have said, telling him exactly what she thought of him. You thought you'd pick a fight with Shōta on the night of the festival, so you all came and

ended our fun. You even beat up poor Sangorō, who wasn't to blame
for anything! And you planned the whole thing, didn't you? Don't
you think you should apologize? Chōkichi was there calling me
'whore, whore!' I'll bet it was you who put him up to that! What's
wrong with being a whore? I'm not indebted to you for the least little
thing. I have a mother and father, and the master of the Daikokuya,
and there's my sister too. I'll never owe anything to a backslider like
you, not even by accident, so why don't you stop calling me 'whore!'
If you've got something to say to me, why don't you stop hiding in
the shadows and muttering, and come over here and say it to my
face. Anytime you want. I'm ready. So, what'll it be? She would have
grabbed him by the sleeve, and hit him again and again; but now she
just hid in the shadow of the gate without saying a word. She wasn't
even able to go back inside. Her heart was pounding. Midori wasn't
her usual self. (257–58)

If Midori is not her usual self, neither is the narrator. This
is not the figure who plays the part of the knowledgeable
outsider calling attention to the customs of the quarter and
pronouncing them *okashi* (strange, funny), her characteristic
posture in the first half of the novella; instead, the narrator
is in complete sympathy with the young Midori and even
stands at her side as an ally. In this passage, the narrator
fuses with Midori, and her discourse becomes inextricably
intertwined with that of her speechless heroine as she puts
Midori's unverbalized anger into actual words.[39] Nonetheless,
there is a prominent gap here between Midori and the person
who would speak for her, a rhetorical gap between a silent,
brooding Midori and a narrator who fills that void with her
own discourse, all the while shifting out of classical Japanese
to mimic her heroine's tone and idiom. It is the juxtaposition
of a young woman who wants to speak but cannot with a
narrator who feels compelled to speak for her that gives the
scene such a sense of pathos.

It is apparent that the prostitute-to-be is haunted by the
word "whore" and that this word is a major source of the
resentment the narrator verbalizes on her behalf. All of this
points back to the fight between the Main Street Gang and
the Back Street Gang in front of the sundries shop, where

Midori is struck with the dirty sandal. In physical terms, the sandal strikes Midori's forehead, thereby marking her body, inscribing in a semi-permanent way the belittling she received at the hands of Chōkichi. Psychologically speaking, Midori is deeply, profoundly affected by the incident: "She could clean the mud from her forehead, but the affront would not so easily disappear, for resentment had gotten under her skin" (243). She refuses to go to school after that and falls into moodiness. Her bitterness is then displaced onto Nobu. She believes (mistakenly) that he orchestrated the entire incident. Her feelings for Nobu grow ambivalent; at the time of the rainy morning encounter, she is still attracted to him, but also upset by what she sees as his cruelty. In retaliation, she calls him *namagusa* (rendered as "backslider" in the previous quotation) in her mind, which is a derogatory word for a priest who eats meat. Such name-calling is part of a larger web of resentment encompassing to a greater or lesser degree all the major characters in *Takekurabe*, as Kamei Hideo long ago demonstrated.[40] In a few remarkable pages, Ichiyō has skillfully yoked together the major themes—resentment, the awkwardness of first love, growing up, and the sex trade—and situated them within a rich double palimpsest in order to suggest and lament that the endpoint of the process of subjection is inevitably the banishment of speech.

This silence is given enormous symbolic weight by Ichiyō, so that the rainy morning encounter yields much more in thematic and symbolic overtones than merely one more moment in the cycle of resentment that so marks the text. In fact, such moments of pregnant silence loudly punctuate the last half of the novella. Yet more than any of these, meaning and significance seem to rush to the rainy morning scene, making the silence here in the encounter between Midori and Nobu almost deafening.

Let me reiterate that silence does not indicate a lack of thought or feeling, but the short-circuiting of speech. Inside views clearly indicate that Midori experiences a range of often conflicting emotions, but she cannot give voice to them. The reader can only know the heroine's thoughts and emotions when the narrator takes us into her mind and articulates them, which she will often do using free indirect discourse, mimicking Midori's own idiom. Thus, the thematization of subjection results in the narrator's discovery of interiority and her excavation of Midori's psyche. It is in this gap between the articulated and the unarticulated, between what Midori can say for herself in the first half of the novella and what the narrator must verbalize on her behalf in the second half, that we must ultimately locate the effect of subjection. Subjection is the mechanism of internal censorship installed in the individual by institutional power after beating back competing claims. The complex of emotions takes flight into the interior of the psyche, where it exists only as unarticulated thoughts. This occurs because of outright physical coercion and regimes of discipline brought to bear on the body, but subjection also involves more subtle and insidious mechanisms, and it is on these that the novella concentrates. The text holds up visuality as emblematic: the prostitute-to-be acquires more and more of the erotic accoutrements, speech patterns, and body language that are associated with the sex trade; and the gaze ever more insistently plays across the body of the heroine, settling precisely on those metonymic details that are invested with erotic significance.

Subjection is not total domination; there is, as Foucault and others have observed, always an unassimilated part of the individual that cannot be fully molded to conform to an institutional norm or ideal, and this is precisely where critics locate sites of resistance to power. Exactly this point is underscored in *Takekurabe* when the narrator takes us into Midori's mind and reveals its contents to be a complicated gamut of thoughts and emotions. Nonetheless, the text is ultimately pessimistic about the possibility of resistance; that which cannot be verbally expressed is represented as being unthreatening to institutional power.

The thematization of such a gap is allied to Ichiyō's literary method in *Takekurabe*, and while the novella offers us yet one more suffering heroine and one more instance of happiness foreclosed, the text does not partake of the sentimental mode as in "Jūsan'ya." In *Takekurabe*, Ichiyō creates an economy of pathos more characteristic of the stories from the second half of her career, including "Nigorie," which we examined in an earlier chapter, and "Wakaremichi," which we will take up next. The sentimentalism of a work like "Jūsan'ya" or of the early stories relies on tears and excess, while pathos is a more subdued form of literary imagination. Pathos relies on the strategic stripping away of select details to leave blank spaces — gaps.[41] This does not hinder interpretation, but multiplies and enriches it. Because the text itself does not provide all the answers, the reader inevitably poses provocative questions: What will happen to Midori? Will she somehow adapt and become a "success" like her sister? What psychological price will she pay in order to become one of the stars of the quarter? Thus, the reader must become an active participant in the reading process, to fill in the gaps, and this makes interpretation of Ichiyō's stories, in part, the construction of plausible narratives.

As if to compensate for these gaps, pathos relies on the subtle linkage of motifs for aesthetic and emotional purposes rather than on explicit commentary. *Takekurabe* has the most well-known example of resonant motifs in Ichiyō's entire oeuvre. During the silence that dominates the rainy morning encounter, the only expression Midori can muster when she sees Nobu's mishap is to throw out to him the piece of cloth she is holding. Her gesture echoes the moment described in the analepsis when she offers the fallen Nobu her red silk handkerchief. The cloth is symbolic of first love, but in the rainy morning encounter it signals the impossibility of consummating this love. The cloth is decorated with an autumnal pattern of red maple leaves; autumn traditionally signals ends, and here it signals an end that never really had a chance at a beginning. Nobu is in no less a dilemma: he longs to pick up the cloth, to acknowledge Midori's gesture of affection, but there are just too many forces restraining him. He leaves it on the ground soaking in the rain—a symbol of what would never be. However, at the end of the story, just before he leaves for the seminary, Nobu leaves a paper narcissus at the gate of Midori's home, which is ultimately his answer to Midori's gesture.

We also see the exploitation of gaps in the discrepancy between the protagonists' partial comprehension of their situation and the reader's fuller awareness of the significance of events unfolding on the page. The narrator constantly shuttles between the minds of Midori and Nobu in the rainy morning encounter, revealing to the reader what each character cannot reveal to the other. Above and beyond this, readers familiar with the classical literary tradition notice that the evocation of desire in the novella is strengthened through the mobilization of classical tropes and topoi, even though nothing will come of this desire. In an economy of pathos, the bonus of pleasure that grows from recognition of these elements is simultaneously a feeling of anguish, even powerlessness, which stems from awareness of the full implications of the non-explicit. Through such figures and devices, the reader realizes that the tragedy of Midori's situation lies not only in a subjection that manipulates her body to conform to the requirements of the Yoshiwara or in foreclosed love, but also in the transformation of a spirited, articulate, even rambunctious girl into a silent, forlorn, dejected woman.

SIX

Fantasies of Success

Aphorisms do not receive very much attention in literary criticism. They tend to be thought of as a banal, "unliterary" form of expression. Indeed, the aphorism represents exactly the kind of automatization of language and habituation of thought against which the Russian Formalists pitted their idea of defamiliarization as the very definition of the literary, and this view has influenced a wide range of later formalist schools. Yet, from the perspective of historicist criticism, aphorisms and stock phrases provide a crucial means by which we can situate a literary text in its historically specific milieu. Aphorisms that circulated widely in late-nineteenth-century Japan constitute a significant, though so far completely unrecognized, component of Higuchi Ichiyō's "Wakaremichi" (Separate Ways, 1896), especially considering what a short piece it is—about ten pages in modern printed editions. Common expressions of the day such as "he who wears another's clothes will never get anywhere in life" (*hito no o-hatsuu o kiru to shusse ga dekinai*, 275) and "all things come to he who waits" (*mateba kanro*, 283), among others, regularly punctuate the speech of the characters. The phrase "fortune will come to greet you in a carriage" (*jōtō no un ga basha ni notte mukae ni kuru*, 276 and 281) even appears twice in the story, thus assuring it a place of prominent visibility.[1] Almost all of these aphorisms revolve around fortune and success, in other words

risshin shusse. This is true, too, for other kinds of stock phrases
that dot the speech of the characters, an example of which
is "you can achieve anything you want if you put your mind
to it" (*mi hitotsu shusse o shitaraba yokarō*, 278), a common exhortatory expression in the period. The Bakhtinian insight that
the speech of any person is woven together from a variety of
discourses, that it is always borrowed from someplace else,
from someone else's mouth, is perhaps nowhere better exemplified in the corpus of Ichiyō's fiction than in this gem, her
last completed story.[2]

That aphorisms and stock phrases linked to discourses on
fortune and success are such prominent features of the speech
of the two protagonists is really not terribly surprising since
"success" is nearly the sole topic of conversation between
them.[3] What was perhaps only a faint murmur in stories such
as "Nigorie" and "Jūsan'ya" — an echo whose full voice had
to be reconstructed — has turned into an uproar in "Wakaremichi." The very structure of this short work seems designed
to cast conversation about success as the text's central concern.
The first and third parts of the three parts of "Wakaremichi"
are both dramatic scenes consisting almost exclusively of dialogue between the seamstress, Okyō, and the shop hand,
Kichizō (or Kichi for short), the only characters to appear in
the narrative present of the story. These two scenes enclose a
short analepsis that gives background on Kichi.[4] Conversation
is the dominant form of action in the first and third parts; it
even carries the burden of moving the story forward and de-
lineating the psychology of the characters. In the first part, the
two talk about the celebration they will have when one or the
other achieves success, though the hopeful quality of their exchange barely conceals the mutual resignation that their desires will never really be fulfilled. The dialogue in the third
part revolves around Okyō's decision to give up her life as a
seamstress to become a kept woman and Kichizō's exasperation and bewilderment over her decision. Okyō halfheartedly
believes that leaving her life as a seamstress for that of a
mistress is success for her — it is fortune coming to greet her

in a carriage—while Kichi is resolute in his insistence that it is a shameful course to pursue. He tries to persuade her that it is much better to remain in the back streets with her needle, taking orders from her regular customers. Thus, when a plot line that moves a woman from a life of respectable poverty as a seamstress to the dubious life of a kept woman is accompanied by spirited debate about the woman's decision, the meaning and significance of "success" is made the central issue in the text.

This is reinforced by the aphorisms, maxims, and stock phrases, which serve to place success in question, for they invariably appear in a context that reveals suspicion toward one of the most powerful of all discourses in Meiji Japan. The first—the aphorism about wearing another's clothes—appears in the following context: when Kichi visits Okyō in the opening of the story, she offers him some rice cakes, but tells him to toast them himself at the *hibachi* since she is rushing to get an order done.

"Why don't you cook those yourself. I have to finish this tonight. It's a special New Year's outfit for the owner of the pawnshop on the corner," she said, taking up her needle again.

Kichi snorted. "That old baldy. What does he need it for? Why don't I break it in for him instead."

Okyō chided him, "Don't be silly. You know what they say: *He who wears another's clothes will never get anywhere in life.* You can't go around putting the blame on others just because life hasn't gone the way you want."

"Success isn't for me anyway, so what does it matter if it's another person's things or not." (275–76; italics added)

The force of the maxim given by Okyō is undermined by Kichi's reply. He is here claiming that the aphorism is patently false, that it has no claim on him. Given the fact that this particular New Year's outfit is being made for the owner of a pawnshop, an exemplary bourgeois profession in the Meiji period, Kichi is also expressing a genuine class resentment over the social gap between himself and the shop owner. Near the end of "Wakaremichi" Kichi uses an aphorism only to place its truthfulness immediately in question himself in the same sentence: "They say '*all things come to he who waits*,' but day after day only bad things come pouring down on me" (283; italics added). Kichi's bitterness is almost palpable here.

The aphorism about fortune coming to greet a person in a carriage is subverted by Okyō near the end of the first part of the story. Kichi says to her, "But you, you used to be well off, so *fortune will surely come to greet you in a carriage*. And I'm not talking about becoming a mistress, or anything, either. Don't make a bad choice like that." Okyō muses, "I wonder. Instead of a horse-drawn carriage, perhaps it will be a carriage of fire. There are quite a few things that pain me after all" (276; italics added). Given the fact that this aphorism makes two appearances in the narrative present of the story, we get the distinct sense that it is often used in the conversations between the two. Here Okyō fills it with irony and expresses grave doubts about its truthfulness by replacing the image of fortune in a carriage with that of a carriage of fire (associating it with hell) and then linking this new image with her own painful experiences in life. The exchange is doubly ironic in that a reader familiar with the plot will observe that it is, in fact, precisely by becoming a mistress that the fantasy of fortune in a carriage is fulfilled for her. Again at the end of the story, after Okyō has told Kichi about her decision to become a mistress, she says to him, "It's no lie. It's just like you said: *fortune has come for me in a carriage*. I won't be living in this back alley anymore. Kichi, I guess I better hurry up and make you that kimono like I promised." And Kichi replies, "I don't want it. I don't want such a thing. You keep saying it's good luck, but aren't you actually going to do something awful?" (281–82; italics added). This time it is Kichi who questions the truthfulness of the aphorism, since he believes that becoming a mistress is a fall from social grace.

Thus, whenever an aphorism is used, its force is invariably undermined by one or the other character. The discourse of the characters invades the letter of the aphorisms, coexists parasitically with the maxims, and blasphemously subverts all stock phrases. In this situation, a term such as "irony" hardly does justice to the phenomenon. Instead we require the specific conceptualization of parody developed by Bakhtin in his exploration of double-voiced discourse. In "Wakaremichi," the aphorisms are inflected by a different accent, and a second voice—that of Okyō or Kichizō—with its own semantic intentions, colonizes the maxims and stock phrases about success. The phrase is not simply something that can be read in two ways. It is a palimpsest of sorts, whereby the reader is meant to hear both the original voice or meaning and a second voice commenting on the first. In parody, Bakhtin conceives the second voice as inevitably being in a polemic relationship with the first voice.

The second voice, once having made its home in the other's discourse, clashes hostilely with its primordial host and forces him to serve directly opposing aims. Discourse becomes an arena of battle between two voices. In parody, therefore, there cannot be that fusion of voices possible in stylization or in the narration of a narrator . . . ; [in parody,] the voices are not only isolated from one another, separated by a distance, but are also hostilely opposed. Thus in parody the deliberate palpability of the other's discourse must be particularly sharp and clearly marked.[5]

The two voices that coexist in the aphorisms in "Wakaremichi" are also not fused. Instead the authority of the first voice, the "official" voice as it were, is contested and undermined by the voices of the characters.

The aphorisms that are parodied in "Wakaremichi" are much more than ingratiating exhortatory phrases; there is quite a bit more at stake here. They circulate within a distinct discursive regime centered on ambition and success. The discourse on *risshin shusse*, which began in the 1870s as a kind of admonishment to study for wealth and honor, had become by the end of the nineteenth century a hegemonic ideology that had insinuated itself into many corners of society and grafted itself onto a number of other discourses. In addition, while the discourse on *risshin shusse* continued to carry its original meaning, it expanded greatly during the ensuing decades to incorporate a more general drive geared toward prosperity and social standing in a society that insisted that anyone, regardless of their socioeconomic status, could achieve success—provided they had ambition.[6] When Okyō and Kichi parody the aphorisms about success, then, their speech also clashes hostilely with the entire discourse on modern ambition, thereby declaring it patently false and subverting it.

Both the protagonists are mutually estranged from the modern discourse on ambition and success. At the same time, though, *risshin shusse* dominates their fantasies, and Okyō and Kichi orient their actions toward success, dream about attaining it, and even promise to celebrate when the carriage of fortune finally arrives. That the two characters are both pulled in these contradictory ways only serves to cement the bond between them. This is apparent in their dialogue, which is characterized by open frankness and mutual emotional support. They listen to each other, respond to what the other is saying, and offer sympathy and consolation. All of this breaks down once Okyō decides to become a mistress. The dialogue between them becomes disconnected. Komori Yōichi has made the observation that, while Okyō and Kichi might converse with each other in the third part of the narrative, there is no real sense of dialogue between them any longer, no sense that a statement by one is predicated on a prior statement by the other or is geared toward the other's response.[7] The exact moment of disconnection can even be isolated: it occurs when Okyō, trying to explain her decision to become a mistress, says that she is weary of the seamstress's life; Kichi responds this time not with sympathy, but with an expression of resentment over being abandoned.[8] Here Kichi tries to escape the pain of separation by withdrawing into himself, into his own thoughts. After this moment, the conversation may continue, but there is no true dialogue, for each character retreats to his or her own corner and stakes out a hardened position in relation to the status of the kept woman.

Suddenly the aphorism "fortune will come to greet you in a carriage" takes on renewed significance once the heroine makes her fateful decision; and at the heart of "Wakaremichi" is the thematization of the kept woman as an ethical problem. Does the phrase "fortune will come in a carriage" apply to a woman who decides to pursue what in mid-Meiji had become a disreputable occupation? Okyō says that her carriage has indeed come, but her words are laced with irony and resignation; Kichi is completely opposed to her choice and considers it a social fall. The frequent references to this aphorism highlight not just the meaning, but also the gender of success. For a woman, this stock phrase is a reference to the fantasy of the wealthy and handsome male suitor arriving in a bejeweled, horse-drawn carriage to whisk the eligible and beautiful young lady away to the comforts of an aristocratic life of marriage, wealth, and leisure. It was closely connected to the fantasy of the "jeweled palanquin [*tama no koshi*] marriage," which occupied such a prominent place in "Nigorie." Female success essentially meant marriage into luxury, that is, marriage to a successful man, while male success involved the acquisition of formal education, which then allowed one to advance up the social ladder via a prestigious job to a life of status and wealth.[9] For a man, phrases such as "fortune coming in a carriage" would have conjured up rather different fantasies of wealth and power, as well as images of top hats, frock coats, and, of course, a horse-drawn carriage in which he might be seen with his beautiful wife, or, if he were really well off, with an attractive mistress.

The hostile critique of aphorisms in "Wakaremichi" ends up willy-nilly reaching deeply into the fabric of social life and thus implicating such fantasies. I want to suggest that the parodic relationship between the speech of the characters and the aphorisms about success finds an analogy in the relationship between the text of "Wakaremichi" and the discursive regime of *risshin shusse*, which by the turn of the century had become imbricated in a complex social fantasy. As the vastness and complexity of the modern discourse on *risshin shusse* is yet to be realized, we will need to construct an interpretive framework in order to perceive the dialogic relationship under discussion here. My focus for this effort will be on the recirculation of old folktales in the late nineteenth century.

ii

The folktale "Issunbōshi" (Little One Inch) resonates with "Wakaremichi" on a number of levels, and thus there are multiple ways of approaching this little yarn in conjunction with a reading of Ichiyō's story. The case for allusion, for example, could be made with some justification by recalling that Kichizō is of short stature and is called "issunbōshi" (little one inch, a common word of teasing) by others. Surely we could argue fairly persuasively that someone as conversant with traditional literature as Ichiyō could be covertly alluding to the story of Issunbōshi. One might well argue that the sewing needle that Issunbōshi uses to defeat the demons in the folktale is transformed in "Wakaremichi" into the needle used by Okyō in her work as a seamstress. Sufficient ingenuity might also allow us to pull a literary-critical rabbit out of our proverbial hat and find Issunbōshi's bowl and chopsticks, which he uses for transportation on the river leading to the capital, displaced from the representational world of "Little One Inch" to the very different representational world of "Wakaremichi." This would produce a reading from within the paradigm of allusion, not at all an unenlightening approach.[10]

In this chapter, though, I propose something different. While I do wish to produce a distinctive reading or interpretation of "Wakaremichi," at the same time I want to suggest how the literary text can be juxtaposed with other social documents as a way of gaining access to a larger, highly contentious dialogue. Using "Issunbōshi" in this spirit will allow us to situate "Wakaremichi" within a greater social or cultural text centered on gender and success and to sketch the story's parodic relationship to a powerful collective fantasy at work in the mid-Meiji period. Uncovering this fantasy is as important to the goals of this chapter as the literary interpretation. The cost of this shift of attention will be a reading that may perhaps seem more loose and fragmentary than those in the other chapters, but the advantage is that we can gain tremendous insight into the multiple, buried cultural transactions between the literary and the social worlds.

The classic, well-known tale of Little One Inch exists in a variety of versions, whether it be as a children's story, as *mukashibanashi* (orally rooted tales), or as the kind of anonymous short fiction of the Muromachi and early Edo periods known as *otogi zōshi* (companion tales). Our primary focus will first be on the *otogi zōshi* version, with some important glances at the *mukashibanashi*, and then on one particular Meiji-period rewriting of the folktale, in which the story of Little One Inch is reincarnated for very modern ideological goals. Taking these two versions together we will be able to construct an interpretive model that links height, gender, sexuality, class, and success, a constellation of elements that, I will argue, form a crucial subtext in "Wakaremichi."

Although the story of Little One Inch is well known, it is worth spending some time dwelling on the plot of the folktale in some detail, so that the changes that are wrought on the story in the Meiji-period version are fully apparent. The narrative of "Issunbōshi" opens at a village in Naniwa in the province of Tsu, where we find a childless couple who pray to the deity of the great Sumiyoshi Shrine for a child. The Sumiyoshi god takes pity on them, and they have a baby boy, whom they name Little One Inch because of his minuscule size.[11] Strangely, the boy eventually reaches his early teens without growing at all, causing the old couple to lament their fate. Their bitter disappointment compels Issunbōshi to leave home and depart for the capital (taking with him a sewing needle for a weapon, a rice bowl for transportation on the river, and chopsticks for use as oars), where a host of adventures awaits him.

He arrives at a certain mansion, which happens to be that of a nobleman called the Sanjō Lord, where he is taken in.

The Sanjō Lord has a beautiful daughter, and Issunbōshi hatches an outrageous plan to make her his own: he frames the girl by spreading some rice on her mouth while she is sleeping, thus making it look as though she ate his offering rice, with which he makes religious observances. The Sanjō Lord becomes enraged by his daughter's alleged actions and ejects her from the mansion, putting his tiny guest in charge of her punishment. Issunbōshi, gleeful that his scheme has worked, puts the dejected woman in a boat and departs from the capital, apparently intending to start a life with the lady back home in Naniwa.

But before they reach their destination a fierce wind sweeps them ashore onto an unknown island, where they are confronted by two *oni* (demon or ogre). One of the *oni* cries out, "I'll gobble you up and take the woman for my wife" and swallows his tiny prey. But the hero appears out from behind the demon's eye brandishing his needle-sword. The demons grow terrified—"This creature is not the ordinary kind" (a phrase often used in reference to Issunbōshi)—and drop all their possessions in their haste to flee. Among these discarded items is a mallet. Apparently sensing that the implement has magical properties, Issunbōshi waves it about and shouts, "make me big," whereupon he instantly grows to normal height. He then uses the magical device to conjure up a celebratory feast and a pile of gold and silver before returning to the capital to take up residence.

"Such things could not be kept hidden," the narrator tells us, and before long, we hear that the emperor himself has gotten wind of these fantastic events and decides to investigate. He discovers that Issunbōshi's father is none other than the son of the Horikawa Middle Counselor, who was banished to the provinces because of the machinations of a political enemy. Issunbōshi's mother is also of no mean rank: she is the daughter of the Fushimi Lesser Captain. After these discoveries, the emperor calls Issunbōshi before him and makes him the Horikawa Lesser Captain and, eventually, the Horikawa Middle Counselor. The filial Issunbōshi seems to bear no grudge against the parents who were so eager to be rid of him many years before, for he brings the old couple to the capital and installs them in his mansion. He then marries the Sanjō Lord's daughter and they have three children. We are told at the end that Issunbōshi's progeny flourished down through the generations.[12]

If "Issunbōshi" is a story about success, as I will argue, this success rests on certain preconditions. The most obvious is the magic of the demon's mallet. Without this power, Issunbōshi could not attain normal height, and normal stature, the narrative implies in the very unfolding of the plot, is necessary for all his other achievements. For our purposes, however, the question of magic is actually the least compelling element of the narrative. Much more important are the issues of social class and sexuality. The tiny hero of the folktale may appear to be of humble birth at the beginning of the story, but the truth of his high station is dramatically revealed at the end of the narrative. Still, most readers of the time would probably not have been deceived by the conceit all the way until the end of the tale, for Issunbōshi is, after all, a "gift" of the Sumiyoshi deity, and the circumstances surrounding Little One Inch and his acts of heroism lead many characters in the story to say of him, "he's someone out of the ordinary" (*tada-mono narazu*). Indeed, the implication of the tale is that Issunbōshi can perform great feats such as defeating two *oni* with a mere sewing needle precisely because he is *really* of high birth as well as affiliated with the world of the gods. Were this not the case, a narrative that saw the emperor make him into a nobleman would, of course, have been ideologically threatening. The fantasy here, then, is less a rags-to-riches kind of story, than the narrative of a hero who, though having several strikes against him, reclaims his high station through heroic feats, climbs up the courtly ladder of success, and ensures the prosperity of his progeny. The old couple may have simply been praying for a child, but the Sumiyoshi deity's ulterior motive seems to be the reinstatement of this family to its former position of social eminence; it is with this in mind that we should probably read the cryptic reference at the end of the narrative to the plan of the Sumiyoshi deity being fulfilled with Issunbōshi's success.

Height has metaphorical significance in that it indicates the attainment of lofty social status. The plot line implies that normal height is a necessary precondition for Issunbōshi to gain the favor of the emperor. It is also a precondition for Issunbōshi if he wishes to marry the beautiful daughter of the Sanjō Lord. Height is inextricably connected to the sexual order here, for the image of a princess towering over her husband would have aroused all kinds of sexual anxieties and would have been just as ideologically threatening in its own way as the story of a man without pedigree who gains high courtly rank. Thus, once the power of the mallet turns Little One Inch into a man of normal stature, and once the emperor discovers his true lineage, the threat to the sexual order and the threat to the social order are thereby dispelled, and the narrative can race to its festive conclusion in a scene of marriage and political success.

"Issunbōshi" is one of those tales that has galvanized the Japanese imagination for centuries. Iwaya Sazanami (1870–1933) — who is widely credited with having created the first children's story in Japan, the vendetta tale *Kogane maru* (titled after the name of its canine hero) in 1891 — included his own version of the story of Little One Inch, complete with illustrations, as the nineteenth volume in his series *Nippon mukashibanashi* (Folk Tales of Japan), published in March 1896, two months after "Wakaremichi" appeared in *Kokumin no tomo*.[13] The fact that "Wakaremichi" was published before this new version of the story of Little One Inch is strategically useful, for it allows us to dispense with any notion of allusion or influence and instead compels us to examine a shared discursive space. Iwaya's version, at over 30 pages, is substantially longer than any premodern version. The preface to the volume, penned by the nationalist Miyake Setsurei (1860–1945), makes it clear that the intended audience for this new series of classic folktales is primarily children, which represents a significant transformation in itself: "Sazanami's series, *Folk Tales of Japan*, takes those tales passed down from of old and creates new stories that the children of the many provinces can have as their companions."[14] Sazanami seems to have had a number of pedagogical goals in mind for his children's stories. One of these was a geography lesson in which the old provincial and city names are mapped onto their contemporary equivalents for young readers: the narrator explains, for example, that Naniwa is modern Osaka and the capital is present-day Kyoto. In addition, there is a real effort to add liveliness to the narration by including extensive conversation between Issunbōshi and the other characters. The narrator does not just recount in summary fashion how the hero got a needle-sword, for example, but includes dialogue in the section where Issunbōshi is forced to leave his parents:

> "Yes father, I will leave as you asked. But first, father, I would like to ask mother to give me one of her sewing needles."
> "Give you a sewing needle? What will you do with it?"
> "I will use it as a sword."
> "I see. Well, of course, it would make the perfect sword for you."[15]

Here Issunbōshi is portrayed as a filial son willing to do whatever his parents ask, just one of his many good qualities, along with honesty and forthright behavior. Sazanami apparently has no desire to make his hero into the devilish schemer of the *otogi zōshi* version, so the scene in the latter in which Issunbōshi frames the daughter of the Sanjō Lord is not utilized. Sazanami avoids this unpleasant moment by referring to the *mukashibanashi* version, which has the princess herself fall in love with Issunbōshi.[16]

The emphasis on filiality and righteousness is as much a part of this new version of "Issunbōshi" as it is of Meiji-period children's literature in general. The intent behind many children's stories from this age was unabashedly didactic: they were intended to instill values. Besides filiality, truthfulness, and such, ambition was the quality extolled above nearly everything else in Japanese children's literature of the late Meiji period. The classic tale of Issunbōshi works very well within this ideological project. The story of Little One Inch, who is born to a mother and a father who do not want him because of his small stature, and who travels to the capital, defeats two *oni*, and thereby achieves recognition and high rank from the emperor, finally marrying a high-born lady, would have been immensely appealing to the creators of children's literature in the Meiji period. Nonetheless, there is a gulf between the "Issunbōshi" that appeared, for example, in the mid-Edo-period collection *Otogi bunko* (Library of Companion Tales) and the *Issunbōshi* recreated by Iwaya Sazanami; between the appearance of these two versions, a span of over 100 years, there has been a seismic shift in the discourse on success, and this is reflected very clearly in Sazanami's rendition for Meiji children.

Sazanami's version generally elaborates upon the *otogi zōshi*. However, in Sazanami's rendering, Issunbōshi encounters the two *oni* while on a pilgrimage to a temple with the Sanjō Lord's daughter, which, like the other exception noted above, follows the *mukashibanashi* version. But the battle in Sazanami's tale includes even more astounding feats of heroism than any premodern version. One *oni* swallows Issunbōshi, who then proceeds to poke the inside of the demon's stomach. This causes the beast so much agony that he spits out his tiny tormentor. The other *oni* then grabs our hero and attempts to swallow him, but Issunbōshi escapes through the demon's nose and begins to stab at his foe's eye with his needle-sword. Having been bested, the two *oni* flee in such haste that they drop the mallet that they were carrying. The princess explains that the mallet is magical and can grant any wish. Issunbōshi, who apparently cannot be made to appear greedy in this version, replies simply, "Hime-sama, there is nothing in particular that I desire except normal height," whereupon the princess makes the wish on his behalf, and he grows into a splendid figure of a man (the accompanying illustration depicts a grown Issunbōshi as a courtier, and the princess looks the very figure of an aristocratic lady).[17] When the emperor hears of these exploits, he calls Issunbōshi to the palace and

Fantasies of Success   195

bestows many gifts on him. The narrator informs us that "just
as he had grown in height, so too did Issunbōshi go on to acquire rank and attain success [*shusse*]. Later he became the
Horikawa Lesser Captain and was admired by all."[18]

The most notable difference between the two versions here
in the closing pages of the narrative is the complete lack of
attention paid to the social status of Issunbōshi's parents (in
fact, they do not even reappear at the end of the narrative
in Sazanami's rendering). There is no discussion of how the
el-derly mother and father are actually high-born aristocrats,
whose own parents were driven to the countryside because
of the machinations of political enemies. As I suggested, this
was mandatory information in earlier versions so that no ideological threat would be posed by Issunbōshi's rapid advancement through the courtly ranks. In contrast, while the Meiji
Issunbōshi is still cloaked in an aura of the otherworldly, there
is nothing in the story that would make the reader think that
his parents are anything other than humble peasants. This is
part of the ideological power of Sazanami's reworking of the
tale for Meiji readers. By the Meiji period, it had become desirable to represent people of humble birth who attain honors,
wealth, and social rank in order to make believable and to
reproduce the ideology of success. After all, in the late nineteenth century, Japan was representing itself as meritocratic.
One supposedly advanced up the social ladder to wealth and
status not because of the accident of birth or because one had
connections, but because one possessed ambition, studied and
worked hard, and accrued the fruits of that labor. Literary
representations of people from the lower classes who attain
success through ambition and diligence became one crucial
means of reinforcing the view of general social equality and
mobility. Even if one were of humble birth, then, fortune could
supposedly be had with hard work.[19] Indeed, another major
difference between the two versions of the tale is that the Meiji
Issunbōshi demonstrates great practical intelligence and labors
to be of service to the Sanjō Lord after he is taken in.[20] These
are not features of premodern versions. Unlike the story of

Little One Inch from the mid-Edo period, many children's stories from the Meiji era were, like Sazanami's *Issunbōshi*, true rags-to-riches stories, and ambition and hard work, among other qualities, were extolled as virtues that could overcome the constraints of social class and the blind luck of birth.[21] To a good Meiji ideologue like Sazanami, the mandatory references to the high rank of Issunbōshi's parents in the premodern versions would have seemed superfluous, probably even archaic, in the new order.

The anxiety of class difference—which, despite this new version of the folktale, was very much a problem in Meiji Japan—may be elided in Sazanami's *Issunbōshi*, but certain structural and ideological elements remain markedly constant across the gulf of time. Chief among these is the relationship between height, success, and marriage. The tangible signs of success, such as wealth and court rank, can only be gained after the hero attains normal height, which in turn depends on the magic power of the mallet carried by the very foes Issunbōshi defeats. The causal relationship here is stated outright in the closing moments of the Meiji-period folktale: "just as he had grown in height, so too did Issunbōshi go on to acquire rank and attain success [*shusse*]." Normal height is also a precondition for matrimony; just as in the *otogi zōshi* version of the tale, the princess's union with a tiny man would have been utterly ridiculous. Such a marriage would invoke a host of sexual anxieties and thereby threaten the fantasies of the masculine mastery of the female in the patriarchal social order. Issunbōshi simply cannot marry a woman who dwarfs him. (As if to emphasize this, the illustration mentioned earlier depicts a grown Issunbōshi standing proudly beside his future wife, who is kneeling humbly on the ground before him.) But by using the demon's magic to make himself normal height, Issunbōshi can reap all the rewards of his heroic exploits. In addition to wealth and status, then, he acquires the maiden prize, the beautiful daughter of the Sanjō Lord. Once gained, all these desirable objects serve a double duty: they are rewards for hard work and heroic exploits, but also function as tangible indicators of a success Issunbōshi has earned and de-serves, thereby helping to reproduce the ideology of *risshin shusse*. In addition, given the part played by the princess in the drama of the hero's rise, this is a success that must now be seen as gendered male. The structural role of the princess is remarkably constant in a story that essentially narrativizes male fantasies of success. The discourse on ambition and success might have changed, but Sazanami's text can reach backward into the past to find prizes that resonate powerfully with Meiji men. If there is such a thing as female success within this male fantasy world, the only space made for it in *Issunbōshi* is *in relation to* the world of male success, wealth, and status. Another way to say this is that in Sazanami's story female success comes about only by marriage to a successful man.

We can go one step further than this. We can read height as having metaphorical significance for Meiji readers as a sign of maturation. This is perhaps why so many stories for children from the period are *bildungsromane* of sorts, which trace the destiny of a person from their early years to success. Small stature—one inch in the folk tale—can be thought of as signifying childhood. By working hard and accomplishing great deeds, the child achieves success, figured by the acquisition of tangible, desirable objects such as material wealth, high rank, and the princess. The attainment of success is also the attainment of maturity—physical, social, and sexual—which is signaled by normal height. In the Meiji period, then, the Issunbōshi legend could function as an exemplary social allegory joining wealth, status, marriage, height, and maturity into a master narrative of success. Such children's tales could provide models with which young readers could begin to learn how to orient their desires toward the right objects. However, in order to create this seamless fantasy, Sazanami's text must elide issues of gender and social class.

iii

In its own way, "Wakaremichi" reveals precisely what Saza-nami's text conceals. It is not my intention here to crudely

equate Issunbōshi and the princess in the folktale with Kichi
and Okyō in Ichiyō's story. However, I am interested in using
Issunbōshi together with other texts in order to shed light on
the dialogic relationship between "Wakaremichi" and the
social allegory we just uncovered. In the next section, which
centers on Okyō, we will examine how gender and class are
implicated in the heroine's decision to become a mistress. In
this section, which focuses on Kichi, I want to explore the
connections between height and normative physicality and
sexuality.

Kichi is a lonely young man, who clearly has no friends
apart from Okyō, especially now that his benefactor Omatsu—
the woman who found him and gave him stable employment—has passed away. In addition, he is teased mercilessly
by nearly everyone around him for his short stature, which
further alienates him from others. As an orphan Kichi longs to
create a kind of kinship bond with Okyō, whose own parents
also seem to have passed away: "Okyō, somehow I just can't
think of you as a stranger. I wonder why?" he asks the seamstress in the manner of open frankness that characterizes their
relationship in the beginning of the story. "Okyō, have you
ever had a little brother?" he inquires. She replies, "I'm an
only child, so I've never had a brother or a sister." "Really?
Well, of course, you don't have any," Kichi exclaims with
obvious relief, "Somehow if I could call you my older sister,
I'd be so happy" (277). And Okyō, too, seems to be perfectly
content thinking about Kichi as her younger brother.

Yet there are moments when this utopian quasi-familial
relationship swims before our eyes, and the connection between the two strains the bounds of a familial bond.[22] There
are many examples in which the relationship is ambiguous:
it could be interpreted as friendship and affection or it could
be read in a more erotic way. Kichi has access to Okyō's living
space whenever he desires, and, in a kind of schoolboy bra-
vado, he even boasts to his compatriots at the shop that, as
Okyō's favorite, he is allowed to visit her anytime he wants,
even late at night when she is in her sleeping attire (280). In

addition, there are several suggestive exchanges of glances: at one point, Okyō "gazes at Kichizō's face" (276); at another moment, Kichi "takes her in from top to bottom" (281). The significance of these looks is somewhat elusive if we think about the relationship between the two protagonists as solely involving feelings of friendship. Furthermore, in a corpus of fiction in which bodily contact between characters is extremely rare, the moment at the beginning of the third section, when Okyō sneaks up behind Kichi, covers his eyes with her calloused hands, and asks him to guess who it is, stands out all the more. Finally, there is the moment at the end of the story when Okyō says that, even though she is leaving the back streets of the *shitamachi*, she plans to visit him again; she then hugs Kichi from behind, a moment of physical contact that has overtones above and beyond an expression of sadness about the imminent separation of two friends.

There is, I would argue, a mutual attraction between Okyō and Kichizō surging just below the quiet pretense of a familial bond.[23] Furthermore, I would propose that the quasi-familial relationship between the two is itself a manifestation of the sublimation of feelings of desire. This is a more adventurous way of reading "Wakaremichi" than is usual, since sublimation is by no means something that is intuitively obvious at the surface level of the text. Instead, sexuality must be introduced into our interpretation of "Wakaremichi" by moving into an inter- and intra-textual reading that takes into account a variety of representations of sexuality in the Meiji period.

We do not have to go very far to begin such an investigation, for the quasi-familial bond that conceals a mutual attraction is one of the most prominent themes in Ichiyō's early fiction, though by the time "Wakaremichi" was written it had become such an extreme form of narrative shorthand that it was rendered largely invisible to the casual reader unfamiliar with her oeuvre. The inspiration for this narrative shorthand cannot be conclusively demonstrated, but the most likely candidate is *Genji monogatari*. In the story of the Shining Genji and his immediate descendants, the original object of Genji's desire is Fujitsubo, who is brought into the emperor's circle of ladies as a replacement for Genji's own mother Kiritsubo. Kiritsubo was driven to death by the slander and machinations of the other court ladies in the imperial harem. Fujitsubo, then, is simultaneously a surrogate for Genji's own mother and the chief object of his desire. However, desire for the maternal body (even that of a stepmother such as Fujitsubo), especially when such a person is imperial property, is taboo, so while Genji eventually does have physical relations with his mother's replacement, his growing desire is usually unfulfilled and hence deflected onto a seemingly endless series of substitutes—Yūgao, Murasaki, Tamakazura, and so on. Indeed, it could be argued that Genji's forbidden desire for the maternal body forms the very motor for the narrative process of the sprawling text, which becomes a well-nigh Freudian tale of frustrated desire and maternal substitutes.

We see the narrative shorthand that has incorporated this aspect of *Genji* in Ichiyō's 1893 story "Koto no ne" (The Sound of the Koto). The protagonist, a nameless young man, was separated from his mother at an early age and finds a "replacement" figure in a beautiful woman who plays the *koto* of the title. But the desire for a substitute mother figure seems to conceal a more physical desire, though one that is never played out in the very brief story. This motif would be made even more explicit the following year in the gothic "Yamiyo" (Encounters on a Dark Night, 1894). In this story, too, the young male protagonist, who goes here by the name Ryōnosuke, loses his mother and finds a substitute maternal figure in the shadowy and mysterious Oran. The two explicitly call their relationship one of brother and sister. Unlike in "Koto no ne," though, the mutual physical attraction is openly acknowledged by both figures in a climactic moment near the end of the story. However, nothing comes of it because the boy is sent out to avenge Oran by attacking the man who abandoned her; he fails in his mission and is never heard from again.[24]

In "Wakaremichi," the theme of substitution is extended beyond a lone female figure, but these women are only mentioned in the analepsis that occupies the middle section of the narrative. The young orphan, Kichi, finds a kind of mother he never knew in the figure of Omatsu, who takes in the young street urchin and offers him a job oiling umbrellas in her shop. Omatsu is a benefactor, not an object of desire, but after she dies, Kichi becomes acquainted with a young woman named Okinu, to whom he seems to have been attracted; she is young enough to be an object of desire, but old enough to function, too, as a maternal or sisterly figure. Okinu, however, commits suicide by throwing herself in a well after her parents try to force her to marry their own candidate for her hand. The last substitute figure (the only one who appears in the narrative present) is Okyō, who is perhaps four or five years older than Kichi, though his short stature seems to make the apparent gap in ages even more pronounced, perhaps as much as eight or nine years. Kichi explicitly connects Okyō to the other women who appeared briefly in his life when he hears Okyō's decision to become a kept woman:

This is terrible, really terrible. I don't know what to say. I've met people who have been kind to me, but then something awful happens. Omatsu at the umbrella shop was a good person, and Okinu, the dyer's daughter, was nice to me too. But Omatsu got sick and died, and Okinu didn't want to marry so she threw herself into a well. And now you're going to abandon me too, Okyō. It's terrible (283).

Read in light of Ichiyō's frequent appropriations of the story of substitutes and frustrated desire in the *Genji*, we can read Okyō as fulfilling a variety of structural roles in the narrative, all with fluid boundaries: as an older, maternal sister in a quasi-familial relationship, as a friend and confidant with whom Kichi can share his dreams and frustrations, and also as an object of desire.

There are other ways desire between the two characters is suggested in the story. As we have seen, Ichiyō often made use of the trope of the well-curb, in which a boy and a girl begin as childhood playmates and then grow attracted to each other. Having no prior experience with the feelings of love and desire, the two often form a relationship in which they treat each other as brother and sister instead. "Yamizakura" (Flowers at Dusk, 1892) is one example of this. Here, in Ichiyō's first published story, the trope of the well-curb is at its most explicit. Two children from neighboring mansions that share a well played together throughout their childhood years. They grow so close that they treat each other as siblings. Eventually the young woman becomes attracted to her childhood play-mate, but she does not understand her new feelings and does not have the language in which to express them; she eventually dies from her internal agony, her love unrevealed, though it is suspected by the "brother" whom she desires. The 1893 "Hanagomori" (Clouds in Springtime), which involves two cousins who grow up together and fall in love only to have their wishes foiled, is another variation on this theme.

Were we to extend our investigations beyond Ichiyō's oeuvre, we would find still other instances of this phenomenon, but these few examples should suffice to suggest the possible presence of desire and sexuality in relationships in Ichiyō's fiction that are cast in the terms of a quasi-familial connection. This is not to say, of course, that the relationship between Okyō and Kichi is not complicated by other feelings of friendship, kinship, and such, only that desire is one component of the bond between them, but one that cannot appear in the open. If sexuality is a shadowy part of the relationship between the two, why does it need to be sublimated? The answer to this question cannot be found in the *Genji* or in Ichiyō's earlier stories. Here it is specific to the narrative of "Wakaremichi" and also connects to the social allegory exemplified in Iwaya Sazanami's reworking of the Issunbōshi legend.

Desire must be sublimated in "Wakaremichi" because Kichi's short stature prevents any kind of open intimacy between him and Okyō. Although Kichi is sixteen years old—the age when many a fictional character, such as *Takekurabe*'s Chōkichi, would make their first visit to the licensed quarter—we are told that he appears no older than twelve or thirteen because he stopped growing during adolescence (275). Short stature is associated with childhood and thus disassociated from sexuality; Kichi cannot be considered a sexual being in the narrative as long as certain notions of normative adult male physicality are widely shared. My admittedly unorthodox view gains some support when we recall that sexuality between Issunbōshi and the daughter of the Sanjō Lord—which is displaced onto less explicitly sexual matters such as marriage and the birth of children—is only possible *after* the hero has used the magic of the *oni* to make himself (or have the princess make him) into a full-sized man. Whether we look at the premodern folktale or Iwaya Sazanami's modern rendition of the legendary figure, sexuality is not possible until the narrative runs its course, even if there is already present at the midpoint of the story an attraction between the characters.

Such a reading gains further support if we situate "Wakaremichi" within the discourse on height and sexuality in Meiji Japan. In February and March 1895 there appeared in the pages of the *Yomiuri News* the first tale in Hirotsu Ryūrō's lurid series of novellas detailing the fictional murders and other crimes committed by deformed, disfigured, or crippled protagonists, all of which use the body as a text for the exploration of social ills. We have it on Ryūrō's own testimony that he was inspired to write the first, called *Hemeden* (Cross-eyed Den), when he heard about the proprietor of a certain liquor store in Yokohama, who, after wasting all of his capital on prostitutes, murdered the owner of a pawnshop in an attempt to get his hands on some extra money.[25] Ryūrō, one of the most prominent writers in the 1890s, took this story and ran with it. His protagonist, Denkichi, who runs a liquor shop in Kanda called the Saitama-ya, is attracted to a woman named Ohama, the daughter of the proprietor of another shop in the same area. Ohama has no interest in Denkichi, though, so in order to satisfy his frustrated desires, Denkichi frequents the Yoshiwara. He is tricked into spending his capital, and his shop is threatened with insolvency. In a desperate attempt to avoid poverty, Denkichi murders a man who operates a pawnshop, but is caught by the authorities. The text is inhabited by contradictory impulses: It wants to put Denkichi behind bars even while expressing sympathy for him, and it also wants to place much of the blame for the tragic events on Ohama, who consistently spurns Denkichi's advances. Throughout the story, Ohama is repulsed by Denkichi because, while he is a respectable businessman and a filial son, Ryūrō has saddled him with all manner of debilities: he is of short stature, has scars on his face, and is afflicted with a strabismus (hence the title, Cross-eyed Den).[26]

But among all these socially coded disadvantages, Denkichi's short stature seems to be the most central to Ohama's rejection of his advances. Despite the title, Denkichi is called *issunbōshi* and *kumo-otoko* ("little one inch" and "spider man" respectively; both are derogatory terms for someone of short stature) as frequently as he is called "*hemeden*." His height is the sole focus of the narrator's description of him when he is introduced in the opening lines.[27] It is only a bit later that we learn of his other debilities (though, naturally, when he is called "*hemeden*" by another character we do get a hint of later descriptions). The sexual anxieties associated with short stature and other socially coded debilities are given explicit representation in a lengthy conversation between Denkichi and his mother. When his mother raises the issue of marriage to her single son, Denkichi protests that no woman would want him: "But mother, you know everyone calls me names like 'hemeden' and 'kumo-otoko.' What woman is going to want me for a husband?"[28] Ultimately it is impossible to clearly separate Denkichi's disadvantages and the name-calling he endures at the hands of others, but the most explicit disassociation of sexuality and short stature comes fairly early in the narrative. One character remarks to another about Denkichi, "Well it seems that someone [a prostitute] has taken that *issunbōshi* for a lover [*mabu*]," and the surprised reply is, "What, taken as a lover? That *issunbōshi*, that *hemeden*?"[29]

We can begin to see how sexuality is inscribed in "Wakare-michi" when we read Ichiyō's story together with texts like

Issunbōshi, Hemeden, and Ichiyō's own early narratives. Furthermore, we can see how sexuality is associated with a certain notion of a desirable, normative male physicality. Because of his short stature—which makes him the brunt of teasing—Kichi cannot be considered a sexual being by Okyō or any other maternal substitute. The desire Kichi feels for Okyō, and the desire that she very likely feels for him, must be sublimated into a quasi-familial relationship, a relationship between "brother" and "sister" that has been charged with erotic energy since Ichiyō's first published story.

iv

If sexuality has been evacuated from the surface of the text in the relationship between the two principal characters, it is, nonetheless, precisely *through* sexuality that Okyō achieves her "success" when she chooses to become a kept woman. Okyō is highly ambivalent about her imminent good fortune, and Kichi is completely opposed to her decision on ethical grounds. Thus, success must always be placed in scare quotes when thinking about "Wakaremichi." As we have seen in the use of aphorisms in the speech of the characters, the idea of success is always filled with doubt, displaced as an illusion even as it serves as the compass by which they orient their ambitions and the balance with which they judge the acceptability or unacceptability of their lot in life. Okyō's decision can, to some extent, be considered a personal one. However, it is more fruitful to consider it a choice made among a certain number of possibilities that exist within the larger sociopolitical order in a system of social constraints and freedoms centered on gender and class. Only by looking at the narrative in this way can we bring to light the highly contentious social issues at the heart of "Wakaremichi" and restore to it some of the force it must have had for contemporary readers.

In order to understand why Okyō makes the choice she does and why Kichi reacts in so hostile a manner, we need to investigate the class background of the characters in more detail. We learn very little about Okyō, and this seems intentional, since it has been demonstrated that Ichiyō stripped away more and more information about her from the narrative with each successive draft.[30] All we know for certain is that the young and beautiful Okyō descended into the back streets of Tokyo some time before the narrative present of the story and now does needlework for those who live in the area. A few stray comments suggest that she led a comfortable life while growing up, and so it is reasonable to suspect that there must have been some personal or family crisis that forced her to move into the alleys of the *shitamachi* and take up the poverty-ridden life of a seamstress. Perhaps her parents died, for she is clearly without kin in the world.[31] In any case, she is a diligent, hard worker, and is thus widely admired in the area.

This is the extent of our knowledge about the heroine. We learn much more about Kichizō since the purpose of the middle part of the story is to provide the reader with background information about him. Kichi is an orphan without any knowledge of his parents, which places him in a line of fiction from Ichiyō that includes "Koto no ne" and "Yamiyo," both of which, as we have seen, feature as characters young male orphans who seek an older woman as a kind of surrogate mother. Kichi now works at oiling traditional umbrellas, but he was not born to the trade. Rather, the proprietor of the shop, Omatsu, found him while she was making the rounds of some temples. Up until then Kichi eked out a living on the streets by doing acrobatics and juggling for money in places like Shin'ami-chō, one of the worst slums in Tokyo at the time.[32] The sagely Omatsu decides to take a chance on the orphan and to provide him with work and a home. Her decision seems prescient, for Kichi turns out to be a hard worker, several times more productive than his compatriots (278–79). Omatsu died a few years after he started working for her, however, and now he does not get along well with either his fellow workers or with the present proprietor of the business. His sole pleasure seems to be stopping in to talk with Okyō, whom he got to know soon after she moved to the area.

Indeed, the opening lines of the narrative make it clear that this pleasure is an evening ritual for them.[33]

Their dreams of success seem to create allies of the two during their evening talks, but their situations are considerably different. Kichi's fortunes are much improved—he has been rescued from the uncertain life of a Dickensian street urchin and given a stable job—while Okyō seems to have sunk from a position as a bourgeois daughter to that of a seamstress in the back alleys of the *shitamachi*.[34] Okyō is growing weary of the life of drudgery and constant work; she wishes to return to the world of material comforts that she seems to have known as a child. Indeed, this appears to be the sole factor in her decision to become a mistress, for she says to Kichi at one point in the story that she cannot take the life of a seamstress anymore and that she will make her way in the world as a kept woman even if the wonderful clothes and material comforts might carry a stigma (282). Kichi, on the other hand, has made a short climb up the social ladder (even if he still clings to rungs near the bottom), yet he seems to desire no further advancement. His reasons for this are never made entirely clear, but he must intuitively know that no further advancement is possible for him given his background and current social position, as well as the way that short stature is socially coded as a debility. Both class and height prevent further success, making any additional ambition largely futile. After achieving a very limited success, he has decided to spend the remainder of his days rooted in a single location: the neighborhood where his benefactor Omatsu died.

Although both Okyō and Kichi can be thought of as laborers in the *shitamachi*, it is important to note that such labor is gendered in "Wakaremichi." As a male worker in an umbrella shop, Kichi, along with his compatriots, has set work hours and set holidays; he gets off work at a certain time every day and gets the same amount of money for each day's work.[35] His evenings are his to spend as he pleases, and he generally spends them in the company of Okyō. His seamstress friend, however, can never let her needle rest, even when she is entertaining visitors. In order to get a subsistence income she must work day and night, constantly taking in new orders, for the pay for needlework at home not only was quite small, it was also disconcertingly variable depending on the number of orders on any given day.[36]

Okyō's choice is to leave this world of subsistence. It is not as if she wants to become a mistress, but she has few options available to her if she wishes to reclaim the life of comfort and economic stability that she knew in her youth. It would be difficult for her to become a maid, since she is a bit too old for this. Marriage would be one option, but she is an orphan without anyone to act as a go-between for a good match. Prostitution is an unenviable option, and most women in Meiji fiction choose the life of a mistress over life in a brothel.

The argument between the two protagonists at the end of the narrative makes it clear that there is an ethical problem involved in Okyō's ultimate decision. Some roles for women were considered morally suspect in mid-Meiji, and the kept woman, like the prostitute, was one such role. This had not always been the case, however. The status of the kept woman underwent a profound and rapid transformation in the early years of the Meiji period, and we can briefly chart this change in a way that is useful to our interpretation of Ichiyō's story.

In the early years of the Meiji period, there was little social or juridical distinction between a wife and a kept woman (*mekake*). The legal codes relating to the family registry that were passed in 1870 gave the *mekake* the same status in relation to the husband as the primary wife — that of dependent — and this was a holdover from Edo-period norms. Furthermore, the children of the *mekake* were given the same status as the children of the principal wife. This relatively open attitude toward the figure of the *mekake* was reinforced three years later in legal directives issued in 1873. Thus, the *mekake* had full legal status, and her name, as well as those of her children by her "husband," were to be faithfully recorded in the family registry. In 1880, however, the *mekake* was suddenly refigured as a social pariah. In the family laws passed in that year, the *mekake*'s legal status was eroded and her children by her patron no longer received legal protection. This is not to say that the *mekake* disappeared from society. The mistress was a presence, even if not a legally recognized one, long after 1880, and the procurement of a *mekake* by a wealthy man came to be almost as ritualized as a meeting between a prospective bride and groom. The mistress was a very visible presence in certain sections of the middle and upper classes. Indeed, she was often considered a trophy of sorts by highly placed males—a symbol of his wealth and social position.[37]

Why the sudden change? The codes that redefined the legal status of the *mekake* in early Meiji were the result of vigorous debate in the Diet during the late 1870s. This debate was itself grounded in a series of influential polemic essays penned in the mid-1870s, which attacked the *mekake* on ethical grounds. One of the earliest assaults on the *mekake* can be found in Mori Arinori's essay "Saishōron" (A Discourse on Wives and Mistresses), which appeared in the pages of the Enlightenment journal *Meiroku zasshi* (Journal of the Meiji Six) in five installments between May 1874 and February 1875.[38] Mori's essay is testimony to the difficulty of distinguishing the kept woman from the wife in the early 1870s, for he spends much of the first installment staking out boundaries and defining terms. He concludes that the wife typically comes to the husband through the mediation of a go-between, but that the kept woman is acquired by the man through direct negotiation with her parents; this transaction was typically accompanied by the transfer of money from the male suitor to the family of the new mistress. "Saishōron" and other essays like it discursively create the figure of the *mekake* in her modern guise. Furthermore, these essays create her as a social outcast from the very beginning. Mori is indignant about the tradition of keeping mistresses, which he sees as a barbaric custom. His attack is launched on moral grounds and is inseparable from his attitude toward wives. His remarks on wives are at once modern and crushingly patriarchal, cast in the rather unromantic legalese of rights and duties, a far cry from the discourse on love and marriage among, for example, the contemporary Romantics. In Mori's view, the wife has the right to demand protection of the husband, and the husband has the duty to offer it; but he also has the right to demand assistance from his spouse, and it is her duty to offer such assistance. To this matrimonial bond the kept woman can bring only trouble. Mori offers a number of reasons for his assessment of the evil caused by the *mekake*—from the emotional pain it causes the wife to the element of ambiguity about family blood (and thus inheritance) that inevitably arises—but these issues can be subsumed within the ideology of monogamy. So powerful was this discourse in the Meiji period that even the emperor himself was forced to submit to it. The discourse on monogamy makes its appearance with the arrival of the Western powers and Christianity, and, like most of the Meirokusha essayists, Mori was shamefacedly looking over his shoulder at the Euro-American states throughout his very polemic piece.

In later years, as Western ideals of family penetrated deeper into social life in Japan, many others, including women's groups, took up the call of these early Enlightenment thinkers. Closer to the beginning of Ichiyō's own writing career another important moment in the ethical attack on the *mekake* occurred: an influential petition (*kenpaku*) calling for monogamy appeared in the pages of the *Tokyo asahi shinbun* (Tokyo Asahi News) in May 1889. This was issued from the recently formed Tokyo Women's Reform Society, whose main business was to rectify degenerate customs in Japan, especially those centering on marriage. Their call for monogamy is a polished ideological gem. It includes as part of its agenda a brief but sharp attack on the kept woman: "Point: In the middle and upper class households in our country there is a custom of keeping mistresses, but a number of evils result from this."[39] The author(s) of the document follow this by attacking the *mekake* from nearly every imaginable angle, listing six "evils" that are caused by the practice of keeping mistresses: it is cruel to the wife, and is sometimes even the reason why husbands and wives live apart; it is a severe disruption of family harmony, the most important aspect of any household; the mistress is a dire threat to the family, for she invariably sets her target on the family fortune and tries to install her own child as the heir to this money; she poses a threat to the education of the family's legitimate children, for the money spent on the mistress could be put to better use; evil customs in the upper classes invariably spread to the entire social body, thereby endangering the state itself; and the son will undoubtedly imitate the evil ways of the father.[40]

I have been brief in my historical sketch because "Wakaremichi" does not reflect these specific lines of attack on the *mekake* per se, but the discourse condemning the kept woman is, I would argue, a necessary precondition for any story that represents the choice to become a mistress as an ethical problem—in the case of our story, through the voicing of Kichi's moral objections to Okyō's chosen path. Furthermore, as I hope my outline of the contentious modern history of the mistress makes apparent, any representation of a woman's decision to become a *mekake* from mid-Meiji onward takes place within a discursive field fraught with conflict, in which the kept woman occupies a highly ambiguous position—a sought-after emblem of success in some parts of the social order and a social outcast in the eyes of others. These mutually conflicting lines are apparent when Okyō tells Kichi about her decision. The two meet quite by accident as Okyō is returning from an errand—probably making final arrangements with her patron—all decked out in her finery. She tells her friend that she has decided to leave. Kichi is taken by surprise by her news and asks if she is joking:

"It's no lie. It's just like you said: fortune has come for me in a carriage. I can't very well live in this back alley forever. Kichi, I guess I better hurry up and make you that kimono like I promised."

"I don't want it. I don't want such a thing. You keep saying it's good luck, but aren't you actually going to do something awful? The other day Hanji told me: 'It looks like Okyō the seamstress is going to go into service in some rich man's mansion. That 'uncle' of hers who does massages over by the Yokochō market made all the arrangements. She's too old to be a maid. She's certainly not going to be giving sewing lessons to some housewife. I bet she's going to be somebody's kept woman, with a tasseled coat and her hair all done up in ringlets. She won't be a seamstress forever, not with that pretty face.' That's what Hanji said. I thought it must be a lie, so I told him he was dead wrong, and we got into a big fight. But that *is* what you're going to do, isn't it? You're going to some rich household, aren't you?"

"Oh, Kichi, it's not as if I want to go. I just don't have a choice. I suppose this means that we won't be able to see each other anymore, doesn't it?"

Kichi very nearly collapsed when he heard these words. "No matter what kind of success you think it'll bring you, you shouldn't go. It's not as if you can't make a living here doing sewing. You have just yourself to feed after all. You have the talent for it. Why go off and do something awful like this? It's too horrible." Kichi bemoaned her lack of integrity. "Don't do it. Don't do it. You can refuse to go."

"I was worried this would happen," Okyō sighed as she came to a halt. "Kichi, I'm tired of washing and sewing. Anything is better, even becoming somebody's mistress. Even spending the rest of my days wearing a tainted crepe kimono is better than these drab clothes." (281–82)

Okyō here couches her decision using metaphors of clothing. As a seamstress, she herself wears nothing but "drab clothes" (*tsumaranai zukume*) as she washes and sews, makes New Year's finery for others, and collects her meager income. As someone who apparently was raised in better circumstances, she finds her life now intolerable: "Oh, Kichi, it's not as if I want to go," she stresses to her young friend, "I just don't have a choice." Okyō knows completely what is involved in the mistress's life and what others will think of her, but she chooses a life of comfort and security. She will wear the metaphorical "tainted kimono," because it is, after all, made of fine material (*kusare chirimen-gimono*). Kichi's language is couched in the diction of social mores and is far removed from Okyō's language—"Aren't you really going to do something awful?"; "Why go and do something awful like this?"—and his words powerfully reflect the derogatory social gaze that falls on the figure of the *mekake* during this period, even as it reflects, too, his feeling of being betrayed by Okyō at the same time. It is in this dramatic moment, as I suggested earlier, that all true dialogue between the protagonists ceases, making their separation all the more painful and the story itself all the more desolate.

I want to conclude by returning once more to the Meiji-period reworking of the Issunbōshi legend by Iwaya Sazanami in light of this reading of "Wakaremichi." We have seen how the folktale would have been immensely appealing to the creators of the new children's literature in Meiji Japan and how a legend like Issunbōshi could be reclaimed within the contours of a new preoccupation with ambition and success. We have seen, too, how the story of Issunbōshi could function as an ideal social allegory linking wealth, status, marriage, height, and maturity into what I called earlier a master narrative of success for the normative modern subject; any combination of these elements could become the focus of a particular text. I do not wish to make the claim here that Ichiyō is responding directly to the recirculation of folk heroes in Meiji Japan (after all, "Wakaremichi" came out before Sazanami's text, although the series as a whole was underway during Ichiyō's writing career). Rather, we have used Sazanami's version of the age-old folktale as a way of gaining access to the social fantasy of which it is one narrative manifestation. I do this in order to read Ichiyō's text in a new light: "Wakaremichi" vigorously resists or parodies the social allegory that Sazanami's tale exemplifies by highlighting that which the narrative fantasy of the allegory elides.

Although Okyō can strive for the material comforts that the life of a mistress brings, there is no fantastic jeweled carriage awaiting her. Her equation of that carriage with the life of a mistress is bitterly ironic, and she herself knows it. She decides to exchange the drab attire of the seamstress for a beautiful kimono, but while that kimono is made from silk threads, it is also stained with social contempt. Security she may attain, but she will never have the kind of success that was seen as desirable for daughters of good families; she will never snare the rich and successful husband and become the princess in the folktale. The new patriarchal order of Meiji, after all, was over the course of several decades persistently reducing the respectable social roles for women to those of wife and mother, and so the success Okyō dreams of and fantasizes about is impossible for her, for any path she chooses at the end of the narrative must be from a very limited set of options that makes her the trophy of male success.

Kichi is an orphan in the working class with no one to help him along now that his benefactor has died. There is no magic mallet to launch him on a course in which his fantasies could be fulfilled. Kichi intuitively knows that his class position forecloses the possibility of achieving anything more than a very small social advancement, so he refuses to struggle any further. He will remain rooted to the spot where his benefactor died, working at the humble occupation she gave him. If we treat Sazanami's *Issunbōshi* as a social allegory, we can also begin to see the importance of normative ideas about male physicality and the way short stature is coded as a debility in the social order of Meiji Japan, both in relation to success and sexuality. Because of his height Kichi cannot achieve success, and his desire for Okyō must be sublimated into a quasi-familial relationship and will never know fulfillment in marriage. He will never acquire that constellation of objects that were indicative of success. He will never be the hero in the folktale.

Both Kichi and Okyō are alienated from the modern discourse on success even as they are compelled, by the hegemonic nature of that discourse in social life, to orient their dreams toward it. That these fantasies were irresistible to the men and women of Meiji is apparent in the children's stories of the period. For men, wealth, social prestige, and a beautiful wife were the tangible desires that could be fulfilled with ambition; among women, a successful husband, luxury, fine clothes, even a "jeweled" carriage were the wishes of many. Okyō and Kichi, however, are not idyllic figures from folktales or children's stories. They are social outcasts, and Ichiyō's later fiction is densely populated by such men and women, the wrack and cinders of the immense, convoluted process of modernization in Japan. There is a certain grim consistency to the cast of characters in Ichiyō's oeuvre, especially the later stories: the prostitute, the mistress, the unhappy wife, the fallen merchant family, the poverty-stricken woman, the orphan, the waif. Had we delved further into other stories we would have encountered still other types of pariahs: for example, Yukiko of "Utsusemi" (The Cicada Shell, 1895) is mentally ill, while Oritsu of the unfinished "Uramurasaki" (Deep Lavender; the first part appeared in print in 1896) is an adulteress. Ichiyō may have limited the players in her later stories to outcasts and social pariahs, but, in looking at her entire oeuvre, the cast is astonishingly varied for a single social category. This has been observed by more than one critic, but the lens of historicist, dialogic criticism allows us to see these characters for who they really are. They are all various manifestations of the Others of the normative modern subject positions being articulated in heterogeneous sites across the late-nineteenth-century landscape, and there is something almost systematic in the way Ichiyō explored the broken dreams and tragic destinies of the forgotten, cast-aside women and men of a modernizing Japan. Taken in its entirety, Ichiyō's oeuvre constitutes a multifaceted critique of modernity. This frail, diminutive writer, who outwardly appeared dauntingly proper and conservative, whose demeanor suggested both wounded pride and a certain stodginess, and who was so soft-spoken before strangers as to be nearly inaudible, found a harder, more critical persona in her fiction, and used it to represent and give voice to marginal figures who might otherwise be socially invisible.

Reference Matter

Notes

Chapter 1

1. Seki Reiko and Kan Satoko, eds., *Higuchi Ichiyō shū*.

2. It is growing increasingly common to refer to the era preceding the Meiji Restoration of 1868 (commonly considered the beginning of modernity in Japan) as the "early modern" period, which Conrad Totman, in his masterful synthesis of existing scholarship, has defined as the 300 years between 1568 and 1868, a period generally called *kinsei* (recent times) in Japanese. See Totman, *Early Modern Japan*, p. xxv. Although I tend to use this term now, its utility is not completely apparent to me, since it essentially corresponds with the older political designation of the "Tokugawa period" (named after the family of shoguns who ruled Japan). It does have some use, however, in referring to a moment in which some of the nascent signs of modernity are visible, but not yet in the foreground. In addition, there is a stream of scholarship—with Burns, *Before the Nation* being the most recent contribution—that stresses two major breaks between the onset of Tokugawa rule and the outbreak of the Pacific War: one during the eighteenth century, which witnesses the rise of a commercial economy that places extreme stress on the old feudal order, and another occurring with the project of modernization in the wake of the Meiji Restoration. For a superb discussion of the inevitability of periodization and the way modernity as a concept inevitably breeds awareness of preparatory breaks earlier in time, see Jameson, *A Singular Modernity*, pp. 17–41. Jameson's conclusion is that "modernity" is best conceived as a trope or narrative category.

3. I am drawing here on Copeland's thoughtful discussion of the gendering of Meiji-era letters. See her *Lost Leaves*, pp. 7–51.

4. Pioneering postwar critics such as Wada Yoshie, Shioda Ryōhei, and Seki Ryōichi were responsible for much of the work that made possible all later Ichiyō scholarship. Kimura Masayuki is a representative practitioner of biographical criticism. See his *Ichiyō bungaku*. Hasegawa Shigure was writing appreciations of Ichiyō's fiction in the 1930s, many of which are devoted to reconstructing the meaning of difficult words and phrases or forgotten allusions, thus indicating that only 30-some years after Ichiyō's death her stories posed substantial challenges even for the educated reader. These essays are collected in *Hasegawa Shigure zenshū*, vol. 4.

5. Important critics in this camp include Maeda Ai, Seki Reiko, Takada Chinami, and Kan Satoko. Even study of Ichiyō's sprawling diary has been "textualized" in the recent work of Seki Reiko and Chida Kaori.

6. There are exceptions to these general trends, of course, and I have profited from the small number of essays in the last few decades that have focused on the influence of classical literature on Ichiyō. Koike stresses the influence of Bakin in his "Ichiyō to kinsei bungaku," pp. 110–16. Kikuta investigates the inheritance from the Heian-era memoirists, especially Sei Shōnagon. See his "Ichiyō no naka no ōchō," pp. 33–39. More recently, Seki Reiko discusses the influence of *Ise monogatari* and *Genji monogatari*, among other works, on Ichiyō. See her "Ichiyō to *Ise, Genji*," pp. 177–97.

7. "My position is that texts are worldly, to some degree they are events, and, even when they appear to deny it, they are nevertheless a part of the social world, human life, and of course the historical moments in which they are located and interpreted." Said, *The World, the Text, and the Critic*, p. 4.

8. de Man, *Blindness and Insight*, p. 148.

9. Harvey, *The Condition of Postmodernity*, pp. 10–38.

10. Harootunian, *Overcome by Modernity*, p. ix.

11. This has been most fruitfully pursued in the context of studies of millenarian movements in the mid-nineteenth century. See Wilson's tersely suggestive book on the Meiji Restoration, *Patriots and Redeemers in Japan*, pp. 77–122. Approaching Japanese literature and culture of the late nineteenth century in the spirit I am outlining allows us to link Japan's experience of modernity with that of Europe, as discussed in Jameson, *A Singular Modernity*, pp. 129–38. I

have profited greatly from the discovery of overlapping concerns with Jameson.

12. Kobayashi Hideo, "Kokyō o ushinatta bungaku," pp. 36–37.

13. Futabatei first published his translation of "Aibiki" in the July and August issues of *Kokumin no tomo* in 1888. He made significant revisions to this translation and included it in *Katakoi* (1896), a collection of Turgenev translations. It was this revised version that Doppo encountered.

14. Kunikida Doppo, "Musashino," pp. 89–110. In 1901, the story was included as the title piece of a short-story collection. My inspiration for the above views comes from Karatani, *Origins of Modern Japanese Literature*, pp. 11–44, and Komori, *Yuragi no Nihon bungaku*, pp. 29–44.

15. Tsubouchi Shōyō, *Shōsetsu shinzui*, pp. 3–58. For the implications of the equation of the *shōsetsu* with the novel, see Ueda, "Meiji Literary Historiography."

16. Komori, *Shōsetsu to hihyō*, pp. 18–27.

17. Here I am drawing heavily on Komori, *Kōzō toshite no katari*, pp. 85–124.

18. I borrow the term "translingual practice" from Liu, *Translingual Practice*, pp. 25–27.

19. The growing body of work on the enigmatic Izumi Kyōka has seriously grappled with his renewal of older practices in the context of a modern literary practice. See Cornyetz, *Dangerous Women, Deadly Words*, pp. 21–95, and Inouye, *A Similitude of Blossoms*.

20. Ichiyō is known to have read Uchida Roan's translation of *Crime and Punishment* (published in 1892) and was acquainted with a Japanese translation of the Bible. She was also familiar with a few translated short stories and at least one of Shōyō's renditions of Shakespeare. This is a far cry from the wide exposure to Euro-American thought and literature among most contemporary male writers in the literary world.

21. For more on this, see Kornicki, "The Survival of Tokugawa Fiction in the Meiji Period," pp. 461–82, and Maeda Ai, *Kindai dokusha no seiritsu*, pp. 34–72.

22. Because of the extensive biographical information on Ichiyō that is available, I have limited my discussion to these few remarks about her artistic education that are relevant to my larger framework. For a full English-language biography, see Danly's excellent book, *In the Shade of Spring Leaves*. For concise but informative biographies in Japanese, see Shioda, *Higuchi Ichiyō*, or, from a feminist perspective,

Seki Reiko, *Ane no chikara*. The most authoritative source of biographical information about Ichiyō is still Shioda's monumental *Higuchi Ichiyō kenkyū*. Useful information about Ichiyō's use of the Tokyo Public Library in Ueno can be found in Takahashi Kazuko, "Higuchi Ichiyō to Ueno toshokan," pp. 37–52.

23. There are good books that reflect on the importance of the third decade of Meiji. Foremost among these is Gluck, *Japan's Modern Myths*, pp. 17–41. Also useful is Pyle, *The New Generation of Meiji Japan*, which remains illuminating even after 35 years. I would also like to call attention to two collections of cultural studies essays put out by the Meiji Sanjūnendai Kenkyūkai: Komori et al., eds., *Media/hyōshō/ideorogii*; Kaneko et al., eds., *Disukūru no teikoku*.

24. See Duara, *Rescuing History from the Nation*, especially pp. 3–82, and Chakrabarty, *Provincializing Europe*, especially pp. 3–113.

25. Chakrabarty, *Provincializing Europe*, p. 43.

26. I am by no means the first person to utilize Bakhtinian thought to interpret Japanese literary texts. Bakhtin has found an important place in the criticism of scholars as diverse as Maeda Ai, Kamei Hideo, Komori Yōichi, James Fujii, and Haruo Shirane. For a discussion of this phenomenon, see Fujii, *Complicit Fictions*, pp. 27–40.

27. The general contours of Bakhtinian thought are widely known in literary criticism, so this is just a brief rehearsal of ideas that will be taken up in more detail in the chapters that follow. The reader unfamiliar with dialogism may wish to consult either of the following: Bakhtin, *Problems of Dostoevsky's Poetics*, pp. 181–204, or Bakhtin's book-length essay "Discourse in the Novel," pp. 259–422. I am also indebted to Komori Yōichi's two books from 1988: *Buntai toshite no monogatari* and *Kōzō toshite no katari*, which extend the Bakhtinian framework in productive and exciting ways.

28. I borrow this mantra from Henry Louis Gates, Jr., *The Signifying Monkey*, pp. xxiv, 51, and 88.

29. With regard to the literature of the 1870s and 1880s, see Mertz, *Novel Japan*. For Sōseki, see Yiu, *Chaos and Order*. For Tōson, see Bourdaghs, *The Dawn That Never Comes*. Ken Ito demonstrates how Meiji melodrama explores contemporary concerns about the family in his "Class and Gender in a Meiji Family Romance," pp. 339–78.

30. Johnson, *Jane Austen*, p. xviii.

Chapter 2

1. Mori Ōgai's review can be found in *Ōgai zenshū*, vol. 23, p. 355. Miyazaki Koshoshi's review can be found in Okada, ed., *Takekurabe, Nigorie*, pp. 225–27.

2. For the Saikaku boom in Meiji, see Oka, "Saikaku to Meiji nijū nendai no bungaku," pp. 43–48, and Maeda Ai, *Maeda Ai chosaku shū*, vol. 3, pp. 325–31. The most authoritative account of the influence of Saikaku on modern writers is Takeno, *Kindai bungaku to Saikaku*.

3. A section of a letter to Ichiyō from *Bungakukai*'s Hirata Toku-boku dated October 19, 1894, is usually cited by scholars as the main evidence for this: "I will bring you *Saikaku zenshū* sometime soon, as I promised." This letter is included in Noguchi Seki, ed., *Higuchi Ichiyō raikan shū*, p. 141.

4. Danly, *In the Shade of Spring Leaves*, p. 132. Danly's analysis of Saikaku's influence on Ichiyō (pp. 109–32) remains the best in print in any language.

5. Maeda Ai, *Maeda Ai chosaku shū*, vol. 3, pp. 313–22.

6. Kamei, "Buntai sōzō no mitsugi," pp. 47–53.

7. Kan Satoko finds in "Ōtsugomori" the culmination of narrative practices that find their roots in earlier stories, thus implicitly questioning the dominant view about Saikaku's influence. See Kan, "'Ōtsugomori' ron," pp. 50–51.

8. Sas, *Fault Lines*, pp. 37–44. Benjamin's use of memory can be found in *Illuminations*, pp. 155–200.

9. Bakhtin, "Discourse in the Novel," pp. 300 and 366 respectively; italics in original.

10. Ihara Saikaku, *Seken mune zan'yō*, p. 381. The phrase also appears in the preface to *Seken*, p. 382.

11. Ibid., pp. 447–52.

12. Ibid., p. 385.

13. Two critics suggest that Omine may have no other choice but to become a mistress or a prostitute if another financial crisis arises. See Kobayashi Hiroko, "Hanten suru moraru," p. 123 and Seki Reiko, "Zōyo to shutaika," p. 24.

14. Okuda, "Jochū no rekishi," pp. 376–410.

15. Okuda provides an excellent discussion of the problem of wages for maids and the rising demand for set hours and set vacation days against the backdrop of industrialization, an expanding

labor market for women, and an emergent middle class. See Okuda, "Jochū no rekishi," pp. 383–89.

16. Ichiyō made a large number of script revisions for the reprint—modifying *okurigana*, changing some *kanji* to *kana*, adding *furigana* glosses, and such—but Nagai Sachiko, in her exhaustive study of the two versions, finds that none of the revisions are major. See her "Higuchi Ichiyō kenkyū," pp. 44–64. Nonetheless, we should keep in mind that the two magazines were geared toward different audiences. *Bungakukai* was the coterie journal of Japanese Romanticism, and its members were part of the educated elite. *Bungakukai* was an austere journal; it included almost no advertisements or illustrations for its fiction, and there were few pronunciation guides for characters. In contrast, *Taiyō* was aimed at a more diverse audience; it featured essays on politics, economics, international relations, science, and family life, in addition to short stories and literary reviews. The stories included *furigana* glosses next to nearly every character, and illustrations were also added to many stories. The *Taiyō* reprint of "Ōtsugomori" includes two illustrations: one depicts Omine talking to Sannosuke on the street; the other depicts Ishinosuke stealthily taking money from a drawer, an event not even explicitly dramatized in the text itself.

17. Maeda Ai, *Higuchi Ichiyō no sekai*, pp. 173–81.

18. Kuniwake Misako, ed., *Kijo no shiori*. Typical of books from this period, consistent pagination does not begin until the body of the text, but the pages I have just described lie between it and the cover in the first volume.

19. Ibid., 1:101. The chapter under discussion (the fourth) covers pp. 101–21.

20. Ibid., 1:115–16.

21. Ibid., 1:116.

22. Ibid., 1:116–17.

23. Ibid., 1:117.

24. The only exception is cleanliness and hygiene; this was a special concern for the Meiji government and a number of social-activist groups, but it is not an issue in "Ōtsugomori."

25. *Kijo*, 1:120–21.

26. In 1893 (Meiji 26), the year before the publication of "Ōtsugomori," the price of an adult ticket to the Kabukiza Theater was almost exactly 4 yen (3 yen 90 *sen*). See Shūkan asahi, ed., *Nedanshi nenpyō*, p. 37.

27. An alternative reading to "re-interiorization" as I have called it can be found in Yamamoto Kinji, "'Ōtsugomori' o yomu," pp. 52–68. He argues that Omine, socialized to be *shōjiki*, experiences a kind of existential crisis when she is forced to steal. She can only recover a sense that she is *shōjiki* by concluding that her mistress is unfeeling. For an argument that filial piety (*kōkō*) is the central moral problem in the text, see Kitagawa, *Ichiyō to iu genshō*, pp. 21–41. Seki Reiko has looked at the story's moral concerns through the lens of economics. See her "Zōyo to shutaika," pp. 22–38.

28. My attention was called to the resonance between "Ōtsugomori" and the *mukashibanashi* "Ōtoshi no kyaku" by a casual remark at a roundtable discussion by Fujii Sadakazu: Yamada, et al., "Kyōdō tōgi," p. 79.

29. Itō, et al., eds., *Yanagita Kunio zenshū*, vol. 5, p. 78.

30. I have found the following books useful: Seki Keigō, ed., *Nihon mukashibanashi taisei*, vol. 5; Seiki Keigō, ed., *Nihon no mukashibanashi*, vol. 3; Nomura, ed., *Mukashibanashi, densetsu hikkei*.

31. Matsuzaka, *Higuchi Ichiyō kenkyū*, pp. 127–32.

32. Brandon, trans., *Sukeroku, Flower of Edo*, p. 75. The entire text of *Sukeroku yukari no Edo zakura* can be found in Gunji, ed., *Kabuki jūhachiban shū*, pp. 59–139.

33. Brandon, trans., *Sukeroku*, p. 75.

34. Although the Sukeroku character can be traced back to Kamigata *jōruri*, he is really an Edo phenomenon. Ichikawa Danjūrō II played the role of Sukeroku three times in his lifetime, and each time the character accrued more of the features that are now associated with him. Danjūrō II first played Sukeroku in 1713 in *Hanayakata aigo zakura* at the Yamamura-za. In this performance an *aragoto* Sukeroku, a man who is both samurai and *otokodate* (a term explained later), fights his nemesis Ikyū on the rooftops of the Yoshiwara, thus establishing the setting and the major characters. He reprised the role in 1716 at the Nakamura-za in a play called *Shikirei yawaragi soga*, in which Sukeroku is portrayed as Soga Gorō in disguise, a convention that has continued to the present day. He softened the character and established his basic costume: snake's eye umbrella, purple headband, black kimono, a *shakuhachi* tucked into his *obi*, and a short commoner's sword rather than a samurai's sword. The springtime setting among the cherry blossoms also finds its roots in this performance. Danjūrō II played the role for the last time in 1749 at the Nakamura-za in a play called *Otoko moji soga monogatari*, in which

Sukeroku became an up-to-date Edokko. Ichikawa Danjūrō IX played the Sukeroku character four times in his lifetime, and it was not even until his performances in the Meiji period that the text of the play stabilized into the one that has come down to us today, *Sukeroku yukari no Edo zakura*. For more details, see Gunji, ed., *Kabuki jūhachiban shū*, pp. 26–30 in Japanese, and Thornbury, *Sukeroku's Double Identity*, pp. 52–73 in English.

35. Kobayashi Hiroko, in a kind of aside, comments that Ishinosuke resembles an *otokodate* character from the kabuki stage. This remark first brought my attention to this aspect of Ishinosuke's character. See her "Hanten suru moraru," p. 121.

36. Maeda Isamu, ed., *Edogo daijiten*, p. 200.

37. Thornbury, *Sukeroku's Double Identity*, p. 66.

Chapter 3

1. Maeda Ai, *Higuchi Ichiyō no sekai*, pp. 194–224.

2. Maeda Ai, *Maeda Ai chosaku shū*, vol. 3, pp. 313–22.

3. Several essays examine these fragments (*miteikō* in Japanese). At the concise end is Matsuzaka, *Higuchi Ichiyō kenkyū*, pp. 149–57; at the detailed end is Kitagawa, *Ichiyō to iu genshō*, pp. 42–71.

4. The letters discussed here are the following: a letter from Ichiyō addressed to Ōhashi and dated August 2 apologizes for having delivered an unfinished product earlier and explains that the pages enclosed with the letter are the ending to the story (see Shioda Ryōhei, Wada Yoshie, and Higuchi Setsu, eds., *Higuchi Ichiyō zenshū*, vol. 4B, p. 900). Ōhashi's response, written in the evening of August 1, states his apologies for having been absent and discusses the work and the payment (see Noguchi Seki, ed., *Higuchi Ichiyō raikanshū*, p. 247). This letter reached Ichiyō only after she sent her letter of August 2, and so she sent another letter to Ōhashi, this one dated August 3 (see *Higuchi Ichiyō zenshū*, vol. 4B, p. 901). The reader who requires more details about the composition of "Nigorie" should consult Hashimoto, *Higuchi Ichiyō sakuhin kenkyū*, pp. 260–68, or Iwami, et al., eds., *Higuchi Ichiyō jiten*, pp. 57–58.

5. These false starts for the final chapter of "Nigorie" are in *Higuchi Ichiyō zenshū*, vol. 2, pp. 90–91.

6. This draft can be found in *Higuchi Ichiyō zenshū*, vol. 2, pp. 91–92 under the label CIV 40.

7. There are a number of investigations into precisely these things

that I wish to avoid here. The reader interested in other approaches to the death scene can consult Seki Ryōichi, *Higuchi Ichiyō*, pp. 337–53; Gamō, "'Nigorie' no ketsumatsu shōkō," pp. 37–44; and Yamamoto Hiroshi, "'Nigorie' no shūshō," pp. 254–81.

8. Let me mention two "intertextual" studies that contrast with my approach. Izuhara Takatoshi has produced an exhaustive inquiry into "borrowed" phrases that appear in Ichiyō's text (see his "'Nigorie' ni okeru 'shakuyō' ni tsuite," pp. 59–77). Suzuki Keiko attempts to equate Oriki and Genshichi with folkloric and religious figures respectively (see her "Kyūsai no nega," pp. 98–119).

9. Jenny, "The Strategy of Form," p. 34.

10. Ibid., p. 45.

11. Jameson, *The Political Unconscious*, pp. 136–50.

12. Ibid., 144. Bakhtin's thoughts on genre can be found in his *Problems of Dostoevsky's Poetics*, pp. 101–80.

13. After critiquing some of Jameson's positions, Thomas Beebee develops a theory of genre along these lines. His position is that genres are fully ideological and that every text incorporates multiple genres. Furthermore, since genres are inherently ideological, "then the struggle against or the deviations from genre are ideological struggles" (see Beebee, *The Ideology of Genre*, p. 19).

14. An entry in Ichiyō's diary dated September 18, 1892, for example, indicates that she was reading these new collections of Chikamatsu's plays (see *Higuchi Ichiyō zenshū*, vol. 3A, p. 175). For an essay that discusses the relationship between Chikamatsu and Ichiyō, see Chikaishi, "Ichiyō to Chikamatsu," pp. 60–70. For an excellent discussion of the canonization of Chikamatsu in the Meiji period, see Lee, "Chikamatsu and Dramatic Literature in the Meiji Period," pp. 179–98.

15. In thinking about Chikamatsu's plays, I have found two books to be useful: Mizuochi, *Bunraku*; and Hirosue, *Chikamatsu josetsu*, especially his superb essay on *Amijima* (pp. 257–81).

16. Torigoe Bunzō, ed., *Chikamatsu Monzaemon shū 2*, pp. 463 and 505, respectively. An English translation, "Love Suicide at Amijima," is available in Keene, *Major Plays of Chikamatsu*.

17. See Tanaka Yūko, *Edo wa nettowaaku*, pp. 78–79.

18. Ibid., pp. 80–83 and 115–19.

19. For a discussion of the *michiyuki* as a "descent into paradise," see Gerstle, *Circles of Fantasy*, pp. 113–53.

20. Saeki, 'Iro' to 'ai' no hikaku bunkashi, pp. 303–7.

21. Isoda Kōichi has argued that the university students in the story must be from the Imperial University in Hongō, suggesting that this particular Shinkai-machi is in the Maruyama-Fukuyama district, where Ichiyō herself lived at the end of her life. If one accepts this argument, it would mean that the factory workers are probably employees of the giant armaments factory in the area (see Isoda, *Isoda Kōichi chosaku shū*, vol. 5, pp. 393–400).

22. Good discussions of the ambiguous position of the *shakufu* can be found in Seki Reiko, *Kataru onnatachi no jidai*, pp. 254–56, and Iwami, "Oriki densetsu," pp. 126–30.

23. A number of essays have noted that "Nigorie" opens with the voice of a character (a rarity in her fiction) and have developed the observation in interesting ways: Kamei, *Kansei no henkaku*, pp. 151–75; Usami, "Higuchi Ichiyō 'Nigorie,'" pp. 61–66; Ikari, "'Nigorie' no kōzō," pp. 87–106; and Ikari, "Oriki no isō," pp. 25–41.

24. This point was made by Komori Yōichi in a conversation about "Nigorie." Genshichi was a *futon* dealer, and the constant flow of people in a newly developing section of the city suggests that he must have had a thriving business. However, within a year he had spent all of his money on Oriki—after all, if he did not monopolize her time with his money someone else might get to her—and his family fell from their secure position in the middle class. Such is the power of the kind of fetishization that rules the district.

25. Kanai, "'Onna' no raireki," pp. 41–45.

26. I borrow the term "verbal friction" from Greenblatt, *Shake-spearean Negotiations*, pp. 88–91. The "language game" (*gengo geemu*) approach was suggested to me during a discussion with Komori Yōichi.

27. Takada, *Higuchi Ichiyō ron e no shatei*, p. 37. The calling card would have the customer's name, address, and business affiliations written on it, and thus Oriki would finally be able to learn the identity of her new patron. I follow Tomatsu's lead in my discussion of photography in the quarter: see "'Nigorie' ron no tame ni," p. 33.

28. Maeda Ai, *Higuchi Ichiyō no sekai*, p. 197. Maeda glosses the ideographs "kikiyaku" with the French word.

29. Several scholars have interpreted this invitation as the beginning of Tomonosuke's status as Oriki's *najimi kyaku*, and even as the first sexual encounter between them. While it is true that the first meeting between the two did not end up in bed, it is unlikely that the relationship remained that way until the sixth chapter.

30. Tomatsu, "'Nigorie' ron no tame ni," pp. 36–37. Karino makes a similar point, but leaves it largely undeveloped (see her "Hiki-sakareta sei no shosō," pp. 8–9).

31. *Chikamatsu Monzaemon shū*, 2:467.

32. These include Aichi, "'Nigorie' ni wataru 'marukibashi'," pp. 75–97; Yamamoto Hiroshi, "'Nigorie' no marukibashi," pp. 30–50; Yamamoto Kinji, "'Nigorie' shiron," pp. 35–45; Minemura, "'Nigorie' goshō," pp. 81–107.

33. Here the essential references are three books by Takeuchi: *Risshin shusse shugi*; *Risshi, kugaku, shusse*; and especially *Gakureki kizoku no eikō to zasetsu*. In English, see Kinmonth, *The Self-made Man*.

34. By means of details in the story, one can calculate that Oriki was born around the time of the Meiji Restoration of 1868. Both her father and grandfather went through their formative years at a time when *risshin shusse* had not yet erupted into the social order.

35. For an essay that historicizes the discourse on insanity and argues for its centrality to the interpretation of "Nigorie," see Kita-gawa, *Ichiyō to iu genshō*, pp. 72–94.

36. Nakanishi, "The Spatial Structure of Japanese Myth," pp. 120–24.

37. See Kubota and Baba, eds., *Utakotoba utamakura daijiten*, p. 787 for more information on this. My attention was called to the image of Maruki Bridge in the classical tradition by Aichi's aforementioned "'Nigorie' ni wataru 'marukibashi'."

38. Ichiko, ed., *Heike monogatari*, 2:267.

Chapter 4

1. Hiratsuka Raichō, "Onna toshite no Higuchi Ichiyō," p. 154.

2. This resonates strongly with one of the three options women have in writing against patriarchy as outlined by Sharalyn Orbaugh: "The first option of women writing fiction against the dominant economies of power" is to "maintain and *describe* the current con-figurations of power, exposing the harm done through them." See Orbaugh, "The Body in Contemporary Women's Fiction," p. 123.

3. In *Hasegawa Shigure zenshū*, vol. 4, p. 134.

4. One example of a contemporary reaction is Uchida Roan (1868–1929). He reviewed the special issue of *Bungei kurabu* devoted to women writers in which "Jūsan'ya" first appeared. Roan devotes over a quarter of the review to "Jūsan'ya" alone, and it is clear that he both responded to it on an emotional level and considered it one

of the best stories in the collection. See Uchida Roan, *Uchida Roan zenshū*, vol. 1, pp. 445–58.

5. Margaret Cohen's work on the nineteenth-century French novel is to my mind one of the most sophisticated studies to date. Cohen discusses women's dominance of the sentimental novel in France prior to the 1830s and then goes on to show how Balzac, Stendhal, and others construed the realist aesthetic as being opposed to sentimentalism, and even relentlessly coded realism positively as masculine and sentimentalism negatively as feminine. See Cohen, *The Sentimental Education of the Novel*. For the English tradition, see McGann, *The Poetics of Sensibility*.

6. Copeland, *Lost Leaves*, pp. 215–29.

7. The readership of *katei shōsetsu* has begun to receive scholarly attention. See Ito, "Class and Gender in a Meiji Family Romance," pp. 345–52.

8. Zwicker, "Tears of Blood," chap. 2.

9. In some ways, the kind of possibility I am investigating with "Jūsan'ya" bears some resemblance to Cohen's idea of the "sentimental social novel" (Cohen, *The Sentimental Education of the Novel*, pp. 119–62), even though Ichiyō could hardly have been aware of such literature given her education in a poetry conservatory.

10. Kōno et al., "'Jūsan'ya' o yomu," part 1, p. 128. Part 2, pp. 169–89 is also useful.

11. Tanaka Minoru makes a similar point, arguing that Harada has achieved his position through learning and ability. See Tanaka, "'Jūsan'ya' no 'ame,'" p. 16. Inoue Yoshie, too, argues that Harada is likely a member of the academic elite, who rose to his current position by acquiring the appropriate academic credentials. See Inoue, "Mugen no yami," pp. 159–62.

12. See especially Takeuchi, *Gakureki kizoku no eikō to zasetsu*, and Kinmonth, *The Self-made Man*.

13. Ambaras, "Social Knowledge," pp. 2–3.

14. As if to emphasize her luxurious surroundings, the original printing of "Jūsan'ya" in *Bungei kurabu* includes a picture depicting Oseki sadly gazing upon the face of her boy (presumably right before she leaves for her parents' home), which is a scene not even dramatized in the narrative present of the story. She wears a sumptuous kimono and has her hair done up in a splendid *marumage* coiffure. Her son sleeps in luxurious bedding. Also in the room are a low table, a lamp, and a clock, all very expensive-looking.

15. Seki Reiko, *Kataru onnatachi no jidai*, pp. 329–30. Takada Chinami has also called attention to the family's social fall and used it to proffer the tantalizing hypothesis that Oseki's parents are actually from a family of dispossessed samurai (*botsuraku shizoku*), a hypothesis that I find provocative, but with which I ultimately do not agree. See Takada, "'Jūsan'ya' nōto," p. 58.

16. For letters of divorce, see Kōno et al., "'Jūsan'ya' o yomu," part 1, p. 129.

17. I should acknowledge a debt to Seki Reiko's excellent essay on this particular story; in it, Seki briefly touches on the issue of female learning and refinement, which gave me the idea of pursuing this issue further in the Meiji archives. See her *Kataru onnatachi no jidai*, pp. 327–28.

18. For more, see Copeland, *Lost Leaves*, pp. 14–49.

19. For these views, I am relying heavily on essays by Takahashi Yūko. See her "Chūbei jidai ni okeru Mori Arinori," pp. 47–71 and "Vikutoria jidai no hōmu," pp. 261–83.

20. For more on this, see Nishikawa, "The Changing Form of Dwelling," pp. 20–23. Also useful is Nolte and Hastings, "The Meiji State's Policy toward Women, 1890–1910," pp. 151–74. See also Sand, *House and Home in Modern Japan*, pp. 21–29.

21. Muta, *Senryaku toshite no kazoku*, pp. ii, 20, and 22.

22. Komori, *Buntai toshite no monogatari*, pp. 279–82. Muta, *Senryaku*, pp. 182–83.

23. I borrow the term "dual structure" from Nishikawa, "The Changing Form of Dwellings," pp. 23 and 33.

24. Iwamoto, "Kazoku no danran," pp. 218–19.

25. Iwamoto, "Katei wa kokka nari," p. 147.

26. Iwamoto, "Joshi no tai'iku," p. 218.

27. Iwamoto, "Haha no mugaku," p. 127.

28. Ibid., p. 131.

29. Iwamoto, "Tsuma no mujō," p. 126.

30. Iwamoto, "Haha no mugaku," p. 130.

31. Takeuchi, *Risshi, kugaku, shusse*, pp. 38–60.

32. This is described in vivid detail in Takeuchi, *Risshin shusse shugi*, pp. 24–31.

33. Iwamoto, "Katei no kankaryoku," pp. 146–47.

34. Iwamoto, "Katei no yūraku," p. 211. See Muta, *Senryaku*, pp. 91–101 and pp. 127–28 for more on these keywords. See also Sand, *House and Home in Modern Japan*, pp. 29–33.

35. Iwamoto, "Katei no fūga," p. 97.

36. Ibid.

37. Iwamoto, "Katei no fūga," pp. 97–98. David Ambaras has pointed out that the new middle class of Meiji, of which Iwamoto was an exemplary figure, made sport of the aristocratic class by calling them lazy, profligate, and unproductive. See Ambaras, "Social Knowledge," pp. 22–23.

38. Iwamoto, "Katei no fūga," p. 98.

39. Ibid., p. 101.

40. Muta, *Senryaku*, pp. 67–68.

41. Ambaras, "Social Knowledge," pp. 25–29.

42. In some ways, the shadow story haunting our text is Genji's courtship of Murasaki—who is one of those hidden treasures at the margins of aristocratic society—in *Genji monogatari*. The Genji-Murasaki relationship turns out to be successful, so it could be argued that Ichiyō shows us the darker possibility in such a match. Seki Reiko raised this point in my discussions with her about "Jūsan'ya."

43. Seki Ryōichi, *Higuchi Ichiyō*, p. 366.

44. This problem (which is so large in Japanese scholarship that it has acquired something of a name, *chichi no settoku, musume no hon'i*) has been at the heart of the vast majority of critical essays on the text, and a number of interpretations and explanations have been offered. For a variety of views see: Yamada, "'Jūsan'ya' no sekai," pp. 19–20; Tanaka Minoru, "'Jūsan'ya' no 'ame,'" pp. 14–26; Tomatsu, "Higuchi Ichiyō 'Jūsan'ya' shiron," pp. 67–83; Kōra, "Higuchi Ichiyō 'Jūsan'ya' to tsuki no anji," pp. 10–15; Yamamoto Kinji, "'Jūsan'ya' ron," pp. 14–21; and Kitagawa, *Ichiyō to iu genshō*, pp. 95–110.

45. Fukui, ed., *Ise monogatari*, pp. 155–56.

46. Saeki, *'Iro' to 'ai' no hikaku bunkashi*, pp. 23 and 39–40.

47. Ibid., p. 158.

48. Rubin, "The Traffic in Women: Notes toward a Political Economy of Sex," pp. 157–210. I am preceded in this line of thought by Komori Yōichi and Seki Reiko. Komori Yōichi has argued that the father has "sold Oseki to Harada Isamu as 'wife' and 'mother.'" See his *Buntai toshite no monogatari*, p. 286. See also Seki Reiko, *Kataru onna tachi*, pp. 322–26.

49. See Saeki, *'Iro' to 'ai'*, pp. 272–321, and Copeland, *Lost Leaves*, pp. 170–77.

Chapter 5

1. The term is from Grosz, *Volatile Bodies*. Toril Moi, though critical of the poststructuralist orientation of Grosz, has used a similar term in a recent essay in which she attempts to reorient feminist criticism around the body and subjectivity rather than around the categories of sex and gender, and this has greatly influenced my own discussion in this chapter. See Moi, *What Is a Woman?*, pp. 3–120.

2. The entry is dated July 20, 1893. See Maeda and Noguchi, eds., *Zenshū Higuchi Ichiyō*, vol. 3, pp. 201–2.

3. This entry is dated August 3, 1893. See *Zenshū Higuchi Ichiyō*, vol. 3, p. 207.

4. I found the following sources immensely productive for thinking about the Yoshiwara: Miyamoto, "Yūri no seiritsu to taishūka," pp. 169–218; Tanaka Yūko, *Edo wa nettowaaku*, pp. 75–140; and Seigle, *Yoshiwara*.

5. The details of the changes in state-demimonde relations can be found in Yoshimi, "Baishō no jittai to haishō undō," pp. 223–58 and Fujime, "Kindai Nihon no kōshō seido to haishō undō," pp. 461–91.

6. The problems of language and narration occupy a good portion of the scholarship on the text, and readers with an interest in such areas are encouraged to consult other essays. Kamei Hideo has convincingly demonstrated that the narrator of *Takekurabe* frequently grafts her discourse onto the character chosen to be the focus for the dominant point of view (see his *Kansei no henkaku*, p. 136). Seki Ryōichi finds borrowings from the theater, especially from kabuki, in the language and imagery employed by the narrator (see his *Higuchi Ichiyō*, pp. 259–84). Robert Lyons Danly has argued that there is a tendency in *Takekurabe* toward a fragmentary style of juxtaposition, which is a technique borrowed from Saikaku, and which Saikaku in turn borrowed from *haikai renga* (see his *In the Shade of Spring Leaves*, pp. 109–32). Christine Murasaki Millet has argued that allusions to classical texts in *Takekurabe* are not straightforward, but inverted (see her "Inverted Classical Allusions," pp. 3–26). Izuhara Takatoshi has argued that the language of the narrator is borrowed as much from Meiji discourses as from classical texts (see his "*Takekurabe* no seiritsu kiban," pp. 1–18). Yamamoto Kazuaki has demonstrated that in the first half of the novella the narrator remains an outside observer, while in the second half the narrator gives the reader inside views of the characters (see his "*Takekurabe* ni okeru katarite no isō," pp.

20–31). For a discussion of the narrator's relationship to the characters and the reader, see Yamamoto Kinji, "*Takekurabe* no hōhō," pp. 1095–121.

7. The opening lines of *Takekurabe* (a single sentence in the original) are among the most celebrated in modern Japanese literature: "Mawareba ōmon no mikaeri yanagi ito nagakeredo, ohaguro dobu ni tomoshibi utsuru san-gai no sawagi mo te ni toru gotoku, akekure nashi no kuruma no yukiki ni hakari shirarenu zensei o uranaite, Daionji-mae to na wa hotoke-kusakeredo, sarito wa yōki no machi to sumitaru hito no mōshiki." The rhetorical texture is quite dense. "Ito" is a pivot word (*kakekotoba*), that is, a word that allows for two meanings: it is an adverb meaning "great" (referring to the great distance to the front of the quarter) and a noun meaning "threads" (referring to the branches of the willow tree). The tree itself was called the "looking back" willow because, on their way out of the quarter, customers were said to turn their heads and look longingly upon it, not at all pleased to be leaving. In addition, the branches themselves almost seemed to wave goodbye to the nocturnal visitors. The Ohaguro *dobu* is the actual name of the moat surrounding the Yoshiwara, but "o-haguro" is also the name of the black dye that was used to darken the teeth of women, black teeth being an emblem of female beauty throughout much of Japanese history. For the sake of illustrating my points I have sacrificed elegance in order to translate the opening lines fairly literally. A more graceful translation can be found in Danly, *In the Shade of Spring Leaves*, p. 254.

8. A point first made by Maeda Ai in his *Higuchi Ichiyō no sekai*, p. 266.

9. This is frequently commented upon in scholarship. The essay that places perhaps the greatest symbolic weight on it is Shigematsu, "*Takekurabe* no aikan," p. 119. See also Kan, "Katararenakatta monogatari," p. 49.

10. See Maeda Ai, *Higuchi Ichiyō no sekai*, pp. 269–71. He goes on to observe that the Senzoku festival is a communal affair unassociated with the Yoshiwara. My discussion of economics in this and the following paragraph is substantially indebted to Maeda's discussion.

11. For more on school songs and recitation of the Rescript, see Takada, "'Onna, kodomo' no shiza kara," pp. 48–60.

12. I am drawing mostly from Foucault: *Discipline and Punish* and *The History of Sexuality*.

13. Butler, *The Psychic Life of Power*, pp. 83–105.

14. Fukui, ed., *Ise monogatari*, pp. 155–56.

15. For more details see Iwami et al., eds., *Higuchi Ichiyō jiten*, pp. 43–44.

16. See Karatani, *Origins of Modern Japanese Literature*, pp. 114–35.

17. Ariès, *Centuries of Childhood*.

18. Iwaya Sazanami, "Kogane maru," p. 225. Both the German and the English are in the original Japanese preface.

19. Karatani, *Origins of Modern Japanese Literature*, p. 124.

20. Hara, *Shikijō to seinen*, p. 1. As is typical of books from this time period, there is one system of pagination for the text proper and one for the front matter. The citations that follow all refer to the body of Hara's book.

21. Ibid., pp. 6–7.

22. Ibid., pp. 8–9.

23. See Kawamura, *Sekushuariti no kindai*, pp. 82–115. I am indebted to Kawamura's study in thinking about the normative sexual subject of modern times.

24. Hara, *Shikijō to seinen*, p. 9.

25. Wada, ed., *Higuchi Ichiyō shū*, p. 423, note 160. I should emphasize that in this chapter, even more than in the others, I have found Wada's notes to the Kadokawa edition indispensable.

26. Ibid., p. 423, note 162.

27. Seki Reiko, *Kataru onnatachi no jidai*, p. 272.

28. Kimata, *Imeeji no kindai Nihon bungaku shi*, p. 24. Kimata details the significance of various kinds of cultural artifacts in this fascinating book.

29. I believe Kamei Hideo was the first to attach much significance to this point. See his *Kansei no henkaku*, pp. 143–46.

30. Although I have not adopted his psychoanalytic framework, Peter Brooks's meditations on the body in the Western narrative tradition have been productive in my thinking about Midori. See Brooks, *Body Work*, pp. 88–122.

31. I have found Laura Mulvey's well-known essay on visual pleasure useful in thinking about this issue. See her "Visual Pleasure and Narrative Cinema," pp. 57–79.

32. Seigle details a number of such customs in her *Yoshiwara*: fashion parades (p. 69), annual events (pp. 106–10), the procession of the courtesan (pp. 65–66, 75, and 225–28), the display of bedding (pp. 187–88), and the presentation of a new courtesan (pp. 184–87).

33. The reason for Midori being paraded around the streets of the neighborhood in this elaborate attire is an object of fierce debate among Ichiyō critics. Until the mid-1980s the scholarly consensus was that Midori had experienced her first period, and the elaborate attire was meant to symbolize her emergence as an adult woman. That comfortable consensus was disrupted in 1985 when Sata Ineko, a writer herself, argued in the magazine *Gunzō* that this view trivializes Ichiyō's novella; Sata argued that the elaborate attire was meant to suggest that Midori had in fact become a prostitute. Maeda Ai responded a few months later with an essay that marshaled a wide range of historical evidence to demonstrate that the old scholarly consensus was correct: Midori had experienced her first period. Maeda went on to argue that this did not trivialize Ichiyō's story because it still functioned symbolically to hint at Midori's eventual fate. Sata responded by sticking to her original thesis, and she was supported by the writer and critic Noguchi Fujio, who expressed some doubts about Maeda's position. The debate was joined over the following years by a large number of critics and writers (which accounts for nearly half the essays on the novella), and a new stability was found, with scholars (both women and men) tending to support the traditional opinion and writers supporting Sata's position. The issue has become so large that anyone who writes on *Takekurabe* is compelled at least to address it and to take a side. My own position is that we are witness to the presentation of a new courtesan, but the focus of discussion needs to be shifted to how Midori responds to becoming the object of the male gaze. For the first round of the debate see Sata, "*Takekurabe* kaishaku e no hitotsu no gimon," pp. 192–96; Maeda Ai, "Midori no tame ni," pp. 204–11; Sata, "*Takekurabe* kaishaku sono go," pp. 4–7; and Noguchi Fujio, "*Takekurabe* ronkō o yonde," pp. 182–88. A useful guide to the immense number of articles that followed these in the *Takekurabe* debate can be found in Aoki, *Ichiyō ronkō*, pp. 278–306.

34. Mulvey, "Visual Pleasure," p. 62.

35. Abe Akio, Akiyama Ken, and Imai Gen'e, eds., *Genji monogatari*, 1:273–336.

36. Fukui, ed., *Ise monogatari*, p. 133.

37. Ryūtei Tanehiko, *Nise Murasaki inaka Genji*, 1:193–209. As far as I know, there is no translation of Tanehiko's novel, but there is an excellent English-language book on Tanehiko's life and works: Markus, *The Willow in Autumn*.

38. This is Maeda Ai's observation, and it is a point with which every analysis of this scene must grapple (see his *Higuchi Ichiyō no sekai*, pp. 280–85). My discussion in this entire section is deeply indebted to Maeda's superb and graceful analysis. His conclusion about this scene in *Takekurabe* is that it offers a glimpse of another kind of growing up outside the influence of the Yoshiwara. While this is not wrong, Maeda places too much emphasis on how freedom and the possibility of an uncontaminated childhood are closed off for Midori. My own view, as I argued in section ii of this chapter, is that any possible life path for Midori is enclosed by regimes of power.

39. Ichiyō typically inserts the speech and thought of characters into the narrative discourse without using punctuation of any kind except for the quotative particle *to* and a comma, and sometimes not even that. I have tried to capture this in English translation by not making use of quotation marks. Harder to capture, however, is the way the classical language of the narrator drifts into colloquial language when she mimics Midori's voice.

40. Kamei Hideo, *Kansei no henkaku*, chapter 6.

41. I am indebted to a rich and suggestive roundtable discussion of "gaps" in Ichiyō's fiction. See Takada Chinami, Seki Reiko, Margaret Mitsutani, and Usami Takeshi, "Tekusuto no 'kūhaku' o megutte," pp. 6–31.

Chapter 6

1. I have used Danly's excellent translations of the aphorisms from his *In the Shade of Spring Leaves*. The translations of other passages are my own.

2. After "Wakaremichi" appeared in print, Ichiyō published the first part of a very promising work called "Uramurasaki" in the February 1896 issue of *Shinbundan*, but never completed it. Shortly before her death, her novella *Warekara* appeared in the May 1896 issue of *Bungei kurabu*, but most critics consider the ending too abrupt for it to be considered a "completed" story. By that time Ichiyō was suffering from the symptoms of the tuberculosis that would shortly claim her life, so she did not have the strength to devote much time to polishing the ending. *Warekara* is an interesting story, however, and is beginning to receive attention.

3. Takitō, *Ichiyō bungaku*, p. 218.

4. I borrow the terminology of narratology—scene and analepsis—from Genette, *Narrative Discourse*, pp. 40 and 94.

5. Bakhtin, *Problems of Dostoevsky's Poetics*, p. 193.

6. See Takeuchi, *Risshi, kugaku, shusse* and the early chapters of Kinmonth, *The Self-made Man*.

7. Komori's remarks were made at a roundtable discussion on Ichiyō's major works: Yamada Yūsaku et al., "Kyōdō tōgi," p. 102. Incidentally, Komori's observation has proven to be one of the most fruitful ways of analyzing "Wakaremichi." Many of the essays cited in this chapter are predicated, wholly or in part, on this reading.

8. I would like to thank Ken Ito for emphasizing the importance of this moment of disconnection.

9. Kan Satoko has written on this in her stimulating essay: "Ichiyō no 'Wakaremichi,'" pp. 29–30.

10. See Yamasaki, "Surechigau monogatari," pp. 178–84.

11. Medieval Japanese did not, of course, use inches or feet as a measurement, but this is the conventional way to translate the title of the story. Technically the baby measures one *sun*, which is about three centimeters.

12. My summary follows the *otogi zōshi* and can be found in Ōshima, ed., *Otogi zōshi shū*, pp. 394–402. This version is the one that appeared in the mid-Edo period collection of 23 stories called *Otogi bunko* (Library of Companion Tales).

13. Iwaya Sazanami, *Issunbōshi*. This series began with the first volume dedicated to *Momotarō*, published in July 1894, and continued for two full years, ending with volume 24. The stories appear to be transcriptions of Sazanami's oral storytelling efforts. The Issunbōshi volume says that Sazanami recited the tale and a man named Azuma Nishimaru transcribed it. All the volumes include extensive illustrations (the one dedicated to Issunbōshi includes illustrations by Kobayashi Kiyochika) and a preface by some Meiji luminary or other (the preface to our story was penned by Miyake Setsurei).

14. Iwaya Sazanami, *Issunbōshi*, pp. i–ii.

15. Ibid., p. 10.

16. This version of the folktale can be found in Seki Keigo, ed., *Nihon no mukashibanashi*, vol. 3, pp. 22–24.

17. Iwaya Sazanami, *Issunbōshi*, p. 28.

18. Ibid., p. 32.

19. See, for example, Takeuchi, *Risshi, kugaku, shusse* and the early chapters of his *Risshin shusse shugi*.

20. Iwaya Sazanami, *Issunbōshi*, pp. 17–19.

21. The archetypical tale here is perhaps Kōda Rohan's mid-Meiji story "Tetsu Sandan," which also works within the framework of modern discourses on ambition and success. See Fukuda Kiyoto, ed., *Meiji shōnen bungaku shū*, pp. 55–56 for this story.

22. I borrow the term utopian familial (or quasi-familial) relationship from Fujii Sadakazu in Yamada, "Kyōdō tōgi," p. 102.

23. The critical essays on "Wakaremichi" began to notice this issue in the 1990s, though they remain largely parenthetical observations at this point. Nonetheless, I am heavily indebted to these initial observations by others. See, for example, Yamasaki, "Surechigau monogatari," p. 187; Tomatsu, "Kōsa shita 'jikan' no imi," p. 101; Chida, "'Wakaremichi' ron," pp. 185–86; Shigematsu, "Kichizō no wakaremichi," pp. 22–23; Takitō, *Ichiyō bungaku*, p. 227; and Seki Reiko, *Kataru onnatachi no jidai*, pp. 372–73.

24. In making these connections using some of Ichiyō's stories I follow Matsuzaka, *Higuchi Ichiyō kenkyū*, pp. 32–53, although I root these stories more firmly in *Genji monogatari* than he does.

25. Hirotsu Kazuo, "Kaidai," *Hirotsu Ryūrō shū*, p. 437.

26. Hirotsu Ryūrō, *Hemeden*, pp. 48–78.

27. Ibid., p. 48.

28. Ibid., p. 50.

29. Ibid., p. 55.

30. Takada, "'Wakaremichi' no isō," pp. 105–15.

31. There is some debate about the mysterious man who arranges for Okyō to become a kept woman. In the text he is referred to as "uncle" (*ojisan*), but the unorthodox characters used to write it suggest that this term refers not to a blood relative, but is instead used in a more general sense to mean an older male acquaintance.

32. Some recent essays have read this reference to Tokyo slums in "Wakaremichi" as being significant. See Yamamoto Kinji, "Deawanai kotoba," pp. 198–201. See also Seki Reiko, *Kataru onnatachi*, pp. 366–70.

33. In technical terms we are given an iterative narrative. Our sense is that the first part gives us a representative sample of a typical evening between the two characters. See Genette, *Narrative Discourse*, p. 116. I owe this insight to Shigematsu, "Kichizō no wakaremichi," p. 22.

34. Seki Reiko, *Kataru onnatachi*, p. 374.

35. It is not entirely clear whether Kichi exists in the world of wage labor. The umbrella manufacturing shop at which he is employed may operate under a more traditional apprentice system.

36. These points about the gender of labor in the text are from Seki Reiko, *Kataru onnatachi*, pp. 379–80.

37. More details can be found in Murakami, *Meiji josei shi*, pp. 283–312 and Arichi, *Kindai Nihon no kazoku kan*, pp. 38–42.

38. Mori Arinori, "Saishōron," pp. 260–63.

39. Cited in full in Arichi, *Kazoku kan*, pp. 58–60.

40. Cited in Ibid., p. 38.

Works Cited

Abe Akio, Akiyama Ken, and Imai Gen'e, eds. *Genji monogatari*. 6 vols. *NKBZ*, vol. 12–17. Tokyo: Shōgakukan, 1970–1976.

Aichi Mineko. "'Nigorie' ni wataru 'marukibashi.'" In Higuchi Ichiyō kenkyūkai, ed. (1996), pp. 75–97.

Ambaras, David. "Social Knowledge, Cultural Capital, and the New Middle Class in Japan, 1895–1912." *Journal of Japanese Studies* 24, no. 1 (Winter 1998): 1–33.

Aoki Kazuo. *Ichiyō ronkō*. Tokyo: Ōfūsha, 1996.

Arichi Tōru. *Kindai Nihon no kazoku kan: Meiji hen*. Tokyo: Kōbundō, 1977.

Ariès, Phillippe. *Centuries of Childhood*. Trans. Robert Baldick. London: Jonathan Cape, 1962.

Bakhtin, Mikhail. "Discourse in the Novel." In *The Dialogic Imagination: Four Essays*. Trans. and ed. Michael Holquist and Caryl Emerson. Austin: University of Texas Press, 1981, pp. 259–422.

——. *Problems of Dostoevsky's Poetics*. Trans. Caryl Emerson. Minneapolis: University of Minnesota Press, 1984.

Beebee, Thomas. *The Ideology of Genre: A Comparative Study of Generic Instability*. University Park: Penn State University Press, 1994.

Benjamin, Walter. *Illuminations*. Ed. Hannah Arendt. Trans. Harry Zohn. New York: Shocken Books, 1968.

Berman, Marshall. *All That Is Solid Melts Into Air: The Experience of Modernity*. New York: Simon and Schuster, 1982.

Bourdaghs, Michael K. *The Dawn That Never Comes: Shimazaki Tōson and Japanese Nationalism*. New York: Columbia University Press, 2003.

Brandon, James, trans. *Sukeroku, the Flower of Edo*. In *Kabuki: Five Classic Plays*. Honolulu: University of Hawaii Press, 1992, pp. 49–92.

Brooks, Peter. *Body Work: Objects of Desire in Modern Narrative*. Cambridge, Mass.: Harvard University Press, 1993.

Burns, Susan L. *Before the Nation: Kokugaku and the Imagining of Community in Early Modern Japan*. Durham, N.C.: Duke University Press, 2003.

Butler, Judith. *The Psychic Life of Power: Theories in Subjection*. Stanford, Cal.: Stanford University Press, 1997.

Chakrabarty, Dipesh. *Provincializing Europe: Postcolonial Thought and Historical Difference*. Princeton, N.J.: Princeton University Press, 2000.

Chida Kaori. "'Wakaremichi' ron: Okyō no gensetsu o megutte." In Higuchi Ichiyō kenkyūkai, ed. (1996), pp. 178–93.

Chikaishi Yasuaki. "Ichiyō to Chikamatsu." *Kokugo to kokubungaku* 42 (1959): 60–70.

Cohen, Margaret. *The Sentimental Education of the Novel*. Princeton, N.J.: Princeton University Press, 1999.

Copeland, Rebecca. *Lost Leaves: Women Writers of Meiji Japan*. Honolulu: University of Hawaii Press, 2000.

Cornyetz, Nina. *Dangerous Women and Deadly Words: Phallic Fantasy and Modernity in Three Japanese Writers*. Stanford, Cal.: Stanford University Press, 1999.

Danly, Robert Lyons. *In the Shade of Spring Leaves: The Life and Writings of Higuchi Ichiyō, a Woman of Letters in Meiji Japan*. New Haven, Conn.: Yale University Press, 1981. Reprint, New York: W. W. Norton, 1992.

de Man, Paul. *Blindness and Insight: Essays in the Rhetoric of Contemporary Criticism*, 2nd ed., rev. Minneapolis: University of Minnesota Press, 1983.

Duara, Pransenjit. *Rescuing History from the Nation: Questioning Narratives of Modern China*. Chicago: University of Chicago Press, 1995.

Foucault, Michel. *Discipline and Punish: The Birth of the Prison*. Trans. Alan Sheridan. New York: Vintage Books, 1977.

———. *The History of Sexuality, Volume 1: An Introduction*. Trans. Robert Hurley. New York: Vintage Books, 1978.

Fujii, James. *Complicit Fictions: The Subject in the Modern Japanese Prose Narrative*. Berkeley: University of California Press, 1993.

Fujime Yuki. "Kindai Nihon no kōshō seido to haishō undō." In *Jendaa no Nihon shi: shūkyō to minzoku, shintai to seiai*. Ed. Wakita

Haruko and Susan Hanley. Tokyo: Tōkyō daigaku shuppankai, 1994, pp. 461–91.

Fukuda Kiyoto, ed. *Meiji shōnen bungaku shū. MBZ,* vol. 95. Tokyo: Chikuma shobō, 1970.

Fukui Teisuke, ed. *Ise monogatari. NKBZ,* vol. 8. Tokyo: Shōgakukan, 1972.

Gamō Yoshirō. " 'Nigorie' no ketsumatsu shōkō: 'Nigorie' ron no tame no oboegaki." *Nihon bungaku nōto* 10 (1975): 37–44.

Gates, Henry Louis. *The Signifying Monkey: A Theory of African-American Literary Criticism.* New York: Oxford University Press, 1988.

Genette, Gérard. *Narrative Discourse: An Essay in Method.* Trans. Jane Lewin. Ithaca, N.Y.: Cornell University Press, 1980.

Gerstle, C. Andrew. *Circles of Fantasy: Convention in the Plays of Chikamatsu.* Cambridge, Mass.: Council on East Asian Studies, Harvard University, 1986.

Gluck, Carol. *Japan's Modern Myths: Ideology in the Late Meiji Period.* Princeton, N.J.: Princeton University Press, 1985.

Greenblatt, Stephen. *Shakespearean Negotiations: The Circulation of Social Energy in Renaissance England.* Berkeley: University of California Press, 1988.

Grosz, Elizabeth. *Volatile Bodies: Toward a Corporeal Feminism.* Bloomington: Indiana University Press, 1996.

Gunji Masakatsu, ed. *Kabuki jūhachiban shū. NKBT,* vol. 98. Tokyo: Iwanami shoten, 1965.

Hara Masao. *Shikijō to seinen.* Tokyo: Maruyama, 1906.

Harootunian, Harry. *Overcome by Modernity: History, Culture, and Community in Interwar Japan.* Princeton, N.J.: Princeton University Press, 2000.

Harvey, David. *The Condition of Postmodernity.* Malden, Mass.: Blackwell, 1990.

Hasegawa Shigure. *Hasegawa Shigure zenshū,* vol. 4. Tokyo: Nihon bunrinsha, 1942.

Hashimoto Takeshi. *Higuchi Ichiyō sakuhin kenkyū.* Osaka: Izumi shoin, 1990.

Higuchi Ichiyō. *Higuchi Ichiyō shū.* Ed. Wada Yoshie. *Nihon kindai bungaku taikei,* vol. 8. Tokyo: Kadokawa shoten, 1978.

———. *Higuchi Ichiyō shū.* Ed. Seki Reiko and Kan Satoko. *Shin Nihon koten bungaku taikei, Meiji hen,* vol. 24. Tokyo: Iwanami shoten, 2001.

——. *Higuchi Ichiyō zenshū.* Ed. Shioda Ryōhei, Wada Yoshie, and Higuchi Setsu. 6 vols. Tokyo: Chikuma Shobō, 1974–1994.

——. "Jūsan'ya." *Bungei kurabu,* special issue on *keishū shōsetsu.* 1895. 10 December, pp. 34–51.

——. "Nigorie." *Bungei kurabu.* 1895. 20 September, pp. 106–42.

——. "Ōtsugomori." *Taiyō.* 1896. 5 February, pp. 162–75.

——. *Takekurabe. Bungei kurabu.* 1896. 10 April, pp. 94–131.

——. *Takekurabe, Nigorie.* Ed. Okada Yachiyo. Tokyo: Kadokawa shoten, 1968.

——. "Wakaremichi." *Kokumin no tomo.* 1896. 4 January, pp. 64–71.

——. *Zenshū Higuchi Ichiyō.* Ed. Maeda Ai, Kimura Masayuki, and Yamada Yūsaku. 4 vols. Tokyo: Shōgakukan, 1979.

Higuchi Ichiyō kenkyūkai, ed. *Ronshū Higuchi Ichiyō I.* Tokyo: Ōfūsha, 1996.

——. *Ronshū Higuchi Ichiyō II.* Tokyo: Ōfūsha, 1998.

Hiratsuka Raichō. "Onna toshite no Higuchi Ichiyō joshi." In *Hiratsuka Raichō chosakushū,* vol. 1, ed. Ōoka Shōhei, et al. Tokyo: Ōtsuki shoten, 1983, pp. 152–72.

Hirosue Tamotsu. *Chikamatsu josetsu: kinsei higeki no kenkyū,* 2nd ed. Tokyo: Miraisha, 1980.

Hirotsu Kazuo, ed. *Hirotsu Ryūrō shū. MBZ,* vol. 19. Tokyo: Chikuma shobō, 1965.

Hirotsu Ryūrō. *Hemeden.* In *Hirotsu Ryūrō shū, MBZ,* vol. 19, ed. Hirotsu Kazuo. Tokyo: Chikuma shobō, 1965, pp. 48–78.

Ichiko Teiji, ed. *Heike monogatari.* 2 vols. *NKBZ,* vol. 29–30. Tokyo: Shōgakukan, 1974–1975.

——. "Kaisetsu." In *Otogi zōshi. NKBT,* vol. 38. Tokyo: Iwanami shoten, 1963, pp. 5–21.

Ihara Saikaku. *Seken mune zan'yō.* In *Ihara Saikaku shū 3, NKBZ,* vol. 40, ed. Tanikawa Masachika, Jinbō Kazuya, and Teruoka Yasutaka. Tokyo: Shōgakukan, 1972, pp. 381–508.

Ikari Tomokazu. "'Nigorie' no kōzō: 'yobikake' to 'manazashi' o jiku toshite." *Shiraume joshi tanki daigaku kenkyū kiyō* 27 (1991): 87–106.

——. "Oriki no isō: 'Nigorie' no kōzō saikō." *Shiraume joshi tanki daigaku kenkyū kiyō* 28 (1992): 25–41.

Inoue Yoshie. "Mugen no yami: 'Jūsan'ya.'" In Shin feminizumu hihyō no kai, ed. pp. 151–76.

Inouye, Charles Shiro. *The Similitude of Blossoms: A Critical Biography of Izumi Kyoka (1873-1939), Japanese Novelist and Playwright.* Cambridge, Mass.: Harvard University Asia Center, 2000.

Isoda Kōichi. *Isoda Kōichi chosakushū*, vol. 5. Tokyo: Ozawa shoten, 1991.

Itō Kanji, et al., eds. *Yanagita Kunio zenshū*, vol. 5. Tokyo: Chikuma shobō, 1998.

Ito, Ken K. "Class and Gender in a Meiji Family Romance." *Journal of Japanese Studies* 28, no. 2 (Summer 2002): 339–78.

Iwami Teruyo. "Oriki densetsu: 'Nigorie' ron." In Shin feminizumu hihyō no kai, ed., pp. 125–49.

Iwami Teruyo et al., eds. *Higuchi Ichiyō jiten*. Tokyo: Ōfūsha, 1996.

Iwamoto Yoshiharu. "Haha no mugaku." *Taiyō* 2, no. 2 (Jan. 1896): 127–31.

———. "Joshi no tai'iku." *Taiyō* 2, no. 6 (March 1896): 217–19.

———. "Katei no fūga." *Taiyō* 2, no. 23 (Nov. 1896): 97–101.

———. "Katei no kankaryoku." *Taiyō* 2, no. 4 (Feb. 1896): 145–48.

———. "Katei no yūraku." *Taiyō* 2, no. 15 (July 1896): 208–12.

———. "Katei wa kokka nari." *Taiyō* 2, no. 5 (March 1896): 145–48.

———. "Kazoku no danran." *Taiyō* 2, no. 11 (May 1896): 217–21.

———. "Tsuma no mujō." *Taiyō* 2, no. 3 (Feb. 1896): 125–28.

Iwaya Sazanami. *Issunbōshi. Nippon mukashibanashi*, vol. 19. Tokyo: Hakubunkan, 1896.

———. "Kogane-maru." In *Kawakami Bizan, Iwaya Sazanami shū, MBZ*, vol. 20, ed. Senuma Shigeki. Tokyo: Chikuma shobō, 1968, pp. 225–47.

Izuhara Takatoshi. "Oriki no tōjō: 'Nigorie' ni okeru 'shakuyō' ni tsuite." *Bungaku* 56, no. 7 (July 1988): 59–77.

———. "*Takekurabe* no seiritsu kiban." *Kokugo kokubun* 60, no. 12 (Dec. 1991): 1–18.

Jameson, Fredric. *The Political Unconscious: Narrative as a Socially Symbolic Act*. Ithaca, N.Y.: Cornell University Press, 1981.

———. *A Singular Modernity: Essay on the Ontology of the Present*. London: Verso, 2002.

Jenny, Laurent. "The Strategy of Form." In *French Literary Theory Today: A Reader*. Ed. Tzvetan Todorov. Trans. R. Carter. Cambridge, Eng.: Cambridge University Press, 1982, pp. 34–63.

Johnson, Claudia. *Jane Austen: Women, Politics, and the Novel*. Chicago: University of Chicago Press, 1988.

Kamei Hideo. "Buntai sōzō no mitsugi." *Kokubungaku: Kaishaku to kanshō* 29, no. 13 (Oct. 1984): 47–53.

———. *Kansei no henkaku*. Tokyo: Kōdansha, 1983. (*Transformations of Sensibility*. Ed. and trans. Michael Bourdaghs. Ann Arbor: Center for Japanese Studies, University of Michigan, 2002.)

Kan Satoko. "Ichiyō no 'Wakaremichi': go-shusse to iu wa onna ni kagirite." *Kokugo kokubungaku* 70, no. 2 (Feb. 1993): 29–42.

——. "Katararenakatta monogatari: *Takekurabe* o yomu." *Joshi Seigakuin tanki daigaku kiyō* 26 (1994): 47–62.

——. "'Ōtsugomori' ron." In Higuchi Ichiyō kenkyūkai, ed. (1996), pp. 39–53.

Kanai Keiko. "'Onna' no raireki: 'Nigorie' ron e no shikaku." *Nakadachi* 5 (1988): 38–52.

Kaneko Akio, Takahashi Osamu, and Yoshida Morio, eds. *Disukūru no teikoku: Meiji sanjūnendai no bunka kenkyū.* Tokyo: Shin'yōsha, 2000.

Karatani, Kōjin. *Origins of Modern Japanese Literature.* Ed. Brett de Bary. Durham, N.C.: Duke University Press, 1994.

Karino Keiko. "'Nigorie': hikisakareta sei no shosō." *Kindai bungaku ronshū* 15 (1989): 1–13.

Kawamura Kunimitsu. *Sekushuariti no kindai.* Tokyo: Kōdansha, 1996.

Keene, Donald, trans. *Major Plays of Chikamatsu.* New York: Columbia University Press, 1961.

Kikuta Shigeo. "Ichiyō no naka no ōchō: sono koten taiken no imi suru mono." *Kokubungaku: Kanshō to kyōzai no kenkyū* 25, no. 15 (Dec. 1980): 33–39.

Kimata Satoshi. *'Imeeji' no kindai Nihon bungaku shi.* Tokyo: Sōbunsha shuppan, 1988.

Kimura Masayuki. *Ichiyō bungaku seiritsu no haikei.* Tokyo: Ōfūsha, 1976.

Kinmonth, Earl. *The Self-made Man in Meiji Japanese Thought.* Berkeley: University of California Press, 1981.

Kitagawa Akio. *Ichiyō to iu genshō: Meiji to Higuchi Ichiyō.* Tokyo: Sōbunsha shuppan, 1998.

Kobayashi Hideo. "Kokyō o ushinatta bungaku." In *Kobayashi Hideo zenshū,* vol. 3. Tokyo: Shinchōsha, 1968, pp. 29–37.

Kobayashi Hiroko. "Hanten suru moraru: 'Ōtsugomori' ron." In Shin feminizumu hihyō no kai, ed., pp. 103–24.

Koike Masatane. "Ichiyō to kinsei bungaku." *Kokubungaku: Kaishaku to kanshō* 43, no. 5 (May 1978): 110–16.

Komori Yōichi. *Buntai toshite no monogatari.* Tokyo: Chikuma shobō, 1988.

——. *Kōzō toshite no katari.* Tokyo: Shin'yōsha, 1988.

——. *Shōsetsu to hihyō.* Tokyo: Seori shobō, 1999.

———. *Yuragi no Nihon bungaku*. Tokyo: Nihon hōsō shuppan kyōkai, 1998.

Komori Yōichi, Kōno Kensuke, and Takahashi Osamu, eds. *Media/hyōshō/ideorogii: Meiji sanjūnendai no bunka kenkyū*. Tokyo: Ozawa shoten, 1995.

Kōno Kensuke, Komori Yōichi, Togawa Shinsuke, and Yamamoto Yoshiaki. "'Jūsan'ya' o yomu," part 1. *Bungaku* 1, no. 1 (Winter 1990): 125–58

———. "'Jūsan'ya' o yomu," part 2. *Bungaku* 1, no. 2 (Spring 1990): 169–98.

Kōra Rumiko. "Higuchi Ichiyō 'Jūsan'ya' to tsuki no anji: chichi no chinmoku, musume no chinmoku." *Jōsai bungaku* 19 (1993): 6–22.

Kornicki, Peter. "The Survival of Tokugawa Fiction in the Meiji Period." *Harvard Journal of Asiatic Studies* 41, no. 2 (Dec. 1981): 461–82.

Kubota Jun and Baba Akiko, eds. *Utakotoba utamakura daijiten*. Tokyo: Kadokawa shoten, 1999.

Kunikida Doppo. "Musashino." In *Kunikida Doppo shū, Nihon kindai bungaku taikei*, vol. 10, ed. Yamada Hiromitsu. Tokyo: Kadokawa shoten, 1970, pp. 89–110.

Kuniwake Misako, ed. *Kijo no shiori*. Tokyo: Ōkura shoten, 1895.

Lee, William. "Chikamatsu and Dramatic Literature in the Meiji Period." In *Inventing the Classics: Modernity, National Identity, and Japanese Literature*. Ed. Haruo Shirane and Tomi Suzuki. Stanford, Cal.: Stanford University Press, 2000, pp. 179–98.

Liu, Lydia. *Translingual Practice: Literature, National Culture, and Translated Modernity – China, 1900–1937*. Stanford, Cal.: Stanford University Press, 1995.

Maeda Ai. *Higuchi Ichiyō no sekai*. Tokyo: Heibonsha, 1978.

———. *Kindai dokusha no seiritsu*. Tokyo: Yūseidō, 1973.

———. *Maeda Ai chosaku shū*, vol. 3. Tokyo: Chikuma shobō, 1989.

———. "Midori no tame ni: *Takekurabe* Sata setsu o yonde." *Gunzō* 40, no. 7 (July 1985): 204–11.

Maeda Isamu. *Edogo daijiten*. Tokyo: Kōdansha, 1972.

Markus, Andrew. *The Willow in Autumn*. Cambridge, Mass.: Council on East Asian Studies, Harvard University, 1992.

Matsuzaka Toshio. *Higuchi Ichiyō kenkyū*, 2nd ed. Tokyo: Kyōiku shuppan sentaa, 1983.

McGann, Jerome. *The Poetics of Sensibility: A Revolution in Literary Style*. New York: Clarendon Press, 1996.

Mertz, John. *Novel Japan: Spaces of Nationhood in Early Meiji Narrative.* Ann Arbor: Center for Japanese Studies, University of Michigan, 2003.

Millet, Christine Murasaki. "Inverted Classical Allusions and Higuchi Ichiyō's Literary Technique in *Takekurabe.*" *U.S.-Japan Women's Journal, English Supplement* 14 (1998): 3–26.

Minemura Shizuko. "'Nigorie' no goshō: 'Marukibashi' no haikei." *Joshidai kokubun* 125 (1999): 81–107.

Miyamoto Yukiko. "Yūri no seiritsu to taishūka." In *Bunka no taishūka, Nihon no kinsei,* vol. 14, ed. Takeuchi Makoto. Tokyo: Chūō kōronsha, 1993, pp. 169–218.

Mizuochi Kiyoshi. *Bunraku.* Tokyo: Shin'yōsha, 1989.

Moi, Toril. *What Is a Woman?* New York: Oxford University Press, 1999.

Mori Arinori. "Saishōron." In *Meiji keimō shisō shū, MBZ,* vol. 3, ed. Okubo Toshiaki. Tokyo: Chikuma shobō, 1967, pp. 260–63.

Mori Ōgai. *Ōgai zenshū,* vol. 23. Ed. Kinoshita Mokutarō. Tokyo: Iwanami shoten, 1973.

Mori Osamu, Torigoe Bunzō, Nagatomo Chiyoji, eds. *Chikamatsu Monzaemon shū* 1. *NKBZ,* vol. 43. Tokyo: Shōgakukan, 1972.

Mulvey, Laura. "Visual Pleasure and Narrative Cinema." In *Feminism and Film Theory.* Ed. Constance Penley. New York: Routledge, 1988, pp. 57–79.

Murakami Nobuhiko. *Meiji josei shi,* vol. 2A. Tokyo: Rironsha, 1970.

Muta Kazue. *Senryaku toshite no kazoku.* Tokyo: Shin'yōsha, 1996.

Nagai Sachiko. "Higuchi Ichiyō kenkyū: 'Ōtsugomori' ni tsuite." *Nihon bungaku kenkyū kaihō* 5 (1990): 44–64.

Nagazumi Yasuaki, ed. *Tsurezuregusa. NKBZ,* vol. 12. Tokyo: Shōgakukan, 1971.

Nakanishi Susumu. "The Spatial Structure of Japanese Myth: The Contact Point between Life and Death." In *Principles of Classical Japanese Literature.* Ed. Earl Miner. Princeton, N.J.: Princeton University Press, 1985, pp. 106–29.

Nishikawa Yūko. "The Changing Form of Dwellings and the Establishment of the Katei in Modern Japan." *U.S.-Japan Women's Journal, English Supplement* 8 (1995): 3–36.

Noguchi Fujio. "*Takekurabe* ronkō o yonde: Maeda Ai shi setsu e no gimon." *Gunzō* 40, no. 9 (Sept. 1985): 182–88.

Noguchi Seki, ed. *Higuchi Ichiyō raikan shū.* Tokyo: Chikuma shobō, 1998.

Nolte, Sharon H. and Sally Ann Hastings. "The Meiji State's Policy toward Women, 1890–1910." In *Recreating Japanese Women*. Ed. Gail Lee Bernstein. Berkeley: University of California Press, 1991, pp. 151–74.

Nomura Jun'ichi, ed. *Mukashibanashi densetsu hikkei. Bessatsu kokubungaku* 41 (1991).

Oka Yasuo. "Saikaku to Meiji nijūnendai no bungaku." *Kokubungaku: Kaishaku to kanshō* 10, no. 5 (May 1965): 43–48.

Okuda Akiko. "Jochū no rekishi." *Onna to otoko no jikū: Nihon josei shi saikō*, vol. 5, ed. Okuda Akiko. Tokyo: Fujiwara shoten, 1995, pp. 376–410.

Orbaugh, Sharalyn. "The Body in Contemporary Women's Fiction." In *The Woman's Hand: Gender and Theory in Japanese Women's Writing*. Ed. Paul Schalow and Janet Walker. Stanford, Cal.: Stanford University Press, 1996, pp. 119–64.

Ōshima Tatehiko, ed. *Otogi zōshi shū. NKBZ*, vol. 36. Tokyo: Shōgakukan, 1974.

Pyle, Kenneth. *The New Generation in Meiji Japan: Problems of Cultural Identity, 1885–1895*. Stanford, Cal.: Stanford University Press, 1969.

Rubin, Gayle. "The Traffic in Women: Notes toward a Political Economy of Sex." In *Toward an Anthropology of Women*. Ed. Rayna Reiter. New York: Monthly Review Press, 1975, pp. 157–210.

Ryūtei Tanehiko. *Nise Murasaki inaka Genji*, 2 vols. Ed. Suzuki Jūzō. *Shin Nihon koten bungaku taikei*, vol. 88–89. Tokyo: Iwanami shoten, 1995.

Saeki Junko. *'Iro' to 'ai' no hikaku bunkashi*. Tokyo: Iwanami shoten, 1998.

Said, Edward. *The World, the Text, and the Critic*. Cambridge, Mass.: Harvard University Press, 1983.

Sand, Jordan. *House and Home in Modern Japan: Architecture, Domestic Space, and Bourgeois Culture, 1880–1930*. Cambridge, Mass.: Harvard University Asia Center, 2003.

Sas, Miryam. *Fault Lines: Cultural Memory and Japanese Surrealism*. Stanford, Cal.: Stanford University Press, 1999.

Sata Ineko. "*Takekurabe* kaishaku e no hitotsu no gimon." *Gunzō* 40, no. 5 (May 1985): 192–96.

——. "*Takekurabe* kaishaku no sonogo." *Gakutō* 82, no. 8 (Aug. 1985): 4–7.

Seigle, Cecilia. *Yoshiwara: The Glittering World of the Japanese Courtesan*. Honolulu: University of Hawaii Press, 1993.

Seki Keigō, ed. *Nihon mukashibanashi taisei*, vol. 5. Tokyo: Kadokawa shoten, 1978.

———. ed. *Nihon no mukashibanashi*, vol. 3. Tokyo: Iwanami shoten, 1957.

Seki Reiko. *Ane no chikara: Higuchi Ichiyō.* Tokyo: Chikuma shobō, 1993.

———. "Ichiyō to *Ise, Genji*: ibunka to no sesshoku toshite." In *Heian bunka no ekurichūru.* Ed. Kawazoe Fusae et al. Tokyo: Bunsei shuppan, 2001, pp. 177–97.

———. *Kataru onnatachi no jidai: Ichiyō to Meiji josei hyōgen.* Tokyo: Shin'yōsha, 1997.

———. "Zōyo to shutaika: 'Ōtsugomori' ron." In Higuchi Ichiyō kenkyūkai, ed. (1998), pp. 22–38.

Seki Ryōichi. *Higuchi Ichiyō: kōshō to shiron.* Tokyo: Yūseidō, 1971.

Shigematsu Keiko. "Higuchi Ichiyō ron: Kichizō no 'wakaremichi'." *Hagi joshi tanki daigaku kenkyū kiyō* 1 (1993): 19–32.

———. "*Takekurabe* no aikan: katarite no shuhō." *Nihon bungaku kenkyū* 27 (1991): 109–20.

Shin feminizumu hihyō no kai, ed. *Higuchi Ichiyō o yominaosu.* Tokyo: Gakugei shorin, 1994.

Shioda Ryōhei. *Higuchi Ichiyō.* Tokyo: Yoshikawa Kōbunkan, 1960.

———. *Higuchi Ichiyō kenkyū.* Tokyo: Chūō kōronsha, 1956.

Shūkan asahi, ed. *Nedanshi nenpyō: Meiji, Taisho, Showa.* Tokyo: Asahi shinbunsha, 1988.

Suzuki Keiko. "Kyūsai no nega: kyōgi toshite no *Nigorie*." In Higuchi Ichiyō kenkyūkai, ed. (1996), pp. 98–119.

Takada Chinami. *Higuchi Ichiyō ron e no shatei.* Tokyo: Sōbunsha, 1997.

———. "'Jūsan'ya' nōto." *Kindai bungaku kenkyū* 1 (1984): 53–65.

———. "'Onna' 'kodomo' no shiza kara: *Takekurabe* o sozai toshite." *Nihon bungaku* 38, no. 3 (March 1989): 48–60.

———. "'Wakaremichi' no isō." *Komazawa kokubun* 25 (1988): 105–15.

Takada Chinami, Seki Reiko, Margaret Mitsutani, and Usami Takeshi. "'Nigorie,' *Takekurabe*: Tekusuto no kūhaku o megutte." *Kokubungaku: Kaishaku to kanshō* 60, no. 6 (June 1995): 6–31.

Takahashi Kazuko. "Higuchi Ichiyō to Ueno Toshokan." *Sagami kokubun* 19 (1992): 37–52.

Takahashi Yūko. "Chūbei jidai ni okeru Mori Arinori to joshi kyōiku kan." *Shikyō* 34 (1997): 47–71.

———. "Vikutoria jidai no hōmu to saisho no joshi ryūgakusei." *Tsuda juku daigaku kiyō* 30 (1998): 261–83.

Takeno Seio. *Kindai bungaku to Saikaku.* Tokyo: Shintensha, 1980.

Takeuchi Yō. *Gakureki kizoku no eikō to zasetsu. Nihon no kindai,* vol. 12. Tokyo: Chūō kōronsha, 1999.

———. *Risshi, kugaku, shusse.* Tokyo: Kōdansha, 1991.

———. *Risshin shusse shugi: Kindai Nihon no roman to yokubō.* Tokyo: Nihon hōsō shuppan kyōkai, 1997.

Takitō Mitsuyoshi. *Ichiyō bungaku: seisei to tenkai.* Tokyo: Meiji shoin, 1998.

Tanaka Minoru. "'Jūsan'ya' no ame." *Nihon kindai bungaku* 37 (1987): 14–26.

Tanaka Yūko. *Edo wa nettowaaku.* Tokyo: Heibonsha, 1993.

Thornbury, Barbara. *Sukeroku's Double Identity: The Structure of Edo Kabuki.* Ann Arbor: Center for Japanese Studies, University of Michigan, 1982.

Tomatsu Izumi. "Higuchi Ichiyō 'Jūsan'ya' shiron: Oseki no 'kesshin.'" *Sagami joshi daigaku kiyō* 55 (1992): 67–83.

———. "Kōsa shita 'jikan' no imi: 'Wakaremichi' ron." In Higuchi Ichiyō kenkyūkai (1998), pp. 93–112.

———. "'Nigorie' ron no tame ni: kakareta shakufu, Oriki no eizō." *Sagami kokubun* 18 (1992): 30–48.

Torigoe Bunzō, ed. *Chikamatsu Monzaemon shū* 2. NKBZ, vol. 44. Tokyo: Shōgakukan, 1975.

Totman, Conrad. *Early Modern Japan.* Berkeley: University of California Press, 1993.

Tsubouchi Shōyō. *Shōsetsu shinzui.* In *Tsubouchi Shōyō shū,* MBZ, vol. 16, ed. Inagaki Tatsurō. Tokyo: Chikuma shobō, 1969, pp. 3–58.

Uchida Roan. *Uchida Roan zenshū,* vol. 1. Ed. Nomura Kyō. Tokyo: Yumani shobō, 1984.

Ueda, Atsuko. "Meiji Literary Historiography: The Production of 'Modern Japanese Literature.'" Ph.D. diss., University of Michigan, 1999.

Usami Takeshi. "Higuchi Ichiyō 'Nigorie': 'onnatachi' no koe." *Kokubungaku: Kaishaku to kanshō* 56, no. 4 (April 1991): 61–66.

Wilson, George. *Patriots and Redeemers: Motives in the Meiji Restoration.* Chicago: University of Chicago Press, 1992.

Yamada Yūsaku. "'Jūsan'ya' no sekai." *Gakugei kokugo kokubungaku* 13 (1977): 15–25.

Yamada Yūsaku, Tomatsu Izumi, Komori Yōichi, and Fujii Sadakazu. "Kyōdō tōgi: Higuchi Ichiyō no sakuhin o yomu." *Kokubungaku: Kaishaku to kyōzai no kenkyū* 29, no. 13 (Oct. 1984): 76–107.

Yamamoto Hiroshi. "'Nigorie' no marukibashi." *Kokugo kokubun* 47, no. 4 (April 1978): 30–50.

——. "'Nigorie' no shūshō." In *Ronshū Nihon bungaku Nihongo*, vol. 4. Tokyo: Kadokawa shoten, 1978, pp. 254–81.

Yamamoto Kazuaki. "*Takekurabe* ni okeru 'katarite' no isō." *Jōnan kokubun* 11 (1991): 20–31.

Yamamoto Kinji. "Deawanai kotoba no 'wakare.'" In Higuchi Ichiyō kenkyūkai, ed. (1996), pp. 195–215.

——. "'Jūsan'ya' ron: Oseki no 'koyoi'/Saitō-ke no 'koyoi.'" *Kokugo to kokubungaku* 71, no. 8 (Aug. 1994): 13–25.

——. "'Nigorie' shiron: Oriki no 'omou koto'." *Ronkyū Nihon bungaku* 57 (1992): 35–45.

——. "'Ōtsugomori' o yomu: 'Shōjiki wa waga mi no mamori' o megutte." *Ritsumeikan bungaku* 540 (1995): 52–68.

——. "*Takekurabe* no hōhō." *Ritsumeikan bungaku* 564 (2000): 1095–121.

Yamasaki Makiko. "Surechigau monogatari: 'Wakaremichi' ron." In Shin feminizumu hihyō no kai, ed., pp. 177–94.

Yiu, Angela. *Chaos and Order in the Works of Natsume Sōseki*. Honolulu: University of Hawaii Press, 1998.

Yoshimi Kaneko. "Baishō no jittai to haishō undō." In *Nihon josei shi*, vol. 4, ed. Josei shi sōgō kenkyūkai. Tokyo: Tōkyō daigaku shuppankai, 1982, pp. 223–58.

Zwicker, Jonathan. "Tears of Blood: Melodrama, the Novel, and the Social Imaginary in Nineteenth-century Japan." Ph.D. diss., Columbia University, 2002.

Index

Harvard East Asian Monographs
(* out-of-print)

*20. Toshio G. Tsukahira, *Feudal Control in Tokugawa Japan: The Sankin Kōtai System*

*21. Kwang-Ching Liu, ed., *American Missionaries in China: Papers from Harvard Seminars*

*22. George Moseley, *A Sino-Soviet Cultural Frontier: The Ili Kazakh Autonomous Chou*

 23. Carl F. Nathan, *Plague Prevention and Politics in Manchuria, 1910–1931*

*24. Adrian Arthur Bennett, *John Fryer: The Introduction of Western Science and Technology into Nineteenth-Century China*

*25. Donald J. Friedman, *The Road from Isolation: The Campaign of the American Committee for Non-Participation in Japanese Aggression, 1938–1941*

*26. Edward LeFevour, *Western Enterprise in Late Ching China: A Selective Survey of Jardine, Matheson and Company's Operations, 1842–1895*

 27. Charles Neuhauser, *Third World Politics: China and the Afro-Asian People's Solidarity Organization, 1957–1967*

*28. Kungtu C. Sun, assisted by Ralph W. Huenemann, *The Economic Development of Manchuria in the First Half of the Twentieth Century*

*29. Shahid Javed Burki, *A Study of Chinese Communes, 1965*

 30. John Carter Vincent, *The Extraterritorial System in China: Final Phase*

 31. Madeleine Chi, *China Diplomacy, 1914–1918*

*32. Clifton Jackson Phillips, *Protestant America and the Pagan World: The First Half Century of the American Board of Commissioners for Foreign Missions, 1810–1860*

*33. James Pusey, *Wu Han: Attacking the Present Through the Past*

*34. Ying-wan Cheng, *Postal Communication in China and Its Modernization, 1860–1896*

 35. Tuvia Blumenthal, *Saving in Postwar Japan*

 36. Peter Frost, *The Bakumatsu Currency Crisis*

 37. Stephen C. Lockwood, *Augustine Heard and Company, 1858–1862*

 38. Robert R. Campbell, *James Duncan Campbell: A Memoir by His Son*

 39. Jerome Alan Cohen, ed., *The Dynamics of China's Foreign Relations*

 40. V. V. Vishnyakova-Akimova, *Two Years in Revolutionary China, 1925–1927,* tr. Steven L. Levine

 41. Meron Medzini, *French Policy in Japan During the Closing Years of the Tokugawa Regime*

 42. Ezra Vogel, Margie Sargent, Vivienne B. Shue, Thomas Jay Mathews, and Deborah S. Davis, *The Cultural Revolution in the Provinces*

 43. Sidney A. Forsythe, *An American Missionary Community in China, 1895–1905*

*44. Benjamin I. Schwartz, ed., *Reflections on the May Fourth Movement.: A Symposium*

*45. Ching Young Choe, *The Rule of the Taewŏngun, 1864–1873: Restoration in Yi Korea*

 46. W. P. J. Hall, *A Bibliographical Guide to Japanese Research on the Chinese Economy, 1958–1970*

 47. Jack J. Gerson, *Horatio Nelson Lay and Sino-British Relations, 1854–1864*

74. Kang Chao, *The Development of Cotton Textile Production in China*

75. Valentin Rabe, *The Home Base of American China Missions, 1880–1920*

*76. Sarasin Viraphol, *Tribute and Profit: Sino-Siamese Trade, 1652–1853*

77. Ch'i-ch'ing Hsiao, *The Military Establishment of the Yuan Dynasty*

78. Meishi Tsai, *Contemporary Chinese Novels and Short Stories, 1949–1974: An Annotated Bibliography*

*79. Wellington K. K. Chan, *Merchants, Mandarins and Modern Enterprise in Late Ching China*

80. Endymion Wilkinson, *Landlord and Labor in Late Imperial China: Case Studies from Shandong by Jing Su and Luo Lun*

*81. Barry Keenan, *The Dewey Experiment in China: Educational Reform and Political Power in the Early Republic*

*82. George A. Hayden, *Crime and Punishment in Medieval Chinese Drama: Three Judge Pao Plays*

*83. Sang-Chul Suh, *Growth and Structural Changes in the Korean Economy, 1910–1940*

84. J. W. Dower, *Empire and Aftermath: Yoshida Shigeru and the Japanese Experience, 1878–1954*

85. Martin Collcutt, *Five Mountains: The Rinzai Zen Monastic Institution in Medieval Japan*

86. Kwang Suk Kim and Michael Roemer, *Growth and Structural Transformation*

87. Anne O. Krueger, *The Developmental Role of the Foreign Sector and Aid*

*88. Edwin S. Mills and Byung-Nak Song, *Urbanization and Urban Problems*

89. Sung Hwan Ban, Pal Yong Moon, and Dwight H. Perkins, *Rural Development*

*90. Noel F. McGinn, Donald R. Snodgrass, Yung Bong Kim, Shin-Bok Kim, and Quee-Young Kim, *Education and Development in Korea*

*91. Leroy P. Jones and Il SaKong, *Government, Business, and Entrepreneurship in Economic Development: The Korean Case*

92. Edward S. Mason, Dwight H. Perkins, Kwang Suk Kim, David C. Cole, Mahn Je Kim et al., *The Economic and Social Modernization of the Republic of Korea*

93. Robert Repetto, Tai Hwan Kwon, Son-Ung Kim, Dae Young Kim, John E. Sloboda, and Peter J. Donaldson, *Economic Development, Population Policy, and Demographic Transition in the Republic of Korea*

94. Parks M. Coble, Jr., *The Shanghai Capitalists and the Nationalist Government, 1927–1937*

95. Noriko Kamachi, *Reform in China: Huang Tsun-hsien and the Japanese Model*

96. Richard Wich, *Sino-Soviet Crisis Politics: A Study of Political Change and Communication*

97. Lillian M. Li, *China's Silk Trade: Traditional Industry in the Modern World, 1842–1937*

98. R. David Arkush, *Fei Xiaotong and Sociology in Revolutionary China*

*99. Kenneth Alan Grossberg, *Japan's Renaissance: The Politics of the Muromachi Bakufu*

100. James Reeve Pusey, *China and Charles Darwin*

178. John Solt, *Shredding the Tapestry of Meaning: The Poetry and Poetics of Kitasono Katue (1902–1978)*

179. Edward Pratt, *Japan's Protoindustrial Elite: The Economic Foundations of the Gōnō*

180. Atsuko Sakaki, *Recontextualizing Texts: Narrative Performance in Modern Japanese Fiction*

181. Soon-Won Park, *Colonial Industrialization and Labor in Korea: The Onoda Cement Factory*

182. JaHyun Kim Haboush and Martina Deuchler, *Culture and the State in Late Chosŏn Korea*

183. John W. Chaffee, *Branches of Heaven: A History of the Imperial Clan of Sung China*

184. Gi-Wook Shin and Michael Robinson, eds., *Colonial Modernity in Korea*

185. Nam-lin Hur, *Prayer and Play in Late Tokugawa Japan: Asakusa Sensōji and Edo Society*

186. Kristin Stapleton, *Civilizing Chengdu: Chinese Urban Reform, 1895–1937*

187. Hyung Il Pai, *Constructing "Korean" Origins: A Critical Review of Archaeology, Historiography, and Racial Myth in Korean State-Formation Theories*

188. Brian D. Ruppert, *Jewel in the Ashes: Buddha Relics and Power in Early Medieval Japan*

189. Susan Daruvala, *Zhou Zuoren and an Alternative Chinese Response to Modernity*

*190. James Z. Lee, *The Political Economy of a Frontier: Southwest China, 1250–1850*

191. Kerry Smith, *A Time of Crisis: Japan, the Great Depression, and Rural Revitalization*

192. Michael Lewis, *Becoming Apart: National Power and Local Politics in Toyama, 1868–1945*

193. William C. Kirby, Man-houng Lin, James Chin Shih, and David A. Pietz, eds., *State and Economy in Republican China: A Handbook for Scholars*

194. Timothy S. George, *Minamata: Pollution and the Struggle for Democracy in Postwar Japan*

195. Billy K. L. So, *Prosperity, Region, and Institutions in Maritime China: The South Fukien Pattern, 946–1368*

196. Yoshihisa Tak Matsusaka, *The Making of Japanese Manchuria, 1904–1932*

197. Maram Epstein, *Competing Discourses: Orthodoxy, Authenticity, and Engendered Meanings in Late Imperial Chinese Fiction*

198. Curtis J. Milhaupt, J. Mark Ramseyer, and Michael K. Young, eds. and comps., *Japanese Law in Context: Readings in Society, the Economy, and Politics*

199. Haruo Iguchi, *Unfinished Business: Ayukawa Yoshisuke and U.S.-Japan Relations, 1937–1952*

200. Scott Pearce, Audrey Spiro, and Patricia Ebrey, *Culture and Power in the Reconstitution of the Chinese Realm, 200–600*

201. Terry Kawashima, *Writing Margins: The Textual Construction of Gender in Heian and Kamakura Japan*

202. Martin W. Huang, *Desire and Fictional Narrative in Late Imperial China*

203. Robert S. Ross and Jiang Changbin, eds., *Re-examining the Cold War: U.S.-China Diplomacy, 1954–1973*

204. Guanhua Wang, *In Search of Justice: The 1905–1906 Chinese Anti-American Boycott*

205. David Schaberg, *A Patterned Past: Form and Thought in Early Chinese Historiography*

206. Christine Yano, *Tears of Longing: Nostalgia and the Nation in Japanese Popular Song*

207. Milena Doleželová-Velingerová and Oldřich Král, with Graham Sanders, eds., *The Appropriation of Cultural Capital: China's May Fourth Project*

208. Robert N. Huey, *The Making of 'Shinkokinshū'*

209. Lee Butler, *Emperor and Aristocracy in Japan, 1467–1680: Resilience and Renewal*

210. Suzanne Ogden, *Inklings of Democracy in China*

211. Kenneth J. Ruoff, *The People's Emperor: Democracy and the Japanese Monarchy, 1945–1995*

212. Haun Saussy, *Great Walls of Discourse and Other Adventures in Cultural China*

213. Aviad E. Raz, *Emotions at Work: Normative Control, Organizations, and Culture in Japan and America*

214. Rebecca E. Karl and Peter Zarrow, eds., *Rethinking the 1898 Reform Period: Political and Cultural Change in Late Qing China*

215. Kevin O'Rourke, *The Book of Korean Shijo*

216. Ezra F. Vogel, ed., *The Golden Age of the U.S.-China-Japan Triangle, 1972–1989*

217. Thomas A Wilson, ed., *On Sacred Grounds: Culture, Society, Politics, and the Formation of the Cult of Confucius*

218. Donald S. Sutton, *Steps of Perfection: Exorcistic Performers and Chinese Religion in Twentieth-Century Taiwan*

219. Daqing Yang, *Technology of Empire: Telecommunications and Japanese Expansionism, 1895–1945*

220. Qianshen Bai, *Fu Shan's World: The Transformation of Chinese Calligraphy in the Seventeenth Century*

221. Paul Jakov Smith and Richard von Glahn, eds., *The Song-Yuan-Ming Transition in Chinese History*

222. Rania Huntington, *Alien Kind: Foxes and Late Imperial Chinese Narrative*

223. Jordan Sand, *House and Home in Modern Japan: Architecture, Domestic Space, and Bourgeois Culture, 1880–1930*

224. Karl Gerth, *China Made: Consumer Culture and the Creation of the Nation*

225. Xiaoshan Yang, *Metamorphosis of the Private Sphere: Gardens and Objects in Tang-Song Poetry*

226. Barbara Mittler, *A Newspaper for China? Power, Identity, and Change in Shanghai's News Media, 1872–1912*